THE ECONOMICS OF URBAN SIZE

The Economics of Urban Size

HARRY W. RICHARDSON

*Director, Centre for Research in the Social Sciences,
University of Kent at Canterbury*

SAXON HOUSE | LEXINGTON BOOKS

First published in Great Britain by
Saxon House, D. C. Heath Limited, 1973

Reprinted 1977 by Teakfield Limited,
Westmead, Farnborough, Hampshire, England.

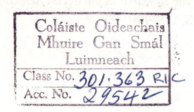
ISBN 0 347 01023 7

Library of Congress Catalog Card Number 73-8050

Printed and bound by Ilfadrove Limited,
Barry, Glamorgan, S. Wales.

Contents

Preface

The purpose of this book is to explore the relationships between various economic phenomena and city size to shed more light on the controversies about whether big cities are bad and whether city size is the arch villain in the so-called 'urban crisis'. In this way this study builds upon and extends previous work, in particular, the study by Neutze published in 1965 (long before urban size became a fashionable topic), a series of papers written by Alonso between 1968 and 1972, and the proceedings of a conference on National Urban Development Strategies organised by Resources for the Future and Glasgow University and held in September 1971 (most of the papers presented were published in *Urban Studies* in February and October 1972). I am grateful to the Editors of *Urban Studies* for permission to use material contained in my contribution to that Conference in Chapters 10 and 13 of this book. I am also grateful to the Editor of *Regional Studies* for permission to use a paper which appears as Chapter 11. I also wish to thank Mrs Sandy Sharples and Miss Glenys Phillips for typing the drafts.

Harry W. Richardson
March 1973

1 Introduction

The problem of city size

The problem of city size has been of recurrent interest ever since the process of urbanisation began. It has commanded equal attention over space as through time, in that it has been recognised as a problem in all countries regardless of their level of development. This does not mean to say, of course, that there has been a fixed view about what is a 'desirable' size for a city. Relative size has been far more important than absolute size. The city size curve in history has been very steep. In the ancient world only a handful of cities reached the hundred thousand mark (perhaps Memphis, Babylon, Thebes, Syracuse, Athens, Alexandria and Rome). The million metropolis is a twentieth century phenomenon,[1] and prior to the growth of London and New York the only earlier cities of this size were found in the Far East (Chang an, Hangchow and Tokyo).[2] The ideal size for Plato, the 5,040 citizens who could pack into a forum, would be regarded as far too small today for the efficient supply of even the lowest level urban functions. As for differences between countries today the concern of certain developing countries with the size of their largest city is not usually based on its absolute size, since in most cases there are many much larger cities to be found in other parts of the world. What may be worrying is the size of the leading city *relative* to the rest of the urban system of which it forms a part, and the inhibiting effects of a primate city on the growth of intermediate size centres. If 'too big' or 'too small' are sensible descriptions only in relative rather than absolute terms, this must complicate the analysis since it then becomes difficult, if not impossible, to offer any observations about city size without outlining the background conditions and institutional environment.

This obstacle has not held back comment on the size of cities. Although there has been some discussion of the minimum viable size of cities, most of the comment has concentrated on the upper end of the urban hierarchy, and much of it has taken the line that big cities are excessively large. However, there is a wide gap between the cautious but inconclusive analysis of social scientists and the wild histrionics of other observers such as environmentalists, some planners, and journalists. Sometimes, the argument becomes an attack on materialism, and a recognition of the fact that cities represent the height of materialism as well as the height of civilisation. This attitude could well be increasing in popularity with the more widespread challenge to affluence reflected in the views of Veblen, Galbraith, Mishan and others. However,

1

the value judgements that these views represent refer far more to the nature of modern living than to city size *per se*, though spatial concentration in the metropolitan city may make the 'grossness' of materialism seem worse.[3]

With the growth of the environmentalist lobby, this attack on metropolis, materialism and technology is occasionally combined either with a wishful retreat into the idea of small rural idylls or a utopian plan to set up neat and regular small self-sufficient communities. *Blueprint for Survival* (1972) expressed this kind of outlook very clearly.[4] After distorting evidence about the relationship of crime and drunkenness to city size, arguing (quite incorrectly) that infrastructure costs increase with city size and that *per capita* distribution costs are much higher in cities than in small towns, and quoting the Greek city states as some kind of ideal, this document puts forward a set of dubious psychological, economic and sociological propositions. These include: that life in a small community is essential for 'individual' expression; that decentralisation is necessary for self-sufficiency, and self-sufficiency is in turn necessary to minimise the burden on the ecosystems; and that 'social elasticity' breaks down in big cities. The proposed solution is one of 'neighbourhoods of 500, represented in communities of 5,000, in regions of 500,000, represented nationally, which in turn as today should be represented globally'. This recommendation is stronger on arithmetical regularity than on practicality.

Although many economists are pessimists[5] in the city size controversy, they are usually much less extreme than those quoted. It is significant that the latter rely on nebulous social psychological and sociological arguments which are much more difficult to test than most of the economic hypotheses.[6] The economists rest their case on negative externalities such as pollution, traffic congestion and long journeys to work, and managerial diseconomies in the public sector. Most recognise the existence of factors on the other side such as external economies of agglomeration so that in the end it all becomes a matter of balance. The diversity of views is considerable. Neutze (1965), for example, is a mild pessimist arguing – without much evidence – that diseconomies predominate in large cities while external economies are more important in small centres (Neutze, p. 27). Many economists, however, adopt either a firm optimistic or an uncommitted line, both of which are useful correctives to the pessimists' emotion. Alonso, for instance, has argued strongly that their is no evidence that large cities have become too big from the point of view of growth and productivity, and that small town life can be as socially objectionable (or as pleasurable) as big city life. Wingo (1972) and Smith (1970, p. 159) have stressed the magnetic attractions of big cities, the externalities in consumption and the variety of opportunities.

The uncommitted view probably remains the majority opinion. For instance, Hirsch (1967) reported to an official US Congress Committee that

2

'there is no study that shows that the social costs of huge urban complexes outweigh the benefits accruing to society'. It is interesting that this outlook is also shared by some sociologists (e.g. Ogburn and Duncan, 1964, p. 147) and geographers (Harris and Ullman, 1945, p. 7).

A major purpose of this book is to try to resolve some of the conflicts of viewpoint between the pessimists and optimists as regards the effects of increasing city size on inhabitants of these cities and on society as a whole. In this task use will be made of the tools of economic theory and the available, though frequently sketchy, empirical evidence. At the outset, however, it is interesting to raise the question of from where the pessimist case, particularly in popular literature and the mass media, derives its strength. A major factor must be the emphasis given to congestion, pollution, crime and urban poverty, and other possible negative net externalities, whereas the positive benefits of cities are more nebulous and less newsworthy. The economic benefits, such as the advantages of specialisation and exchange, the variety of employment opportunities and other labour market economies, and other external economies of agglomeration, are difficult to measure and of little public interest, while the social benefits such as externalities in consumption are either taken for granted or not perceived as being function-ally related to city size.

A naive extension of the same kind of outlook is to associate all the prob-lems and social evils that are found in big cities with the direct effects of city bigness itself. This is easy to do, not because these problems do not exist in smaller towns but because they are more noticeable, perhaps as a result of a higher degree of spatial concentration, in the larger cities. Yet there is very little evidence for the hypothesis that these problems are due to excessive city size rather than being a reflection of society as a whole. In Webber's words (1968, p. 1093): 'Neither crime-in-the-streets, poverty, unemployment, broken families, race riots, drug addiction, mental illness, juvenile delin-quency, nor any of the commonly rated "social pathologies" marking the contemporary city can find its causes or its cure there', or, more succinctly (Alonso, 1971b, p. 6): 'The problems of poverty and race in cities are problems *in* cities, not problems *of* cities'. If we hold city size constant and make cross-cultural comparisons, this becomes obvious. All large cities are locations for social problems, but not necessarily the same set of social problems, and their incidence in the big cities is higher merely because cities as the focus of civilisation mirror society at large, perhaps in a magnified form. The freedom to walk the streets of London and Madrid at night compared, say, with New York and Detroit is a reflection on European versus American society not on city size.

Decrying large cities is made easier because little research has been undertaken into examining the social costs of small towns. Indeed, much of the argument is distorted by a deep-rooted size bias. The disadvantages of large cities are frequently exaggerated while their benefits are ignored; conversely, life in small towns is regarded as idyllic, while its social costs are neglected. In fact, as strong a case can be made against the small town as a living environment as against the large city. True, pollution may be (though not inevitably) much lower, there is less congestion, access to open countryside is easier, and there is a possibility (no more than that) of a stronger sense of community. On the other hand, the economy of the small town may be much more unstable, the incidence of poverty may be much greater, the scope for a full social life is much more restricted by lack of amenities, and the 'closeness' of small town society may be more stifling than comforting. Furthermore, many of the benefits of small town life, such as almost rural living or the 'village atmosphere', may be obtainable in the large metropolis because of the great variety of life styles that a well-designed city may offer, ranging from downtown high-rise apartment living at one extreme to a very low density quasi-rural life at the metropolitan fringe at the other.

This last point raises the much broader question of whether it is possible in modern society to abstract city size and treat it as an isolated variable. The most striking characteristic of recent urbanisation is that cities have been able to alter their spatial structures by outward expansion, polinucleation and, in the extreme case, by the growth of megalopolis. The distinction between large and small size becomes blurred when cities are conceived as multi-centric rather than as monocentric systems. Such systems reflect a desire to maximise scale economies and other advantages of concentration without destroying the capacity to provide livable environments. Thus, 'Smaller metropolitan · areas within megalopolis draw many of the benefits of agglomeration without many of the penalties of large size. From the point of view of the advantages and disadvantages of urban size, they may, in a way, have their cake and eat it too' (Alonso, 1970b, p. 11.) The implication of this is that the issue of pro-size or anti-size may, in itself, be irrelevant. Of far more importance may be the questions of optimum density, the efficiency of spatial structure and the variety of opportunities for different styles of living both within and between cities.

These comments should not be interpreted as suggesting that the pessimists' case stands solely on bias and distortion or that the optimists have clear-cut evidence in their support. Even if we could accept that it is permissible to focus on size itself, and even if we could unequivocally demonstrate that the benefits of urban scale exceeded the costs throughout the urban hierarchy, the optimists' viewpoint would still not be confirmed. Some analysts (e.g. Edel, 1972 and Kirwan, 1972) have argued that what counts is not the absolute magnitude of benefits relative to costs but their

4

distribution. Edel argued that many of the net benefits of agglomeration are capitalised in the land values and accrue regressively to landowners. There is some justification for the belief that the benefits of agglomeration accrue to the landowner, the entrepreneur and the upper-income household while the poor bear a disproportionate share of the costs. It is difficult to test these propositions with available evidence, but it is clear that it needs money power to take advantage of the variety of opportunities that large city life offers (including externalities in consumption) and that the city poor may find themselves 'locked in' inside urban ghettoes with severely restricted choices for living and working. On the other hand, in all countries migration to the large cities has offered the sole escape from rural or small-town poverty, and regardless of the distribution of income and welfare in the metropolis in-migrants are usually better off in terms of wages, regularity of employment and living conditions than at their previous location.

Defining urban areas

A recurrent and almost insoluble problem in urban and regional economics is how to delimit spatially the units of study. This problem becomes even more critical in an analysis of urban size since the measure of city size (e.g. population) depends directly upon how the urban area is defined. For example, it makes a considerable difference whether we use a central city or a metropolitan area definition. It might not matter much in relative terms (i.e. in city size distribution discussions) if the size of the central city was a constant proportion of the size of the metropolitan area. Unfortunately, this is not the case. The ratio of central city to metropolitan area population varies widely from place to place[7] and within each urban area over time (as suburbanisation proceeds).

The arbitrariness of all attempts to delimit cities casts some doubt on the value of the concept of city size. Frequently for analytical purposes it is necessary to work with administratively defined urban areas since these form the basis upon which data are provided. These vary widely from country to country. In the United Kingdom the only areas are local authority areas (apart from a few conurbations made up of contiguous urban areas), and these bear little relation to any kind of economic or functional criteria.[8] The minimum cut-off size for urban status varies widely from one country to another.[9] In the United States, several classifications are used. At the lowest level there is the *urban place* defined as any concentration of at least 2,500 people. Since an urban area usually contains many urban places, the latter has little meaning for the economist. Next comes the *incorporated city*, again more than 2,500 inhabitants, which has a separate political entity. A much

5

more meaningful level is that of the *urbanised area* which is centred on one central city (or occasionally two) of 50,000 population or more and the surrounding settled area (the urban fringe). The urbanised area does not conform to any political boundaries but rather includes the physical extent of the city. The fourth level, and the one that figures most prominently in the empirical analysis of this book,[10] is the *standard metropolitan statistical area* (SMSA). Each SMSA contains at least one central city with 50,000 or more inhabitants or two cities having contiguous boundaries and constituting, for general economic and social purposes, a single community with a combined population of at least 50,000, the smaller of which must have a population of at least 15,000. To this nucleus is added the county in which the central city is located and adjacent counties that are metropolitan in character and economically and socially integrated with the county of the central city.[11] For a county to be defined as 'metropolitan' in character it must satisfy certain criteria: contain 10,000 non-agricultural workers, or 10 per cent of the non-agricultural workers of the SMSA, or at least 50 per cent of its population residing in areas with a population density of 150 or more per square mile and contiguous to the central city. In addition, non-agricultural workers must make up at least two-thirds of the total employment population of the county. The integration criteria are based on commuting (15 per cent of workers in the outlying county must work in the central-city county) and telephone communications (calls per month to central-city county at least four times that of the number of the subscribers in the outlying county). However, a SMSA may cross State lines. Since SMSAs are made up of whole counties they include non-urbanised parts of contiguous metropolitan counties. In some parts of the United States, particularly in the West, this means that SMSAs may contain large, sparsely populated tracts of land. This may distort interpretation of SMSA data for some purposes, but not to a great extent in city size analysis. The reason is that sparsely populated zones within SMSAs yield low scores on other variables that we may wish to correlate with population size (e.g. income, crime rates, externalities, etc.). The largest urban concept recognised in the United States is the *standard consolidated area* consisting of several contiguous SMSAs, i.e. New York/north-eastern New Jersey and Chicago/north-western Indiana.[12]

There have been other suggestions for delimitation. Following upon the research of Fox (e.g. Fox and Kumar, 1965) into the concept of *functional economic areas*, based upon several criteria but especially urban labour market commuting areas, the US Bureau of the Census have explored the possibility of urban areas based upon labour markets. This involved delimiting FEAs for all counties containing central cities greater than 50,000, with the main criterion for allocation of a county to a FEA being that the proportion of resident workers commuting to a given central county should exceed the proportion to any other central county. Where marked cross-commuting occurs[13] between FEAs it was suggested that these might be merged to form consolidated urban regions (CURs). These criteria enable almost 96 per cent of the US population to be assigned to urban regions.

Another possibility, implicitly favoured by Mills (1972c), is based on the idea that the distinctive feature of an urban area is its higher population density than elsewhere.[14] This suggests that the density gradient might be used as a method of delimiting cities in that the boundary may be drawn where the height of the gradient approximates to rural densities. Though useful from a conceptual point of view, this approach has serious practical limitations. First, in some densely populated urbanised regions there may be no true measure of rural density, though the extent of urbanisation is unlikely to be so continuous as to justify the designation of the whole region as one urban area. Second, the urban area defined in population density terms will not conform to the urban area definition that forms the data base. Urban empirical analysis invariably demands compromise with theoretical ideals. Despite these drawbacks, urban population densities are a useful measure. Since many externalities, both positive and negative, are associated with spatial concentration, there is a good case for arguing that urban densities are at least as relevant a variable as city size.[15]

A potential solution to the data problems arising from defining sensible urban areas for operational purposes is reform of national data collection systems. A common suggestion (Hägerstrand, 1968) is to collect data for spatial units consisting of small squares (standard quadrat units) each of which can form a building block that can be used for virtually any kind of areal configuration. In the United Kingdom the General Register Office is making small area (grid square) statistics available for the first time in the 1971 Census, though subject to limitations imposed by disclosure rules.

As far as this book is concerned, it has been necessary to measure city size in terms of data availability. This means that most of the US analysis refers to SMSAs rather than to urbanised areas. City size is not measured as central city population unless expressly stated. Empirical analysis on British data has to be based on local authority areas which do not correspond to economic definitions of urban areas. These strictures may blur interpretation but are unavoidable.

Is city size an intervening variable?

A question which must be asked is whether city size is a true independent variable when we examine the relationships between certain economic and social phenomena and city size. For instance, the observed association between crime and city size in the United States *might* obscure a stronger relationship between crime and race with the concentration of blacks in big cities being explained by factors other than the size of these cities. Similarly, the tendency for incomes to be higher in big cities might be due to an association between income and industrial structure where an economic structure favouring high incomes develops in big cities for reasons not directly connected with their size. On the other hand, in this particular case it is probable that the economic structure of large cities reflects to some degree the market potential of the city (which is a function of metropolitan population weighted by income) so that city size *per se* could be important after all.

This problem is not peculiar to this topic alone. It is related to the familiar identification and specification problems that plague many empirical, particularly econometric, applications in the social sciences. To a degree the problem may be handled by feeding all the relevant variables into a multiple regression analysis and allowing significance tests to isolate the key factors, but in many practical cases (such as those described in the previous paragraph) this simple procedure may be invalidated by high intercorrelation among the independent variables. The methods of getting round this difficulty are only partially successful. Nevertheless, this type of approach may reveal more, and certainly will obscure less, than the bivariate analyses favoured in many city size discussions.

The upshot of these observations is that city size may in at least some cases be what is called an *intervening variable* that forms a statistical link between one variable and another and may stand as a surrogate for one of them but is not the real independent variable itself. If this were so, it could mean that an analysis of the economics of city size could be littered with mis-specified problems and might cast doubt on the relevance of such an analysis as a valid exercise. This argument is not without merit, and despite the scope of this book I have some sympathy for it. However, there are some economic phenomena which are a direct function of city size itself (e.g. urban services with a critical population threshold). Also, and perhaps more important, the emphasis on city size has been brought into the forum of academic and public debate by planners, social scientists and national urban policy makers. Discussion of the problem of city size is necessary if the claims of those who recommend a city size control policy are to be scrutinised. The alternative is to let these claims pass by default. As it happens, such a scrutiny may well reveal that in many cases the intervening variable thesis is justified. In some instances city size analysis only seems to work because city size is a surrogate for city population density; the obvious example is where externalities are a function of spatial concentration rather than of urban scale. Another problem that is of some relevance here is that city size is a static concept yet may reflect dynamic influences to the extent that it is a surrogate for past growth.[16] Similarly, city size fails to reflect space as well as time. Yet the influence of the size of a city is very much affected by its location in space. For instance, a suburb of 150,000 fifteen miles from a million-plus metropolis can hardly be compared with a central place of the same size located in the heart of a large rural region.

These considerations stress the serious difficulties in interpreting the influence of city size. It is hard to avoid the conclusion that those who have prescribed city size control strategies have done so on the basis of implicit value judgements and casual (and frequently biased) empiricism. Despite the major role of value judgements in the literature on city size, a role which is to some extent made inevitable by the nature of the problem, there is some scope for a more detached approach to its theoretical and empirical aspects. In Duncan's (1956) words: 'The problem of optimum city size originates in the realm of values and, ideally, eventuates in action. Only the middle term of the translation of values into action is open to scientific procedures, for the choice of values and the decision to act are intrinsically beyond the scope of science. Nevertheless, both valuation and action should profit from an occasional summing up of the evidence and its implications.' This is the ultimate justification for this book.

Notes

[1] In 1850 there were only 4 cities of one million plus, by 1900 19, but by 1960 there were 141.

[2] See Regional Plan Association (1967).

[3] This view has been expressed most forcibly by Mumford (1961, especially p. 242). Some planners share the same opinion, e.g. Osborn and Whittick (1969).

[4] It is quite astonishing that distinguished scientists should associate themselves with such an unscientific and, indeed, rather silly, tract.

[5] I define a pessimist in this context as someone who believes that very large cities generate negative net social benefits.

[6] This is not to imply that empirical testing of the economic hypotheses is easy. As we shall see, the data constraints are very severe.

[7] For instance, there are several cases where the ratio is higher than 80 per cent and others where it is below 25 per cent. See *Statistical Abstract of the United States, 1971*, Section 33.

[8] The modifications and consolidations of the local government reorganisation scheme do not alter this conclusion.

[9] A minimum of 10,000 population is defined as urban in Switzerland and Spain, but 250 persons count as urban in Denmark.

[10] The reliance on the SMSA concept merely reflects data availability *not* an assumption that it is a more relevant economic unit than the urbanised area.

[11] In New England the units comprising the area are towns rather than counties.

[12] The common concept of megalopolis, frequently applied to the cities of the Atlantic seaboard, is unofficial.

[13] This is defined as when at least 5 per cent of the resident workers in one FEA commute to the central counties of another.

[14] It is interesting that in the United States the average density of urbanised areas is about ten times as great as that of SMSAs.

[15] See pp. 132-5

[16] See Alonso (1972, p. 15): 'Our present theories and rhetoric deal primarily with size. This derives on the theoretical side from the static equilibrium bias of most social science, and on the rhetoric side from the traditional utopianism of ideal size. But size and growth must be distinguished.'

2 The Theory of City Size

The theory of optimal city size

A conceivable approach to the theory of city size is to examine how costs
and benefits vary with city size. This may help us to derive an optimal city
size where marginal benefits equal marginal costs. To play this game,
however, requires some cavalier assumptions. Among these we might mention: measurement of city size in terms of urban population; aggregation of
non-additive benefits, e.g. externalities in consumption and agglomeration
economies for business; neglect of the importance of spatial variables in
urban efficiency; the assumption of identity of interests of all citizens;
and a static framework abstracting from shifts in production functions and
changes in consumer tastes and preferences. Even with assumptions of this
kind, however, the models have to be crude since our degree of ignorance
is so great that we cannot even be sure about the shape of cost and benefit
functions. For this reason, there is little point in precise mathematical
models, and the use of simple diagrams is appropriate.[1]

A fairly typical set of benefit and cost curves is shown in Fig. 2.1. Because
of the shortage of empirical evidence whether the curves shown are of a

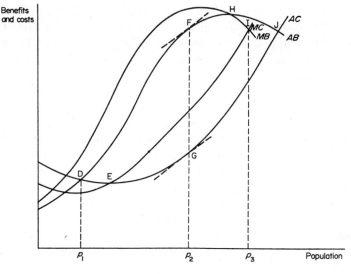

Figure 2.1

11

reasonable shape is a matter of conjecture. It might be possible, for instance, to have gently upward sloping cost curves combined with benefit curves which never turned down (or at least did not turn down within the range covered by existing cities), and on these assumptions there would not be any optimal city size at all. However, most urban analysts might be reasonably satisfied with the curves of Fig. 2.1; a U-shaped cost curve with minimum cost at a relatively low population level and a S-shaped benefit curve where benefits *per capita*, though initially increasing faster than city size, soon rise at a diminishing rate and eventually turn downwards.

To derive any conclusions we have to assume that all items of costs and benefits (monetary and non-monetary) can be added together and that they face decision makers with uniform preferences. Perhaps the easiest way to conceptualise this is to consider the costs and benefits facing the individual prospective migrant. Costs will include items such as rent and other costs of living, taxes for service provision, commuting costs, psychic costs of noise and other forms of congestion, the risk of damage from air pollution, and all other costs associated with city size. Benefits include not only incomes, but the benefits of scale economies in the provision of public goods, external economies of consumption (e.g. shopping, theatres, sports and leisure opportunities, access to hire purchase facilities), and the increased opportunities for interaction compared with a smaller urban place. For simplification, let us consider the individual city in isolation from a wider urban system.[2]

There are several city sizes of interest in Fig. 2.1. Not all of these are optima, and even those which are optimal are so only from a particular point of view; the concept of an unambiguous optimum is, in fact, false. To examine the critical city sizes from left to right, the point D ($AB=AC$; AB rising, AC falling) represents the minimum city size p_1. Below a population of this size the city is not viable. Even if we had a large sample of cities each with its own cost and benefit curves we would expect D to cluster around the same population level to reflect the fact that in a specific institutional environment and at a given level of technology there tends to be a minimum urban population size required to perform urban functions efficiently. This is not the same as the least cost city size (represented by the point E). There has been so much emphasis in the literature on the variation of costs with city size that the population level corresponding to E is frequently labelled an optimum. Assuming that there are some benefits of urban scale (confirmed both by detailed empirical evidence, e.g. higher incomes, and casual observation), this is clearly wrong. Net returns to urban scale (benefits costs) can almost always be increased by expanding cities beyond the least cost level.

The population level p_2 is more critical, because this represents the city size which maximises net benefits *per capita* $(AB-AC)$, i.e. the point where the tangent to AB (at F) is parallel to the tangent to AC(at G). Beyond p_2 the citizens have a vested interest in keeping out migrants. However, it does not necessarily follow that the whole of the net benefit $(AB-AC)$ accrues to the individual resident. If there is competition for urban locations, e.g. if the supply of land is inelastic and migration is very elastic in respect to net benefits, part of the difference between AB and AC may be absorbed in surplus rent. Although this could be represented by an upward shift in the cost function, it is perhaps easier to conceive as an additional payment out of the net returns to urban living to monopolists who hold the control of the one necessary prerequisite for access to urban life, i.e. an urban location. The degree of competition in the land market will determine how much of the net benefit the individual is allowed to retain.

The next city size of some interest is found at H. Here gross average benefits are at a maximum. As in the least cost case, this is not an optimum and to treat the maximum *gross* benefits value as having any special significance is to take a view of the urban economy as one-sided as that which concentrates solely on costs to the exclusion of benefits. The point I is much more important. Here the urban population level, p_3, is at its optimum from a social planning point of view, assuming that the opportunity costs of locating the marginal increments of population below p_3 are zero. At p_3 the total net benefits generated by the city are maximised. However, there is no guarantee that p_3 will be achieved automatically via the operation of market forces. The costs and benefits percieved by the potential migrant will be average rather than marginal, and migrants will continue to be attracted into the city so long as $AB > AC$. If the urban land market is purely competitive (so that no surplus rents accrue to landlords), market equilibrium will be attained at J where $AB = AC$. However, not only is each citizen worse off than if the urban population were p_3 but also the total net benefits corresponding to J are less than at I (the maximum level). Moreover, beyond I the marginal cost and benefit curves diverge rapidly so that the costs of non-intervention are very high. Given the difficulties in the way of pricing urban goods and services at marginal social cost and the degree of ignorance about the behaviour of the marginal benefits curve (particularly at high population levels), this analysis represents the case for the familiar argument that unconstrained market forces result in big cities becoming too big. However, it should be noticed that the analysis depends upon the assumptions made about the shapes of the cost and benefit curves, and in particular upon the hypothesis that there is some relevant city size where the MC curve cuts the MB curve from below. Without this assumption the analysis would fall to the ground.

The relevance of this model, therefore, depends upon empirical questions, and as we shall see the evidence is thin and unclear. Nevertheless, the hypothesis of a cross-over point is not unreasonable, though some might argue that the city size corresponding to this point has not yet been reached anywhere in the world. A more worrying feature of the model is whether or not it makes sense in theory. Is urban population a good proxy for city size, and if so how can it be defined unambiguously? Do cost and benefit curves of this kind have any operational value in view of the facts that they aggregate non-pecuniary variables with monetary values and that the curves facing firms would differ from those facing householders (not to mention differences between groups of households according to income, occupation or social class)? How can we identify the cost and benefit curves in a dynamic world in which technology and tastes are more or less continuously changing? Does the concept of city size have any meaning in an urban system where polinucleated and megalopolitan structures are more common than the monocentric city surrounded by a rural hinterland? In other words, does the introduction of space negate the value of this kind of analysis; for instance, urban densities may be more important than population size and optimal size may be a function of location (i.e. proximity to both larger and smaller centres)? To what extent is political decentralisation possible, and does not the feasibility of this destroy the logic of a city size restriction policy since any large city can be broken down into a family of smaller, linked cities? Is an analysis based on uniform cost and benefit functions facing a representative household misconceived in that it abstracts from the fundamental distributional questions raised by urban growth? Does the individual city model represent a myopic view which underplays the systemic functions of cities and detracts from exploring the more interesting problem of how to distribute total population efficiently over the national urban hierarchy as a whole? The answers to these questions will not be considered here. Some are discussed elsewhere,[3] and in any event many of the answers are self-evident. What is clear is that once these issues have been raised the value of the type of model summed up in Fig. 2.1 is much more restricted than it appears at first sight.

Externalities and city size

One of the most influential studies in the theory of city size is a somewhat fugitive paper by George Tolley (1969). The framework of his analysis is simple general equilibrium theory in which the total economy is conceived as a system of interdependent cities linked by commodity and factor flows. To facilitate the analysis, this system is reduced to two 'regions' – one city (City A) and the rest of the economy represented as some kind of average of all other cities. His model is derived from two sub-models. First, he develops a theory of interurban money (and real) wage differentials where these differentials reflect the presence of externalities, and in which people move in response to wage differentials. Second, he explains the association between externalities and city size on the assumption that there are increasing negative externalities due to pollution and congestion, and that these negative externalities are an increasing function of city size. He then brings the two elements together to show that in a situation where no action is taken to tax externalities interurban migration will result in a situation where big cities are too big.

The wage model stresses the interdependence between wages and prices. If wages are higher in one city than another, production costs will also be higher and this fact is likely to make for higher prices. These higher prices reinforce the higher wage level, since living costs increase thereby raising the wage necessary to attract labour. It is also assumed that the scope for a cost effect of wages on prices is greater for local commodities (non-traded goods)[4] than for goods traded between cities, on the grounds that the latter are produced under more competitive conditions. In addition, the presence of negative externalities will also raise costs and have an impact upon wages. These factors explain why wages differ between cities, but at the same time workers will move between cities in response to these differentials thereby tending to eliminate them. Under certain assumptions equilibrium is attained when real wages are at the same level in each city. However, there may be non-pecuniary benefits and costs attached to living in particular places, and Tolley does allow for a component to reflect 'the amount of money people are willing to take to live in one place as opposed to another after correcting for pricing differences between places'. This implies that the presence of workers in some cities earning less in real terms than elsewhere does not necessarily indicate suboptimality. Also, apart from their effects on money costs negative externalities may push up wages because workers in cities suffering from these externalities may demand more income in the form of 'compensation payments'. The hypothesis that higher wages in large cities primarily reflect compensation payments has been examined at some length by Hoch (1972).

The relationship between externalities and city size can be most easily illustrated by reference to Fig. 2.2 where City A (assumed to be a large city) is compared to the rest of the economy, whose marginal product curves are drawn on the assumption that they are the averages of marginal products for cities of different size. If there are increasing negative externalities with city size due to pollution and congestion, then the vertical difference between the *MPP* (marginal private product) and *MSP* (marginal social product) curves will increase as employment in City A expands. Also, the marginal

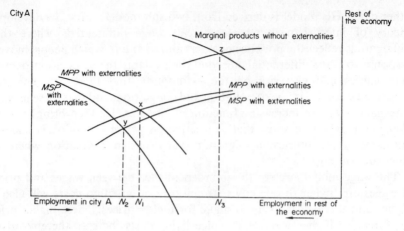

Figure 2.2

product curves in City A will fall off rather steeply. As far as the rest of the economy is concerned, however, since this includes small as well as large cities, the slopes of the marginal product curves will be flatter and the vertical difference between *MPP* and *MSP* will increase only slightly as employment in the rest of the economy expands. The reason for this is that negative externalities are weaker in the rest of the economy than in City A.

In the absence of intervention and assuming the mobility of labour in response to wage differentials, the equilibrium solution will be obtained at x where the marginal private products are equalised, and employment in City A equals N_1. However, this means that City A is much too large, given the presence of negative externalities. The benefit of locating the marginal project at a location other than City A can be expressed as $(MPP - MSP)$ in City A minus $(MPP - MSP)$ in the rest of the economy. It is, therefore, possible to improve the allocation of resources by switching factors from employment in City A to the rest of the economy. If wage levels were related to marginal social rather than private products total social product would be maximised at y (where employment in City A is N_2). A policy of wage taxes and subsidies to bring interurban wage levels into line with marginal social products would, therefore, lead to a better allocation of resources and reduce the size of large cities (such as City A).

However, the wage tax-subsidy solution still leaves the negative externalities intact. A more radical – and more efficient – solution would be to take action to eliminate those externalities altogether. This might be done by legislation, decree or (perhaps more efficiently) by taxation. The idea would be to impose a tax (e.g. a pollution or congestion tax) on the activities of firms that shift unfavourably the production functions of other firms. An

16

optimum tax would result in a situation where the marginal social and private product curves coincide. The curves for City A shift upwards more than for the rest of the economy because of the assumption that externalities are greater in City A. This means a new equilibrium z where City A is, in fact, larger than when externalities were present (employment in City A equals N_3). The imposition of pollution and congestion charges raises costs, but the situation shown in Fig. 2.2 implies that these higher costs are more, than offset by shifts in production functions.

This analysis suggests the possibility that measures to eliminate externalities would lead to big cities becoming bigger, and that this would be economically beneficial. 'Large cities would have cleaner air and low rent gradients, and money wages would not be as high relative to wages in smaller cities as now. More manufacturers of labour-intensive transportable goods would locate in big cities instead of being driven to places of lower wages as they are at present' (Tolley, p. 32). Also, the gains from eliminating externalities accrue locally as well as nationally, so that there is an incentive for local measures to combat them. The failure to take such action could be due to ignorance, conflicts of interest and administrative difficulties in the way of imposing new types of charges.

The main drawback of Tolley's model is that its prediction, that in the absence of intervention big cities are too big, depends vitally on the model's assumptions, and in particular on the assumption that all externalities are negative and are an increasing function of city size. Although this is later qualified since it is stated that there are 'gains from spatial reallocation as long as there are differences in external effects *of any kind* among cities' (my italics; *ibid*, p. 38), a superficial reading of the analysis appears to give strong ammunition to the 'optimal city size' protagonists. However, there is no specific mention of the positive externalities of increasing city size. These are less obvious and even more difficult to measure. The crucial question is whether *net* externalities are positive or negative and how these vary with city size. Even if pollution and congestion increase with city size, net externalities may nevertheless be positive and if this were the case market equilibrium would lead to big cities being too small rather than too big. This complex question can only be resolved empirically. Tolley's model can cover the general case, but the tone and bias of his analysis is insufficiently supported by the facts.

An aggregate agglomeration economy – congestion cost function?

If it were possible to measure all external economies and diseconomies of scale, and in a way which enables the values of each to be aggregated, we

17

could derive a *net* agglomeration economies index $A=(\Sigma E-\Sigma D)$ where A=net economies, and E and D represent economies and diseconomies. The impact of city size on net agglomeration economies could then be measured by examining the relationship between A and a city size variable. The most common size measure would be SMSA or city population, but it is arguable that a more appropriate choice might be population potential or density. For example, population density may be a more precise size measure than urban population in the analysis of certain individual economies and diseconomies such as traffic congestion.[5]

Following an idea of Baumol's (1967), an initial hypothesis might be

$$A=k \cdot P^2 \qquad (2.1)$$

where k=constant and P=city size. Baumol suggested this in relation to an individual external diseconomy such as air pollution or road congestion, but the idea can be generalised to refer to all externalities, both positive and negative. Its rationale is that if each action imposes external costs or benefits on every other, and if the scale of costs borne (or benefits gained) by each individual is roughly proportional to city size then, because the costs (benefits) apply to each individual, the total external costs (benefits) will vary in proportion to P^2. Equation (2.1) extends this theory to apply to aggregate *net* externalities.

This model is rather too restrictive. The assumption that external costs and benefits are proportional to city size is too arbitrary. The aggregation of separate externalities implies that either net economies *or* diseconomies must always predominate regardless of city size if the proportionality between A and P^2 is to hold. A more satisfactory *a priori* hypothesis would be that total *net* external economies tend to be positive up to some critical city size (which may or may not have been reached in the real world) and then become negative.[6] If the agglomeration function is capable of measuring both economies and diseconomies the relationship must be non-linear. It is also unnecessarily restrictive to assume that the square of the population determines externalities.

There are two obvious ways of generalising this framework. First, the exponent may be treated as a parameter which is itself a function of city size and the strict proportionality assumption may be dropped, i.e.

$$A=f(P^\alpha) \qquad (2.2)$$

where

$$\alpha=f(P) \qquad (2.3)$$

For net external economies to become negative at some high level of city size, the slope of the function described by eqn. (2.3), $d\alpha/dP$, must eventually become negative. Second, a possibly superior formulation is to make the function an inverted U as described by a quadratic, i.e.

$$A=f(b_1 P-b_2 P^2) \qquad (2.4)$$

Although both these approaches are more satisfactory theoretically, they

18

remain very difficult to operationalise. The problem is: can we measure A? By their very nature, externalities cannot be assigned direct monetary values on the basis of market prices since they, for the most part, fall outside the scope of the price mechanism. Even if an approximate value could be placed on each individual externality, it is not certain that they can be aggregated together. They may be interdependent rather than independent so that simple aggregation may give a misleading result. Moreover, the distributional incidence of each economy and diseconomy may vary so widely that crude aggregation is nonsense (this is a direct attack on the validity of the concept of optimal city size).

The most fruitful approach from the point of view of operational analysis would be to find some residual variable which captures both the costs and benefits of agglomeration. Edel (1972) has argued that economies of agglomeration and diseconomies of congestion are capitalised in land values. Thus, the change in land values with city size gives some indication of the net benefits of living in cities of a particular size. The elasticity of land values with respect to changes in city size tends to decline as city size increases, falling below unity between the 250,000–500,000 level, declining sharply up to the million mark, but then returning to above unity in cities larger than three million. Land values *per capita* thus peak about the 300,000 level apart from in the very large cities where Edel argues that corporate and hierarchical managerial functions sustain the increase in land values. The latter fact does not generate net social benefits because heavy congestion costs are incurred for the maintenance of the hierarchy while the benefits of large size are distributed regressively.[7]

Whereas Edel's analysis lends itself too readily to pursuit of the optimal city size myth[8] and his disposal of the 'net benefits of large cities' case is unconvincing, his suggestion that land values *per capita* may represent a measure of the net average effect of agglomeration economies and congestion costs is ingenious. It is also useful in that it permits the relationship between A and P to be tested rather than left in the limbo of empty theory. Assuming that households and firms perceive economies of agglomeration and congestion costs correctly, then competition for urban land in cities of different size should lead to these economies and diseconomies being reflected in land values. On the other hand, if it is impossible for individual actors to appraise these benefits and costs or if they underestimate them because of undervaluation of external effects, or again if monopolistic elements are strong in the urban land market, then the analysis loses much of its force. Despite the heroic assumptions and the qualifications, the problem deserves further research.

Notes

¹ For similar treatments see Edel (1972), Barr (1972), von Böventer (1970), Alonso (1971a) and Smith (1970). The slightly different version of Tolley (1969) is discussed separately and specifically; see pp. 14–17.

² This assumption is clearly unrealistic. Firms and migrants face many alternative opportunities when they decide where to locate, and the cost and benefit curves will vary from city to city. Particularly from the point of view of national planners, the $MB=MC$ criterion should be modified to include the opportunity costs of locating increments to population and new firms in other, more attractive cities. Another way of dealing with this is to make the benefit and cost curves net of alternatives. In terms of Fig. 2.1 this would imply that all curves shift downwards to the right (probably intercepting the horizontal axis).

³ See below, pp. 120–131.

⁴ Wages must be raised by the multiplier $1/(1-w_s S)$, where w_s=share of wages in nontraded goods production and S=share of total expenditures devoted to nontraded goods, to compensate for the higher costs of nontraded goods due to higher wages.

⁵ Of course, population, population potential and central city densities are all highly correlated with each other.

⁶ The jackpot question is where the turning point occurs. Neutze (1965) assumes that it occurs at a relatively low city size: 'If we could correct the imperfections of the price mechanism to compensate for external effects the result would probably be a less concentrated pattern of location.... Where there are external diseconomies from growth they appear to be more important in large centres, while external economies appear to be more important in small centres'. (p.27).

⁷ Edel (1972, p. 62) suggests that the principal use of land value measurement may be in the study of distribution rather than in the measurement of aggregate social welfare cost (either gross or net of positive agglomeration economies).

⁸ Lave (1970) has argued that equality of external economies and external diseconomies does not imply efficient resource allocation or, by extension, an optimal city size. Resource allocation may be improved (and city size altered) by subsidising the external economies and taxing the diseconomies.

3 Negative Externalities

The congestion cost model

It is argued that many of the negative externalities associated with city size derive from the heavy spatial concentration of population in large cities. According to this view, pollution, traffic congestion and strain on public service facilities are all manifestations of urban congestion (Rothenberg, 1970; Mills and de Ferranti, 1971). If this is the case a useful if simple approach to analysing this problem is via a congestion model first used to deal with traffic congestion but capable of being generalised (Walters, 1961 and 1968; Johnson, 1964).

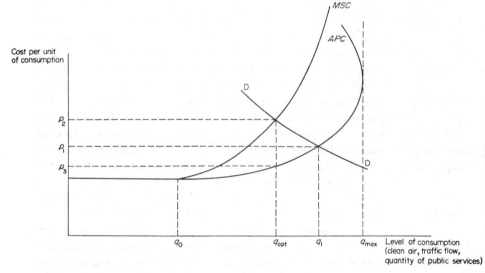

Figure 3.1

The model is illustrated in Fig. 3.1. It is expressed in traditional supply and demand terms, except that its special feature is the shape and interpretation of the supply curve. It is assumed that citizens pay only the average unit cost for the service in question (per unit of traffic flow, or of public service, or the unit of cost of achieving a volume of clean air), and that this meets the full cost of supply up to a certain level (q_0). Beyond q_0 congestion develops. Average costs rise which each individual perceives and bears.

However, he imposes costs on others; these he does not take into account. The costs which fall upon others are an external diseconomy of his action. They are represented by the more steeply rising marginal cost curve. This is merely a slight revamping of the elementary microeconomic axiom that if average costs are rising, marginal costs must be above them. In Fig. 3.1 the average costs curve represents private costs (hence it is labelled APC), while the marginal cost reflects the social costs (MSC). Beyond q_0 the true cost of achieving a particular level of service is greater than the cost actually borne by consumers. The other interesting feature of the APC curve is that it ultimately bends back (at q_{max}). An essential characteristic of the phenomena with which we are dealing (a transportation facility such as a road, an environmental medium such as the air above a city or its water supply, or a public service establishment such as a hospital) is that they have a *maximum* physical threshold beyond which congestion is so acute that the level of service supplied declines *absolutely* despite higher and higher average unit costs.

To complete the analysis we introduce a demand curve DD. The only restriction we need to impose on DD is that it slopes downward in the normal way, i.e. demand is an inverse function of price. In some circumstances (travel demand, demand for hospital treatment, etc.) demand may be a function of time-price as well as money-price. This could be important in a policy context since it suggests the possibility of an efficient pricing policy characterised by a mix of queuing and congestion tolls. The location of the demand curve reflects the influence of city size. If it is too far over to the right so that it does not intersect the supply curve at all the city is too big and/or the capacity of the facility too small; an outward shift in the supply curve via an expansion in capacity is needed. If the DD curve is located far to the left so that it intersects the horizontal section of the supply curve there are no congestion costs at all. The equilibrium is efficient from the point of view of the individual city though not from that of the urban system as a whole if there are congestion costs in other cities. However, in normal circumstances there is a mutual adjustment between demand and capacity over time so that the demand and supply curves intersect in the rising section of the APC curve. If DD intersects the backward bending portion of the APC curve it is always possible to achieve the same level of service at a lower cost by inducing a downward shift in the demand curve so that it intersects on the positive slope of APC via imposition of a congestion levy.

The standard case occurs when DD crosses APC on its positive slope, as in Fig. 3.1 where private market decisions result in an equilibrium level of consumption q_1 and consumers pay the average cost of supply, p_1. However, this involves substantial congestion costs due to external diseconomies which are not taken into account by individual decision makers. The true social

22

equilibrium will be achieved at q_{opt} where the appropriate supply price is p_2. To achieve this it is necessary to choke off some of the demand by rationing the use of the facility. The appropriate theoretical solution is to impose a congestion toll, $(p_2 - p_3)$, equal to the external diseconomy at the socially efficient equilibrium. This reduces use of the facility by the amount $(q_1 - q_{opt})$, and each consumer then pays the true cost per unit of consumption, i.e. $APC+$the congestion levy.

The use of a model of this kind has several implications. First, it depends upon the validity of the assumption that social costs are an increasing function of city size and/or density.[1] For instance, to take pollution, it is necessary to assume 'that the damage per resident of an urban area from health, aesthetic and other effects of pollution is an increasing function of the number and density of people in the urban area' (Mills and de Ferranti, 1971, p. 341). Some evidence on this question is presented elsewhere (pp. 30–5), but many other factors, e.g. industrial structure and climate, influence the level of pollution besides city size. Nevertheless, most forms of pollution become a problem only under conditions of a high degree of spatial concentration. The equivalent assumption in urban transportation is perhaps more difficult to uphold, since there are many determinants of traffic congestion apart from city size. It is essential, for example, to distinguish between congestion resulting from general density of traffic and that due to network bottlenecks (Vickrey, 1969). Although the latter are obviously influenced by the through-flow of vehicles they are primarily explained by deficiencies in the design of the transport system. Even more important, the congestion model assumes that the automobile is the universal transport mode. Big cities have an increasing advantage in the supply of public transit facilities (in the United States over a third of trips are by public transport in the multi-million city size class as compared with less than 2 per cent in towns below 25,000; Schnore, 1963) and offer a wider choice of transport facilities so that transfer between modes may mitigate the effects of congestion. On the whole, however, these qualifications do not alter the substance and general validity of the model.

There is a difference between knowing that congestion and pollution costs are an increasing function of city size and being able to identify and trace the precise path of the function. It might be argued that the congestion model is non-operational because we cannot estimate marginal social costs. Reasonable attempts have been made in respect to traffic congestion since congestion reveals itself in ways easy to measure such as time spent in traffic delays. Conversion to monetary values is rather more controversial because of the dispute about the valuation of travel time. But congestion costs in other areas, e.g. air pollution, are far harder to measure. Again, we have some idea what to look for: damage to health and effects on mortality, corrosion costs and cleaning expenses, and disturbance to amenity. But separating out what is due to air pollution and what is the result of other variables, and then converting to a common monetary measure, are in this case virtually intractable problems. It is for these reasons that Baumol and Oates (1971) argues that it is impossible to set optimal pollution taxes, and instead suggest that charges should be fixed that achieve specific environmental acceptability standards and that the latter should be determined via the political process.

A more radical extension of the same argument has been developed by Buchanan (1969). He draws a distinction between costs objectively measured and costs that influence choice. The analyst may make an objective measure of costs on the basis of resources used, time and so on, but this measure is not the same as that which influences choice. Costs which influence choice are able to modify behaviour only at the moment of choice. These costs are determined subjectively. They are never realised and they cannot be measured after the fact. Buchanan argues that this distinction invalidates the meaning and utility of the Pigovian allocative criterion that marginal private and social costs should be equated and its policy implication that a levy should be imposed to modify the behaviour of the individual decision maker so as to achieve 'efficiency': 'This Pigovian framework provides us with perhaps the best single example of confusion between classically-derived objective cost concepts and the subjective costs concepts that influence individual choice' (Buchanan, 1969, p. 71). To estimate the level of the corrective tax the external costs would have to be measured objectively. But this is impossible: 'Since the persons who bear these "costs" – those who are externally affected – do not participate in the choice that generates the "costs", there is simply no means of determining, even indirectly, the value that they place on the utility losses that might be avoided' (*ibid.*, p. 72). In regard to air pollution, for instance, clean air may be defined physically. It is also possible to estimate the outlays needed to clean up the air. But this is by no means an estimate of pollution damage. Such an estimate cannot be made because clean air cannot be exchanged or traded between people in a market.[2] The costs of foul air can be assessed only by those bearing the costs and when confronted by a choice.

Another problem with the congestion model is that there are doubts about the accuracy and relevance of the explicit assumption that private decision makers in a market-oriented urban economy pay only the average and not the marginal costs of congestion and the implicit assumption that those affected by external diseconomies are helpless and can do nothing but bear them. The compensating payments hypothesis (see pp. 15,48–9), on the contrary, implies that individuals subjected to pollution, long journeys to work, noise and other external diseconomies will demand and get higher wages to compensate them. Thus, higher wages are necessary in large cities to attract migrants and to keep them there. To the extent that these are due to external diseconomies, some of the latter are being passed back to employers in the form of higher labour costs which have some influence on location decisions. In other words, although the diseconomies may be external to the individual, firm or activity generating them, they are internal to the urban economy as a whole and they do fall upon firms (and households) whose decisions influence city size (Hoover, 1971).

The congestion model is, of course, incomplete because offsetting economies of agglomeration are ignored. It is impossible, therefore, within the framework of this model to know whether or not congestion costs are offset by agglomeration economies. An exact offset would occur only by chance. Even so, equality of external diseconomies and economies does not imply efficient resource allocation. For example, in a situation where economies of agglomeration still existed but where there were substantial congestion costs, the appropriate solution would be to subsidise immigration and simultaneously to impose congestion tolls to reduce traffic congestion. Both taxes and subsidies would have to be levied separately to achieve efficient resource allocation (Lave, 1970).

Even if marginal social costs could be measured, the optimal corrective tax prescription is not the sole solution. Johnson (1964) suggested a combination of both time and money taxes as an efficient and feasible method of controlling congestion. Smolensky, Tideman and Nichols (1971) supported this strategy even more strongly. They point out that queues function in certain competitive markets in the private sector despite the existence of prices, and that this fact suggests that queues may be consistent with efficiency in both the private and public sectors. Queues or time charges have the special advantage that they discriminate among consumers because the valuation of time differs according to income. Time charges are attractive from an equity point of view because time is more equally distributed than money. Money charges retain a role but not as a punishment to those who generate negative externalities but to widen consumer choice. Combinations of money charges and constant time charges (equivalent to variable money charges) offer more choice to consumers, and in particular the queues ration users with a high opportunity cost of time, shifting them to less time-consuming substitutes with a higher money cost: 'the private sector accommodates queuing as a part of a process of product differentiation so as to respond efficiently to the fact that the opportunity cost of time varies among consumers' (Smolensky et al., p. 45). The argument is that there is a lesson here for the public sector and for the treatment of congestion costs.

In terms of the model outlined in Fig. 3.1, there are other methods of

25

dealing with the divergence between the *APC* and *MSC* curves apart from pricing strategies. These solutions are capable, in theory, of getting rid of congestion altogether, unlike the pricing strategy case where some congestion (in the sense of rising *APC*) always remains. However, it is doubtful whether this feature of these alternative policies is an advantage since some degree of congestion is quite compatible with the efficient allocation of resources. The two main alternative strategies are reducing the size of the city (a left-ward shift in DD) and investment in more capacity for the congested facility[3] (an extension to the right in the horizontal section of *APC*).[4] Measures to reduce the size of the city, though quite consistent with the views propounded by optimal city size protagonists, would be utterly inappropriate in this case. If population were the only flexible variable in the congestion problem, and if there were no offsetting economies of agglomeration, a smaller city size would relieve the congestion. But neither of these conditions holds, and employing instruments to control city size is to use a sledgehammer to crack a nut (admittedly, quite a big nut). In any event, except in the case of small towns, urban population size is very 'sticky' downwards. It is doubtful whether in a mixed economy there are instruments available to reduce city size to the levels needed to eliminate (or even markedly improve) congestion. Also, the congestion–city size relationship is not so clearly defined as such a strategy might suggest, and our knowledge of the shape and location of the congestion function too imperfect for fine-tuning of the demand curve via changing city size. Although this last argument applies to pricing strategies as well, the reversibility of congestion levies gives the policy maker scope for experiment which is denied to city size adjustment policies.

The investment in new capacity strategy is a much more sensible solution, and in a dynamic framework a mix of congestion levies and public investment in expanding capacity may be included in the optimal solution. However, investment of this kind (extending a public transit system, building more urban motorways, pollution abatement equipment, new hospitals, etc.) is expensive, and in a world of resource scarcity it will be the exception rather than the rule for facilities to be expanded so much that the horizontal section of *APC* cuts the demand curve. The question arises of how much investment should be undertaken. Whatever criterion is chosen it will be necessary to have some estimate of the gains achieved via the reduction in social costs. A specific expansion in a facility (e.g. an indivisible extension to a public transit system) may be assessed as an individual project via use of traditional cost-benefit techniques. The more general criterion, however, is not to predetermine the scale of the investment but, once we have calculated the potential gains of investment increments from social cost reductions, to use the opportunity costs of investment resources in order to equate the

26

marginal social costs of investment with its marginal social benefits. How broadly opportunity costs are defined depends upon the level at which the policy decision is taken and upon how transportable the resources are. However, Tolley (1969) and others have argued that there are gains to the metropolitan community from adopting such a strategy locally.

Finally, it cannot be specified beforehand whether this type of strategy for dealing with congestion will result in a greater, smaller or the same city size. Investment in new capacity will in many cases embody a degree of technical change so that the *APC* curve not only shifts outwards but slopes upwards more gently. In such cases, therefore, it will involve not only an expansion in capacity but a measure of control over external diseconomies. The net impact on city size depends upon the parameters of the model, and in particular on how the demand curve adjusts to the changes in supply conditions. This feedback effect of expansion of supply on demand is particularly marked with respect to improvements in the road system. In many circumstances, the equilibrium city size will be larger rather than smaller. Whether, after all the adjustments have occurred, there is a net improvement in allocative efficiency depends upon how the curves shift. Hopefully, there will be an improvement – after all, this is the objective of the strategy, but the results cannot easily be determined *a priori*.

Congestion costs and transportation expenditures

A commonplace in the city size literature is that traffic congestion is one of the major social costs generated in large cities. This is very plausible. It is well known that congestion can be regarded as an inverse function of speed (Walters, 1968), speed is inversely related to total vehicular flow (for a given road width), and flow can be expected to be a direct function of city size. Hence, congestion is positively associated with city size. Although this chain of reasoning is probably correct, the analysis is much more complicated and the evidence contradictory. For example, can the above hypothesis be squared with the empirical finding that the share of transportation expenditures in household consumption tends to *decline* with increasing city size (Clark, 1967, p. 369)? Another complication is that many models of residential location are based on a close degree of substitutability between housing and transportation expenditures (Richardson, 1971, pp. 18–28). If the unit cost of housing and transport varies with city size, and if the average distance between home and work also varies with city size, then transportation expenditures depend upon how household location decisions adjust to the relative prices of housing and transportation. Congestion costs and urban spatial structure are linked via a complex set of interdependencies

27

that can only be unravelled with the aid of a general equilibrium urban model (e.g. Mills, 1972c). Although the variations of housing and transportation costs with city size are discussed elsewhere as components in the urban cost of living (see pp. 54–60), it was decided that it was inconvenient, if not impossible, to include the valuation of travel time in the cost of living index. Since time delays are the main external effect of traffic congestion, this provides some justification for treating congestion and longer journeys to work as social costs. But the evidence for such costs is clearer for transport costs connected with firms than for households, since firms have either to bear the costs or move out of the city whereas households have other opportunities for adjustment (changing location of home, switching transport modes, changing jobs, etc.).

That large cities have the potential to generate heavy social costs of transportation is beyond doubt. Increasing city size will be associated with greater extent of the urban area and/or greater densities; the former means a longer journey to work (unless jobs decentralise as fast as homes) while the latter implies, *ceteris paribus*, increasing traffic congestion. Both survey data and computed estimates show that the mean distance from home to place of work increases with city size (Voorhees, 1966). Similarly, the radius of the CBD tends to be larger in bigger cities.[5] Also, the travel time involved in work trips increases regularly with city size (Voorhees, 1966; Morgan *et al.*, 1966). Even using a low valuation of travel time, the cost differential between adjacent city size classes in the United States due to this factor may be about 1 per cent of income (Hoch, 1972). Travel time increases faster than distance with city size because of the greater concentration of vehicles. The peak density of vehicles in the CBD is about 50 per cent greater in cities larger than 250,000 than in smaller cities. However, CBD traffic densities decline in some cities over the million mark. The reason is that economies of scale in public transportation make mass transit systems viable in large cities (Schnore, 1963; Clark, 1967, p. 366), and quality of service and incipient congestion switch some of the transportation demand away from private to public modes.[6] The road congestion effects of city size can be exaggerated; studies reported by Meyer, Kain and Wohl (1965, p. 452) showed that the peak hour corridor traffic was surprisingly low in large American cities (apart from New York). Also, the number of vehicles *per capita* entering the CBD declines strongly with increasing city size.

The other piece of evidence, perhaps the most puzzling of all, that conflicts with the 'more congestion in big cities' hypothesis is that on transportation expenditures. Their share in consumption declines with increasing city size (though expenditure on *public* transportation is higher in the larger cities), while the BLS cost of living data for the United States (see pp. 56–7, and Hoch, 1972) also show an inverse relationship between transport expenditures and city size. However, the latter can be explained partly by the nature of the BLS data. They refer to the money costs needed to attain a constant level of utility, and are consequently not an estimate of *actual* expenditures. On the other hand, they support the view that unit money costs of transport are lower in bigger cities. But they take no account of the value of travel time. Moreover, Hoch's (1972) regression results suggest that the inverse relationship between transport expenditures and city size was not statistically significant,[7] and the fit was rather poor.

If the money and time costs of commuting are higher in some cities than others, then these must be compensated for (if the cities are still to attract population) by higher wages and/or lower housing costs. We know that the former are higher in large cities. The trade-off models of residential location (between housing and transport costs) place reliance on the latter. Yet housing costs (both for rental and owner-occupied housing) are positively associated with city size (see pp. 56–9; Hoch, 1972). Does this imply that the brunt of the compensation for commuting costs must fall on higher wages? Although this seems to be the case at first glance, closer inspection reveals that this is not necessarily the case. If transport costs and rents are treated as joint costs, they increase with city size when taken together. Since incomes are higher in bigger cities and the income elasticity of demand for housing is positive, this permits higher levels of expenditure on housing with increasing city size. At the same time, the higher housing and lower transport costs will induce households to substitute longer journeys to work for dearer close-in housing (given the fact that house prices and rents decline with distance from the city centre). Thus, once it is remembered that the transport cost measures in relation to city size tend to ignore the travel time component, longer journeys to work, travel time and congestion are not incompatible with the finding that transport costs decline and housing costs rise with increasing city size. Comparing households receiving *the same level of income* in cities of different size, we would expect the household resident in the larger cities to consume less units of housing[8] and more of transportation, and therefore to live further out. This is consistent with the hypothesis that the elasticity of substitution between housing and transportation is fairly high.[9] It is not inconsistent with the observed tendency for transportation's share in consumption expenditure to fall with increasing city size, given that incomes are positively associated with city size, if the income elasticity of demand for transportation is relatively low.

To sum up this brief discussion of a very complex question, increasing city size probably does generate higher traffic congestion costs. However, this social cost is not as serious as it appears at first sight, except perhaps for non-residential businesses tied to the CBD. Mitigating factors include: a shift of transportation demand to public transit in very large cities; the opportunities for households to adjust their location to variations in housing and transportation costs[10]; and the fact that a worktrip cannot be regarded in isolation as pure disutility since it is one element in a complex residential choice which offers a variety of choices for work, education, leisure and amenities, housing environment and life style. Residence in a large city can easily involve a household in more and longer journeys, but many of these journeys are taken for pleasure and to widen the opportunities for living. To elevate the minimisation of transport costs to a guiding social principle would unduly narrow down and restrict the quality and variety of life. However, this argument is a qualification to not a denial of the social costs of traffic congestion. Finally, congestion costs rise rapidly as road use (demand) increases in relation to design capacity (supply). If congestion costs tend to be higher in bigger cities, this may not only indicate improper pricing of transportation services but also reflect chronic underinvestment in the capacity of the transportation system.[11]

Air pollution

Air pollution would seem to be a good illustration of the kind of external diseconomy positively associated with city size, and perhaps the most obvious example with the possible exception of traffic congestion. Air pollution is a long-standing external diseconomy familiar to nineteenth century cities, and long recognised as being due to spatial concentration.[12] The generation of pollutants is an increasing function of population size and density and of industrial concentration, and their effects on the quality of the air are cumulative and complex depending on the quantity and kind of pollutants emitted, the rate of dispersion of pollutants (which depends in turn upon their level and upon climatic conditions), and on chemical and physical reactions which change pollutants in the air. The adverse effects of air pollution include damage to health, disturbance to amenity – particularly visual disturbance, and direct economic costs such as medical costs, cleaning costs, and anti-corrosion and replacement expenditures. A major reason why the analysis of the effects of air pollution is complex is that different pollutants have differential effects under each of these headings.[13] Of the materials discharged into the atmosphere the five quantitatively important and most likely to have adverse effects on man, vegetation and materials are carbon monoxide, sulphur dioxide, hydrocarbons, nitrogen oxides and particulate matter. Motor vehicles, commonly regarded as the main scourge, generate almost all the carbon monoxide, two-thirds of the hydrocarbons and almost one half of the nitrogen oxides in the United States. Sulphur dioxide and particles arise primarily from the burning of coal and fuel oils.

Variations in the generation rate with city size differ considerably from one pollutant to another, and this is a further complicating factor. There is a general impression that air pollution has become appreciably worse in recent decades. This could easily be explained by the increasing use of motor vehicles, the growth of industrialisation and rapid urbanisation. Although the evidence does not support the deterioration hypothesis for the very recent past, the social costs of a given volume of pollutants are probably increasing as a consequence of wider public concern about pollution and a reduction in the minimum tolerance level associated with increasing affluence.

Regardless of the empirical findings on the relationship between air pollution and city size, it is clear that other determinants are very important. First, since what counts is not the volume of pollutants so much as their concentration, it is arguable that population density is more critical than city size, and that any correlation between size and pollution levels is largely due to the tendency for the biggest cities to be the most densely populated. The main defect in any average pollution level comparison with city size is that the average does not mean very much because of very wide local variations even within a small geographical area. Second, the tendency for pollution levels to be associated with urbanisation and higher in big cities can be obscured by factors such as climate (especially in a country of wide climatic variations such as the United States) and by industrial structure. 'Temperature, precipitation, air movement, wind direction, cloudiness, relationship between upper and lower strata of air and their relative temperature and moisture contents, as well as topographical obstacles to the movement of air – these are factors which influence the intensity of air pollution' (Kapp, 1963, p. 49). A particular problem is the role of 'thermal inversion' in preventing the dispersion of pollutants. The excess death rate in London in early December 1952 and to a lesser extent in early January 1956 was largely explained by the effects of severe fog and temperature inversion in retarding the dispersion rate of pollutants. Industrial structure effects can also be more important than city size influences. In Bedfordshire, although the county is not exceptionally urbanised or densely populated, there are heavy emissions of sulphur dioxide, smoke, fluorides and organic sulphur compounds largely due to the chain of brickworks between Bletchley and Bedford. In the United States, sulphur dioxide emissions are concentrated in a diagonal belt east of the Mississippi River. Much of the nation's industrial activity is concentrated there, and coal and fuel oils are the chief sources of energy.[14] Since both climate and industrial structure can be, to a large extent, subsumed under regional differences, this helps to explain a familiar finding that regional variations in air pollution tend to be wider than variations in city size.

Turning to the empirical evidence, and considering the United States first, the relationship between air pollutants and city size is obscure for the above reasons. There is some tendency for average levels of suspended particulate matter (smoke, dust and fumes particles and droplets of viscous liquid) to be higher in the larger cities. For instance, 10 out of 15 cities >700,000 had average levels in excess of 100 $\mu g/m^3$ (micrograms per cubic metre) as opposed to 57 out of the 171 smaller cities sampled. But 6 cities had concentrations greater than 180 $\mu g/m^3$, and none of these was in the million-plus size class. Also, the variations around the average are enormous, for example, the maximum concentration in the Atlantic region is about seven-and-a-half times the maximum concentration in the desert region. A more clear-cut finding is that the average level of suspended particulates in urban areas is about two-and-a-half times that in rural areas. There is no doubt that the distinction between urban and rural areas is much more obvious than within the city size distribution where the rankings of city size and particulate pollution levels deviate widely. Yet the association with city size is stronger for this type of pollutant compared to, say, ammonia or nitrogen dioxide where there are no signs of any relationship at all. Sulphur dioxide levels exhibit a more definite relationship, particularly because New York is ranked one and Chicago ranked two, while Newark, St. Louis, Baltimore, Pittsburgh and Washington also figure prominently, but there are definite exceptions (Detroit, Buffalo, Denver, Milwaukee) where sulphur dioxide concentrations are very low. As suggested above, the type of industrial structure is a more significant variable than city size. The data for carbon monoxide levels do not extend to a large sample of cities, but they must follow the intensity of use of motor transportation very closely. Of the six cities for which detailed data are available (Chicago, Cincinnati, Denver, Philadelphia, St. Louis and Washington), Chicago is much the worst with Denver and Philadelphia following. With almost all the pollutants, the seasonal variations within a city are very striking.[15]

The published evidence available for the United Kingdom is much less complete. A National Air Pollution survey was mounted in the period 1961–71 to evaluate the effects of the Clean Air Act of 1956, and the limited scope of the survey meant that the pollutants covered were much fewer than those measured in the United States. The survey revealed that the pollution of an urban area depends markedly on the region in which it is situated, and in particular that the highest standards were achieved in the South East Region (with the exception of sulphur dioxide concentrations in London). This finding suggested a *prima facie* case that high pollution standards do not necessarily conflict with economic prosperity and, in view of increasing urbanisation in the South East, casts some doubt on the postulated relationship between air pollution and city size. However within the South East town sites had sulphur dioxide pollution levels, on average, almost double those found at country sites.

Nationally, the most striking feature of the situation in the UK is the drastic improvement in both smoke and sulphur dioxide pollution since the early 1950s. Smoke emissions declined from 2.42 million tons in 1950 to 0.77 million tons by 1970, and the rate of decline was much sharper for industrial than for domestic use. Between 1954 and 1970, smoke emissions fell by 65 per cent despite a 9 per cent increase in population and 29 per cent increase in energy consumption. Although sulphur dioxide emissions increased between 1950 and 1962, they have remained constant in the last ten years and declined by almost 30 per cent in urban areas. This is in spite of weak legislation since the Alkali Acts are the only general legislation affecting sulphur dioxide emissions and the Acts apply only to registered works. The practice of high chimneys has been a prime factor in ensuring dispersion. Given the deficiencies in national legislation, local restrictions may be necessary. For instance, the City of London (Various Powers) Act of 1971 prohibited the use of fuel oil containing more than one per cent sulphur. Grit and dust deposits have remained virtually unchanged over the last decade.

In comparing smoke and sulphur dioxide, a marked dissimilarity has been London's performance in controlling the emission of the pollutants. Smoke concentration fell from $250 \, \mu g/m^3$ in 1954 to less than $45 \, \mu g/m^3$ in 1970–1, a faster decline than elsewhere. Sulphur dioxide concentration in London, on the other hand, is as high as in the industrial north. For instance, 11 out of 15 national sites with winter averages of sulphur dioxide concentration in the $300–350 \, \mu g/m^3$ range were in London. This differential pattern reflects the greater success of the Clean Air Act of 1956 than other pollution measures.

An important element in the air pollution problem revealed in detail from the National Survey is the intraurban variation in emissions. Broadly speaking there is a marked tendency for pollution to vary directly with distance from city centres and inversely with density. This finding applies to all three types of pollutant (smoke, sulphur dioxide and grit and dust) and is most evident in the Greater London Area.[16] Smoke concentration in Inner London is two or three times greater than in outer London, and the range in the winter of 1966–7 varied from $161 \, \mu g/m^3$ in part of Westminster to $34 \, \mu g/m^3$ in Wimbledon. Local variations depend very much on type of area, being very high in the central high-density residential and commercial zones and in industrial areas and lowest in low-density residential areas with a great deal of open space. The pattern for sulphur dioxide was not much different: the highest concentration in Central London, fairly high in commercial and industrial areas and not much lower in high-density residential areas. In this case the range varied from $491 \, \mu g/m^3$ in Lambeth to $69 \, \mu g/m^3$

Table 3.1

Variations in air pollution by type of area, Greater London

Type of area	Median values for sites ($\mu g/m^3$) (Winter 1966–7)		Median values for sites (mg/m^2) (1958–9)	
	Smoke	Sulphur dioxide	Type of area	Grit and dust
Low-density housing with open space	46·5	137	Industrial	238
Lower-density housing: built-up	56	131·5	Mixed industrial/other	132
High density housing	75	181	High density housing	116
Central London	73	337	Low density housing	70
Industrial	65	200	Commercial centres	90
Commercial areas (high density)	84	237	Central zone	172
Commercial areas (low density)	57	125·5	Open ground within built-up area	79
			Outskirts	66
			Mixed non-industrial	102

in Ruislip.[17] The grit and dust distributions were even more varied with the highest distributions not unexpectedly in industrial areas and with a range of 406 mg/m² (milligrams per square metre) in Greenwich to 31 mg/m² in West Drayton.[18] The results by type of area are summarised in Table 3.1. The significance of these wide intraurban differentials (not to mention the marked divergence between winter and summer readings) is that they warn against too facile an interpretation of interurban differences in general and city size differences in particular. This evidence also suggests that population density is far more important than population size. Independent confirmation for this point has been provided by Hoch (1972) in that the t values for regression coefficients in equations with air pollution as the dependent variable were higher for central city densities than for either central city population or urbanised area population.

These considerations suggest that it would be futile to tamper with city sizes as a method of dealing with air pollution since it would be necessary to alter radically and simultaneously the density and structure of urban areas. A more fruitful approach, if it is desired to influence the spatial distribution, is to encourage the decentralisation of high-pollutant industries, or more generally to take account of air pollution costs in selecting among alternative sites for production plants. To deal with prevailing pollution levels in cities more direct measures are necessary. There is something to be said for nationally-determined environmental regulations such as the Clean Air Acts of 1956 in Britain and of 1963, 1965 and 1967 in the United States or the emission standards set for US motor vehicles by 1975. For those who believe in market incentives a preferred solution will be emission fees and taxes of polluters, perhaps combined with subsidies for pollution abatement investment for the adoption of low-polluting production methods. The difficulties involved in measuring the social costs of air pollution and in fixing the correct taxes could mean that setting the charges needed to achieve predetermined environmental standards (Baumol and Oates, 1971) is an appropriate, feasible and not inefficient strategy.

Whatever measures are adopted, the need for control of air pollution is beyond doubt. Lave and Seskin (1970 and 1971) estimated that a 50 per cent reduction in air pollution would lower the economic costs of morbidity and mortality by 4.5 per cent and increase life expectancy of a new-born child by 3–5 years. Other studies (e.g. Ridker and Henning, 1967, and Jaksch, 1970) have shown that air pollution is reflected in lower property values. Similarly, Stanback and Knight (1970) have argued that amenities are an important locational attractor for new industry, and that pollution-free air may be a higher priority than, say, local taxes. Increasingly, the quality of air is becoming an influence on migration decisions. This suggests a significant incentive for air pollution control at the local, as well as the national, level.

Notes

[1] According to Rothenberg (1970), income growth is a twin villain to urban concentration: 'a system which begins with no congestion problems (with air and water and beaches uncongested, unprotected free goods) will gradually move toward greater and greater congestion of all such natural media by the sheer growth and affluence of the society, especially when these occur in a context of greater spatial concentration (urbanization). ... The problem creeps up on the society that is doing nothing differently, only more and better – creeps, and then gallops' (p. 118). Similarly, Kapp (1963 and 1970) has drawn upon the cumulative causation concept to explain these non-linearities.

[2] A possible exception is where the removal of pollutants changes the production functions of firms. In this case the effects will show themselves in the form of changes in output and prices which can be measured.

[3] In the case of pollution, this means more investment in pollution abatement facilities to increase the absorptive capacity of the medium for a given level of population and economic activities.

[4] Another alternative – investment to promote technical change – will show itself as downward shifts in the cost curves.

[5] On the other hand, the *relative* size of the CBD to the metropolitan area (or population) as a whole declines with increasing city size.

[6] A subsidiary explanation is the growth in the importance of secondary sub-centres outside the CBD in very large metropolises.

[7] On the other hand, regional variables (for the North Central and Southern regions) were statistically significant.

[8] 'Less units of housing' here mean a smaller quantity and/or poorer quality (where quality includes, *inter alia*, accessibility).

[9] For a relevant theoretical analysis see Muth (1969, Chapter 2).

[10] However, since the ability to adjust is a function of income, it is arguable that the relatively poor in the big city are found to live either in very poor quality central slum housing or in cheap housing at the periphery of the metropolitan area but at the cost of being forced to endure very long and expensive journeys to work.

[11] For instance, consider a congestion cost function of the type

$$c = f[(d_t/s_t)^\mu]$$

where c = congestion cost, d_t and s_t represent the demand for and supply of transportation, and μ = congestion cost exponent. Even if μ rises with city size, the key determinant of increasing congestion will not be the value of this parameter but whether the ratio of demand to supply (d_t/s_t) is greater or less than unity. Also since transportation demand and supply will vary at different locations within the city, this might explain the differential incidence

36

of congestion particularly with distance from the CBD (see Mills, 1972c, Chapter 7).

[12] Engels, for instance, ascribed harmful effects on the health of London workers to '250,000 fires crowded upon an area 3 to 4 miles square' (F. Engels, 1892, p. 64).

[13] The coverage of the data varies widely between countries. Detailed urban data in the UK refer only to sulphur dioxide, smoke and grit and dust (see Warren Spring Laboratory, 1972). The United States have a much wider spread (*Air Quality Data* periodically published by the Department of Health, Education and Welfare): sulphur dioxide, other sulphates, suspended particulates, benzene-soluble organics, benzopyrene, beta radioactivity, nitrates, a wide range of metals and minerals (e.g. lead), nitrogen oxides, carbon monoxide, hydrocarbons and ammonia.

[14] See the map in Department of Health, Education and Welfare (1968, pp. 24–5).

[15] The *Air Quality Data* reports provide a large quantity of information much too detailed to be summarised effectively here.

[16] See the maps in Warren Spring Laboratory (1972), pp. 164, 173 and 188.

[17] Lower concentrations in some other suburbs were considered unreliable.

[18] The grit and dust data refer to a much earlier year (1958–9).

4 Economies of agglomeration

Introduction

Several of the more important advantages of large urban size – higher incomes, scale economies in the public sector and a stable, diversified and progressive economic structure[1] – are examined separately elsewhere in this book, and other agglomeration economies such as externalities in consumption and communication economies have been mentioned incidentally. The aim here is to provide an approximation to a comprehensive list of agglomeration economies, to discuss one in particular – the innovation-creating and diffusion potential of large cities – in a little more detail, and to offer some brief comments on the conceptualisation and measurement of agglomeration economies.

Many of the external economies of large cities accrue to business firms. These include: access to specialised business services, access to sources of capital,[2] labour market economies (larger pools of and more varied skills, a greater elasticity in labour supply, superior training facilities, better organised placement services), a larger supply of managerial and professional talent and the presence of facilities likely to attract these,[3] opportunities for specialisation offered by the large market (product specialisation, technical externalities such as input-output linkages and transport cost savings), economies in water supply and the possibility of other economies of scale in the public sector, communication and information economies – especially opportunities for face-to-face contact, the greater adaptability and flexibility of fixed investments, particularly structures, and the presence of business entertainment facilities. The market scale economies factor may be particularly important. Ullman (1962) notes that the ratio of internal to external trade rises markedly with the logarithm of city size. Thus, large cities are more self-contained and hence more efficient in the sense that this saves transport costs to and from other places (and between production and distribution centres). Transportation cost advantages may be another external benefit. Many transit improvements, particularly in relation to use of the truck and associated technical changes such as container terminals, have benefited the large urban area, and big cities are almost always the main beneficiaries from public transport improvements. Also important are the scale economies in executive transport services e.g. airport services. How far these advantages are reduced by higher congestion costs in large cities is unclear. With regard to all the externalities mentioned above there is a dearth of precise knowledge about how each varies with city size,[4] the distance range of each economy[5] and on whether the benefits are restricted to particular types of firm (by industry or by size). For instance, how true is the well-known generalisation that external economies are more important to small than to large firms, since the latter in many instances have opportunities for 'internalising' them. Another group of external economies of scale, though benefiting the national economy and regional economies rather than city residents, refers to the systemic functions of big cities – their incubation of new industries and innovations and their subsequent 'filtering-down' and diffusion to other smaller cities in the urban hierarchy. This is discussed separately below.

Other external economies are enjoyed by households rather than firms (consumption externalities). These cover opportunities for earning higher incomes and a wider choice in jobs, shopping facilities, and variety in housing. Also, there are threshold city sizes for the efficient provision of educational facilities, transportation, hospitals, leisure and entertainment opportunities and for most types of social infrastructure. On the other hand, these benefits do not necessarily increase continuously with city size, and there may be some levelling off in the medium size range. Moreover, if we accept Stanback and Knight's (1970) definition of amenities as 'environmental factors such as favourable climate, attractive physical surroundings and access to parks and recreational facilities, as well as the availability and quality of educational, medical, financial, entertainment and retail services', it is clear that some of these (e.g. climate) have no relationship to city size at all. Yet amenities figure prominently among consumption externalities.

This brief summary suggests that while it is easy to identify external economies it is very difficult to measure them and we know very little about the precise variation in each potential economy with increasing city size. Our ignorance in this respect rivals our lack of knowledge about the variation of social costs and external diseconomies with city size. This ignorance reinforces the recurrent argument of this book that it is premature, if not dangerous, for policy makers to attempt to influence city sizes in pursuit of an unattainable optimum.

City size, innovation and growth diffusion

One of the most important of the agglomeration economies created in the largest cities benefits not the citizens but the economy as a whole. This refers to the systemic functions of the largest cities, and more particularly to their rate of innovation (interpreted widely) and its subsequent diffusion to smaller cities and to other parts of the economy. If these systemic functions are important, as the evidence suggests, policies to limit city size based on the evaluation of the social costs and benefits of urban scale to residents could have adverse repercussionary effects on the growth of the economy and on the income levels of people living elsewhere.

Ogburn and Duncan (1964) noted that of 600 major innovations recorded in the period 1900–35 in the United States over 50 per cent occurred in 25 cities with a 1930 population greater than 300,000. Also, the ratio of patents to city size varied strongly with the urban hierarchy. Hägerstrand's (1966 and 1967) inductive studies in Europe showed that innovations tended to be introduced first in the capital city or other major metropolis, and then spread hierarchically. The close communication networks and strength of private and personal contacts between big cities meant that new ideas flowed directly from one to the other, bypassing smaller urban centres located between them. Similarly, a country's largest cities were the first absorbers of innovations imported from abroad. Schultz (1953) found that agriculture operated more efficiently near large urban centres, explaining this in terms of better information flows, less uncertainty and stronger cultural adaptation to change and economic development. Thompson (1965 and 1968) argued that large cities have the skills, technology and institutions to acquire growth industries first, which are subsequently filtered down to smaller, less skilled and low wage urban areas. Madden (1958) presented striking evidence (though based on central city rather than SMSA-equivalent urban definitions) that new cities grew much faster than old, and suggested that an important explanation of this is that new cities present a much more attractive environment for innovation.[6] Berry et al. (1969) argued that the process of polarised development and subsequent diffusion can be analysed in the United States as a system with New York at its centre, with the rate of innovation spreading outwards from the manufacturing belt and down the urban hierarchy. In a later study Berry (1972) showed that the market penetration of TV sets was largely hierarchical with city population a good proportional surrogate for market size. Generalising the argument, Haggett (1968) argued that the impetus of economic change is normally transmitted from large to smaller cities in the urban hierarchy. On this view, continued innovation in large cities remains critical for extending growth through the economy as a whole. The capacity of smaller cities to adopt innovations made elsewhere depends primarily on their location and on their communication links with the major cities of the system; for instance, a location on the main transportation axis between two big cities may be much more favourable to a high innovation rate than at a nearer but less accessible site.[7]

If the generalisations that innovations are first made in the largest cities and then diffuse hierarchically (*hierarchical filtering*) are valid, the interesting questions are why this process occurs and how strong is the impact of city size itself. Berry (1972) suggests four alternative (or complementary) explanations: a 'market-searching' process in which an expanding industry exploits market potential opportunities in a larger-to-smaller sequence; a 'trickle-down' process in which industries faced with rising wages in large cities relocate in low wage, smaller towns (i.e. Thompson's 'filtering' model); an 'imitation' process in which entrepreneurs and innovators in small cities imitate the behaviour of those in large cities; and a simple probability mechanism in which the probability of adoption declines with city size. This last hypothesis has been formalised in a hierarchical diffusion model by Pedersen (1970). The probability of adoption in a given city depends upon the chance of a potential innovator receiving information about an innovation and acting upon it. This is strongly associated with city size for several reasons: exposure to information is a function of information flows, and these can be described with a gravity model which gives due allowance to city size; for many innovations adoption depends upon scale (e.g. market size) and agglomeration economies, the importance of which can be measured by a *threshold city size* for each type of innovation: the presence and incidence of entrepreneurs and potential adopters depends on characteristics such as expected profitability, socio-economic structure and the availability of capital which are all direct functions of city size; finally, the rate of participation in diffusing information is itself a function of city size. As the use of the gravity model implies, the urban hierarchy as a diffusion mechanism must be examined in spatial as well as in size and functional terms. Thus, the innovation potential of a centre is a function of its own rank in the hierarchy and of its location relative to other cities that have already adopted the innovation.[8]

There are many empirical generalisations emphasising the association between innovation potential and city size. The formal communications network is an interurban network with the denser flows between larger cities. The social structure of and prevailing psychological attitudes in larger cities are more favourable to the adoption of new ideas, fashions and innovations. Similarly, the national innovation-adoption elite (scientists and technologists, R and D specialists, managers, etc.) is distributed unequally in favour of the upper levels of the urban hierarchy. This distribution is reinforced by the role of urban agglomeration economies as locational attractors since consumption externalities attract the innovating elite while business agglomeration economies attract the R and D laboratories, growth firms and other corporations that promote a high innovation rate. Hierarchical diffusion is also fostered by the fact that the industrial organisation of advanced economies is based on a hierarchical spatial structure of large multiplant corporations (cf. Edel's, 1972, view that the economic success of the largest cities is based on the fact that they are corporate cities). A related fact is that where innovations are diffused via distributors, this reinforces hierarchical diffusion since the national spatial network of distribution centres is itself structured hierarchically (Brown, 1969). Furthermore, to the extent that technical progress is embodied, innovation diffusion will tend to be superimposed on the interurban capital flow matrix which is itself polarised heavily in favour of the large cities.[9] Finally, Berry (1972) suggests that the income effects of innovations decline over time, and that this helps to explain higher and rising incomes in larger cities.

If these arguments are correct, the policy implications are fairly obvious. The innovation potential of the system and the diffusion rate through the hierarchy tends to be directly related to the size of the top levels in the hierarchy (i.e. the size of the system's largest cities). Accordingly, policies to hold down the growth of the large metropolises are destructive from the innovation and growth point of view. If other measures for dealing with the social costs of big cities can be devised that do not involve controlling city size itself, these should be adopted. In a regional policy context, an important prescription for backward regions is to promote the growth of their largest urban centres to raise their rank in the national urban hierarchy. This strategy should increase the capacity of the region to adopt innovations, first introduced higher still in the hierarchy, sooner and at a more rapid rate.

Conceptualisation and measurement

In Chapter 2 (pp. 17–19) the feasibility of an aggregate agglomeration economy/congestion cost function is analysed. This is concerned with an attempt to specify the relationship between agglomeration economies and diseconomies and city size, as measured by population. The difficulty with this approach is to discover an appropriate surrogate for the benefits and costs of agglomeration. Edel's (1972) suggestion that they are capitalised in land values is ingenious, and deserves further research. In some situations, it may be desirable to treat agglomeration economies separately from congestion and other social costs. How can this be done?

A simple method of handling external economies of agglomeration is to assume that each producer has, on top of his individual fixed costs (f), a *pro rata* share in the overall community fixed costs (F) for the location (Hoover, 1970). The latter will be inversely proportional to the number of firms (x) at that location, and the producer's total costs will be equal to $(\int_o^Q c\,(Q)\,dQ + f + F/x)$, where c = marginal cost and Q = output. This approach has the advantage of emphasising the direct relationship between the force of agglomeration (as measured by the number of producers) and reductions in costs for the individual firm, but it is not entirely satisfactory. It implies that a doubling of firms at the centre of agglomeration halves the cost savings due to agglomeration, and there is no theoretical or empirical justification for this assumption. Also, it is obviously capable of dealing only with those agglomeration economies that are reflected in lower costs for business firms.

A more general treatment, though again emphasising externalities to business firms, is presented in an analysis by Barr (1972), in which he deals with agglomeration economies by including an 'efficiency function' of total urban employment in the production function of the individual firm. A firm's production possibilities are given by

$$Z_i = G(N) F(L_i, K_i, N_i) \qquad (4.1)$$

where F is linear homogeneous in L_i, K_i and N_i which represent the firm's land, capital and labour inputs, and $G(N)$ is the efficiency function of total urban employment, N. It is assumed that $G'(N) > 0$, and that $G''(N) < 0$. Since each firm's labour demand is small in relation to the aggregate labour market, changes in employment in the individual firm will not affect its own efficiency through $G(N)$. On the other hand, if all firms increase their output and employment – in other words, if there is an increase in city size – then greater efficiency is obtained in the goods industry, stimulating further increases in activity by each firm. This specification has two important advantages. First, it introduces a size externality into the goods industry in the form of increasing returns to scale for the industry but constant returns for the competitive firm. In this way, the model may approximate representation of the economies of increased specialisation by individual firms as city size increases. Second, the efficiency function has similar results to production in conditions of neutral technical change and is regressive in periods of declining urban employment. This means that the framework may be of more general use for analysing the process of urban growth and decline in the same way as the agglomeration economy/congestion cost function mentioned above is a general model. These characteristics give rise to further implications. For instance, a monopsonist producer is capable of 'internalising' the external effects of $G(N)$. This reflects the empirical observation that city size economies are usually far more critical for small than for large firms. Moreover, the model implies that changes in cost conditions (e.g. reductions in transport costs) may trigger an urban growth process, but this will be damped since $G''(N) < 0$. On the other hand, regressive disturbances, such as increasing costs or higher social costs, may have cumulative downward impacts on output and employment which may require policy intervention to reverse them.

44

Although both these approaches have a useful conceptual value, they are difficult to make operational. Moreover, they are confined to analysis of one aspect of agglomeration economies. A less neat, but more practical method is to break down agglomeration economies into their individual components. This involves drawing a distinction between agglomeration economies for society at large[10] (social agglomeration economies), for households (household agglomeration economies) and for firms (business agglomeration economies). These subdivisions take account of the multiple functions of agglomeration economies: to boost the rate of innovation and productivity, to improve the efficiency of the spatial structure, to attract industry and capital, and to attract (or retain) households. Social agglomeration economies include economies of scale in urban services (and public service efficiency generally) and the systemic functions of urban centres. Household agglomeration economies include income benefits, choice in employment opportunities, the quality of social and personal services, amenities, leisure and cultural facilities and other consumption externalities. Major problems in measurement arise from three sources: how to impute a cost of *not* having facilities that require a high threshold city size in smaller cities; how to assign weights to each component in the household agglomeration index; how to allow for the fact that the appropriate 'mix' of household agglomeration economies varies according to social class (income, occupation and other status variables). Business agglomeration economies cover Weberian locational agglomeration advantages (e.g. industrial complex analysis),[11] labour market pools, the local availability of capital and banking services, the presence of local business services (e.g. computer consultancies, advertising agencies, accountancy and legal services), market potential economies, public utility costs and other external benefits. Indeed, the list is so long that the critical question is how to identify which economies are the most important for attracting mobile industry to the metropolis. Principal components analysis or some similar technique may be useful for specifying the key business agglomeration economies. Attempts to measure agglomeration economies and their functional relationship to city size by disaggregation on these lines are more clumsy but more productive than the neater and more elegant aggregate external economy function.[12] Also, they are not devoid of policy implications since the results of this kind of inquiry may throw light on the key locational attractors that can pull in migrants and industry to cities of particular sizes.

Notes

[1] See pp. 71–83.

[2] This may be a question of greater availability of information about sources of finance rather than cheaper costs. Smith (1971, p. 38) quotes studies by the Fantus Company of the annual average financing cost in a sample of North American cities. Over three-quarters of the sample fell in the range 8.3–8.6 per cent, and the largest city in the sample (Chicago) had the same financing cost as the smallest town.

[3] These include 'a high quality of physical environment, a range of efficient services and a lively cultural life' (Cameron, 1970, p.29).

[4] Chinitz (1961) has argued that many external economies, such as the supply of entrepreneurs, access to local capital and environmental quality, are more a function of industrial structure than city size. Neutze (1965) argued, though on the basis of judgment rather than firm evidence, that most of the external economies for business firms could be gained in cities of 500,000 population, or even of 200,000.

[5] Some may be enjoyed in smaller urban centres provided that these are close to large cities.

[6] For a similar view see Berry *et al.* (1969). It should be noted that this evidence may cut across the city size-agglomeration economy hypothesis, switching attention to the age of settlement.

[7] These generalisations may be applicable only to western societies. In India, for instance, many middle-size cities are administrative rather than economic in origin and are poor transmitters of growth.

[8] This point is a recurrent theme in this book: that location matters as well as size.

[9] For further elaboration of these arguments and a more detailed discussion of hierarchical diffusion see Richardson (1973a, pp. 126–32).

[10] This is rather vague since it could mean the metropolitan community as a whole or the national interest.

[11] Neither of these is a direct function of city size, but is a consequence of the spatial concentration of industrial establishments which could be heavy even in or near a small urban area.

[12] For further elaboration of this approach see Richardson (1973a, pp. 182–96).

5 Income and Welfare

Income

A main plank in the argument of those who favour large cities in the city size controversy is the variation of wages and personal incomes with city size. It is argued that incomes are much higher in larger cities, and that this fact illustrates the benefits of city bigness both from the social and individual points of view. The social case is that higher incomes must reflect higher productivity and are therefore indicative of the fact that big cities are more productive economic units than smaller urban areas. As for individuals, the higher wages and salaries obtainable in large cities merely reflect the advantages to individual households of living and working in big cities. The strength of this argument depends upon the answers to two key questions. Does the empirical evidence support the hypothesis that personal income per household (or *per capita*) is positively associated with city size? If the answer is yes, how sound are the theoretical implications to be drawn from this evidence about the advantages of big cities? As we shall see, these implications are subject to qualifications. The qualifications and caveats cast some doubt on the force of the arguments, but they do not destroy them. Much depends, however, on the scale of the increase in incomes with city size. The wider the *per capita* income gains as we move up the urban size hierarchy the more difficult it becomes to quarrel with the 'advantages of large size' hypothesis.

Before examining the empirical evidence, it is appropriate to comment on the theoretical points. What about the social benefits of large cities in terms of their higher incomes? To demonstrate that higher wages in big cities are evidence of higher productivity it would be necessary to show that the assumptions of perfect competition are justified. In fact, market imperfections are much more widespread in urban industries than in agriculture while the sizeable geographical distances between cities confer a certain degree of monopolistic protection. Secondly, higher wages may reflect non-homogeneity characteristics such as the impacts of education, age, industry and occupational differences, race, degrees of risk and the life-cycle variation of wages according to occupation. These differences are quite consistent with long-run equilibrium because efficient resource allocation merely requires the equalisation of the marginal productivity of labour in each industry, and since wages, in practice, bear a closer relationship to average rather than marginal products equilibrium can coexist with wide variations in average products (and hence wages) between industries and cities.

Third, wage differentials between cities may reflect disequilibrium in the sense of a failure of interurban migration to equalise the marginal products of labour.[1] This could mean simply that we can no more assume perfect competition in the spatial allocation of factors than in urban production. The mere existence of migration costs, for instance, implies wage differentials, though (as we shall see) the evidence frequently points to wage differentials much wider than migration costs. It is also pertinent to ask why any disequilibrium should not be eliminated in the long run. A possible answer is that the urban system may be subject to periodic disturbances (e.g. technical innovations) which prevent equilibrium from ever being attained. To account for persistently higher wages in large cities, however, it would be necessary to argue that these disturbances, though possibly random in their distribution over time, were systematic in their incidence in space (i.e. always tended to occur in larger cities). The theory of the spatial concentration and hierarchical diffusion of innovations and technical progress might be used in support of such a case. Finally, to argue that higher incomes *per se* are socially beneficial implies something about the nature of the social welfare function. This may not be concerned so much with maximising personal income as with the distribution of income.[2] Thus, higher average incomes in large cities may be undesirable if achieved at the expense of equity. Furthermore, a social welfare function laying a great deal of stress on distributional and equity goals might well suggest a policy to reduce the income gap between cities by measures to hold down the expansion of *per capita* incomes in large cities.

From the point of view of the individual, the higher incomes that may be earned in large cities do not necessarily imply a higher level of welfare. For instance, there are sizeable interurban cost of living differences with some tendency for the association between living costs and city size to be positive. However, to anticipate the results of the review of the empirical evidence, although living costs generally change in the same direction as income, their variation with city size is much narrower so that adjusted real incomes still tend to be higher in larger urban areas. Much more speculative, and more difficult to test, is the hypothesis that employers in large cities have to offer higher wages to compensate workers for the negative externalities (pollution, congestion, noise, etc.) associated with life in big cities. This 'compensating payments' hypothesis has been argued most strongly by Edel (1972) and Hoch (1972). After noting that interurban income differences have converged over time, Hoch observed that persistent differences nevertheless remained and suggested that the failure of equilibrating forces (i.e. migration) to wipe them out supports the view that they are due to compensating payments. This is a feasible but not the only explanation; intermittent

48

disturbances of the equilibrating process via shifts in production functions are an obvious alternative. A counterargument to the compensating payments hypothesis is that if the wage differential in favour of large cities was entirely absorbed as compensation for the unpleasantness of big city life, how could we explain the continued attraction of large metropolitan areas for migrants? In fact, there are several satisfactory explanations: the ignorance of *some* migrants and their incapacity to discount negative externalities sufficiently; the possibility, especially in an underemployed economy *or* where migrants come predominantly from rural areas, that migrants respond to employment opportunities rather than prospective income gains; interurban migration may be due to non-economic influences (such as positive externalities in big cities that exist only for certain groups, e.g. the 'friends and relatives effect' so common in migration studies).

Although there is some merit in almost all of these qualifications, they are unlikely to be of sufficient weight to offset substantial interurban wage differences. Accordingly, this is a convenient moment to turn to the empirical evidence. The data available are frequently not very satisfactory, but they all – regardless of country or time – tend to confirm the hypothesis that incomes rise sharply with city size.[3] For example, Lösch (1954) quoted statistics suggesting that unskilled wage levels were 31 per cent higher in the one million-plus cities than in the smallest ($< 10,000$) settlements in Germany in 1941, while more recent evidence (1964) on output per head indicated that its level in the million-plus cities was 20–25 per cent higher than in other urban areas and 17 per cent greater than in the next size class ($500,000 < 1$ million). Swedish data indicated that average income per employee (1967) was one-third greater in Stockholm than in smaller towns, and about 12 per cent greater than in the other main metropolitan areas. The Japanese evidence quoted by Mera (1970) relates average *per capita* incomes (1965) not to population size but to population density: incomes in the 3000+ persons per square kilometre category were over 20 per cent higher than in the next density class ($1,000 < 3,000$) and 70 per cent higher than in the sparsely populated areas of less than 500 persons per square kilometre.

The most thorough studies and most disaggregated data refer to the United States. The basic sources are the income estimates available from the Census of Population and for intercensus years the estimates obtained from the Office of Business Economics surveys (see *Survey of Current Business*, 1969–72).[4] The most detailed individual study incorporating extensive standardisation procedures on the raw 1960 Census data is by Fuchs (1967). The SCB tables enable time series analysis to be made of the movements in urban income *per capita* at ten year intervals between 1929 and 1959 and for selected years in the 1960s. They show that incomes have been consistently above the US average in SMSAs greater than 1 million population, around the national average in Northern SMSAs below 400,000 and about 15 per cent below this average in Southern SMSAs. There has been convergence since 1929, particularly between Southern and Northern cities but even more between SMSAs and non-SMSAs.[5] Nevertheless, even by 1967 the larger SMSAs (2 million plus) had average *per capita* incomes 20 per cent and the 1–2 million SMSAs almost 15 per cent above the US average (for analysis of the 1950 data see Duncan and Reiss, 1956, p. 105).

Table 5.1
Average Hourly Earnings by City Size, United States, 1959
($ per hour)

Size and type of area	Total	South	Non-South	South White	South Non-White	Non-South White	Non-South Non-White
SMSA							
1 million and over	2·84	2·62	2·87	2·86	1·54	2·96	1·96
½<1 million	2·56	2·34	2·67	2·54	1·37	2·71	2·18
¼<½ million	2·43	2·31	2·50	2·46	1·28	2·52	2·13
<¼ million	2·39	2·15	2·54	2·34	1·13	2·56	1·90
Urban places							
10<100,000	2·23	1·94	2·39	2·14	0·99	2·40	1·84
<10,000	2·12	1·82	2·30	1·98	0·99	2·31	1·62
Rural	2·00	1·71	2·22	1·80	1·06	2·22	1·80

Source: Fuchs (1967), Table 5.

The raw data of Fuchs' analysis are summarised in Table 5.1. These show a marked tendency for earnings to increase with city size for all workers, white and non-white, and in both the South and the non-South. Average earnings in the 1 million-plus SMSAs were one-third higher than in the small urban places (<10,000) and 19 per cent higher than in the small SMSAs (<250,000).[6] The one exception to the clear-cut positive association between income and city size is for blacks in cities outside the South, where SMSAs in the ½–1 million range offered higher money incomes than either the larger or smaller SMSAs.[7] Table 5.1 also indicates the sizeable income gap between blacks and whites and, to a lesser extent, between the South and the non-South.

The main achievement of the Fuchs study was to standardise the earnings data for more effective comparison by adjusting for differences in labour force composition due to colour, age, sex and education, for regional mix and for unionisation and size of employer. He found that these adjustments did not alter the conclusions in substance; for instance, the city size differential in average earnings was about the same at all levels of education. The general conclusions were 'that the relationship between earnings and city size is large, persistent, and cannot be explained by correlation between city size and other variables' (Fuchs, 1967, p. 31) and that 'Standardised hourly earnings in the SMSAs of one million and over are typically 25 to 35 per cent higher than in the areas outside SMSAs within the same region, and about 15 per cent higher than in SMSAs of less than one million. The city-size gradient is steeper in the South than in the rest of the country' (*ibid*, p. 33).

Thus, though it is important in theory to standardise income comparisons, in this particular case it makes little difference in practice to the results. This is fortunate for it is not clear what should be included and what should be excluded from the standardisation procedure. For example, if the aim is to isolate the effects of city size, it is doubtful whether we should adjust for educational differences if there are marked economies of scale in education (e.g. educational benefits which could be provided only in cities exceeding, say, one million). Also, even Fuchs' elaborate adjustments do not take into account all labour quality differences, e.g. variations in the *quality* of education, more or better job training, and possibly the most important and least measurable factor of all – the selective in-migration into big cities of the more hard-working and the more ambitious.

Poverty and income distribution

It might be argued that average income data give a misleading impression of the links between welfare and city size because opportunities for higher incomes can be expected to be higher in large cities than in small. Thus, so the argument runs, this inflates the average estimates and is also indicative of a more inequitable distribution of income. The implication of these views is that more attention should be paid to the incidence of poverty and to income distribution, and how these vary with city size. As with so many empirical questions in urban economics, the evidence has to be drawn from the United States where the population census provides disaggregated income estimates. As far as Britain is concerned, we know very little. The Inland Revenue data suggest that the distribution of income in the London area is similar to that in the rest of the country, but with the level of income an average of 10–12 per cent higher. Pahl (1971) argued that the poor were heavily concentrated in cities in the United Kingdom because of the dominance of low paid workers in the urban service sectors, but the chain of evidence linking this very reasonable hypothesis to the argument that there are *relatively* more poor in large cities is weak. Much public attention has been focused on the problems of London's poor, particularly the badly-housed and the homeless, but the evidence on the incidence of poverty in London and how it compares with other British cities and smaller towns is very skimpy.

The United States evidence on the nature of the link between poverty and urban life in general and city size in particular is clear-cut, though here too the myths are hard to dispel. The incidence of poverty is inversely associated with urban scale. It is true that precise conclusions are made more difficult by the crudity of measurement of the official poverty line: the annual cost of a nutritious diet for low income families of various sizes multiplied by three (on the assumption that low income families spend about a third of their incomes on food), a definition which also fails to allow for interurban cost of living differentials. Nevertheless, this does not lead to too much distortion in the analysis, and its results are supported by other measures of poverty less direct than those based on personal income. The incidence of poverty (i.e. the proportion of population with incomes below the poverty line) is two-and-a-half times greater in non-metropolitan than in metropolitan areas. Two-thirds of the population live in metropolitan areas, but little more than one-half of the poor; for blacks the differential is even better. Of course, poverty is more prevalent among blacks (37 per cent of the black population as opposed to 11 per cent of the white), but this is heavily influenced by black rural poverty in the South. Urbanisation has been a more powerful force in improving incomes and employment opportunities for blacks than for whites.

The myth about urban poverty and its concentration in large cities is primarily explained by the absolute numbers of the poor in these cities and the fact that they are so noticeable because they are spatially concentrated. This spatial concentration is accentuated by the tendency for spatial differentiation (in residences as well as in other types of activity) to become stronger with increasing city size, and may *appear* heavier because the non-white ratio in the poverty areas is much higher than in cities as a whole. This reflects the failure of the black population to suburbanise. The result is that the black ghettoes in the central city of the great metropolises become the symbol for poverty in the United States. This impression is misleading. The incidence of poverty is much greater in rural areas, but because they are scattered the poor are less noticeable. Similarly, within urban areas the incidence of poverty is greater in the smaller towns and the gap between the small town and the large city is greatest at the lowest income level. Evidence for this has been presented by Orshansky (1965) and Ornati (1968).[8] In Ornati's words (1968, p. 343): 'In large cities the fall in the

52

incidence of poverty, however defined, is as clear as is the rise in median income. Although poverty declines in successively larger urban groupings, the rate of change is uneven. The most marked and dramatic change takes place at the very top. Cities of more than a million show a substantially lower incidence of poverty than cities of 250,000 to one million.'

Of course, since all incomes both of rich and poor are positively associated with city size, it might be possible, in principle, at least, to argue that poverty, or even near-poverty, may appear much worse in large cities because of the 'demonstration effect' – ill effects due to observing the expenditure patterns and life styles of the better off.[9] There are flaws in this argument independent of evidence, e.g. that ghetto traps make direct observation of how the rich live very unlikely, and that anyone with a TV set, wherever he lives, can suffer from the gap between expectations and the actual standard of life. Nevertheless, if this kind of reasoning can be made at all it implies a switch of attention from the incidence of poverty to the distribution of income. It is arguable that the gains from larger city size increase with higher incomes and socio-economic status. An obvious example in the labour market is that large cities offer more job opportunities for highly qualified man and wife job-seekers in joint supply (Thompson, 1972). Similarly, it could be the case that the diseconomies of urban scale may set in sooner for the urban poor than for the well off.

There is little evidence to support most of these assertions. In regard to negative externalities, if concern with pollution, noise and congestion is a product of affluence, we would expect the rich to gain more than the poor from improvements in the environment. As for the distribution of income itself, although the problem has been grossly neglected in the urban context (despite the fact that US Census income data has been much more useful for this purpose since 1960 with the introduction of extended income ranges), income inequality appears to be smaller in large cities than in small towns. Duncan and Reiss (1956, p.107) showed this to be true with the 1950 Census where the Gini coefficients fell steadily with increasing city size,[10] and the more precise data available from the 1960 and 1970 Censuses confirm their findings. Some evidence using 1960 data is shown in Table 5.2. To the extent that a high/low income ratio can be used as a surrogate for measuring income distribution, it is clear that inequality decreases as we move up the urban size hierarchy, both for blacks and whites. It is also noticeable that there is a big change in income equality at the one million size for whites and the 500,000 size for blacks. Even more striking, though not unexpected, is the vast difference in income distribution between whites and blacks. Above the one million mark, however, the variation of income inequality with size is much less clear. Using a different, though equally crude, measure – the interquartile variation[12] – Murray's (1969) analysis

Table 5.2

Ratios of High Income to Low Income Families
by SMSA size Class, 1960[11]

Size of SMSA	Total	White	Black
3m and over	1·830	2·341	0·266
1–3m	1·605	2·085	0·190
½–1m	0·956	1·200	0·159
¼–½m	0·828	1·018	0·061
100,000 to 250,000	0·703	0·925	0·043
Less than 100,000	0·670	0·805	0·028
Total SMSAs	1·239	1·579	0·143

of the 15 largest SMSAs, all of them larger than one million, did not point
to definite conclusions. The rank correlation coefficient between the interquartile variation and population size was 0.4133, a value which is statiscally
insignificant.

Of course, the positive association between income equality and city size
does not imply a direct causal connection. The most plausible explanation
is that income equality is functionally related to the average income level
(the Kuznets thesis; see Kuznets, 1955), and, as we have seen, average
incomes are strongly correlated with city size. A regression analysis on 207
SMSAs by Frech and Burns (1971) confirmed that a very high proportion
of the variance in income inequality (as measured by the Gini coefficient)
could be explained by the income level.

Cost of living

The evidence for the hypothesis that money incomes are positively associated
with city size is strong. However, it does not necessarily follow that households are better off in real terms living in larger cities. Much depends on the
relationship of the cost of living to city size. Unfortunately, knowledge of
this relationship is very imperfect for two reasons: the nebulous character
of the cost of living concept and the shortage of data on living costs. To
deal with the latter point first, the most thorough urban living cost index,
and this is very limited in area coverage, is the US Bureau of Labour
Statistics (BLS) index for 1966 (Brackett and Lamale, 1967; updated to 1971
by Ruiz, 1972). This provides cost of living estimates for three living standards (low, moderate and high) for a four person family (an employed
husband, aged 38, a wife at home, an 8-year-old girl and a 13-year-old boy).

Unfortunately, the estimates refer only to 39 SMSAs of varying size and to certain non-metropolitan areas. The items covered, apart from total expenditure, include food, housing, clothing, transportation, medicare expenses, social security payments and personal taxes.

What should be included in the cost of living is a trickier question. The BLS data attempt to deal with many of the more obvious problems such as the variation in costs of living requirements with income and family size, but it still defines the cost of living very narrowly. Some argue that the concept of real income should take into account all influences affecting human welfare, i.e. should attempt to measure the 'quality of life'. This view is hopelessly impractical, but it still raises the question of where the lines should be drawn. Should the definition include amenities? Also, what about negative externalities such as pollution and noise?[13] It is true that the utility people obtain from their environment is part of their real income or welfare, and it may be possible, theoretically, to impute a monetary value to these items by working out the cash sum households would prefer at the margin to a given change in their environment. It would not be fruitful, however, to attempt to take account of these in an overall cost of living index. Yet they must be included among the factors that influence the advantages and disadvantages of living in cities of different size. The wisest methodology would appear to be to delimit the influences affecting welfare very widely but to adopt a 'social indicators' approach listing all the non-measurable criteria separately rather than to attempt to combine them all into a single aggregate social welfare index.

A more borderline case is the travel time needed to get to work. This is not included in conventional cost of living indices unlike the monetary costs of the journey to work. Travel time is not only a variable which is frequently monetised in transportation cost-benefit analyses but one which can be expected to vary systematically with city size. This expectation is supported by available evidence (Branch, 1942; Bostick et al., 1954; Voorhees et al., 1966; and J. N. Morgan et al., 1966). For instance, Morgan's study (Morgan et al., 1966, p. 80, Table S-3) showed that journey to work travel time fell from an average of 68 minutes a day in New York to 59 minutes in the next 12 largest metropolitan areas, to 42 minutes in other metropolitan areas down to 25 minutes in the outlying districts outside metropolitan areas. Whether the length of journeys to work is to be treated entirely as a 'cost' is not clear, since an important attraction of large cities is the wider choice of employment opportunities, and to take advantage of these workers must be prepared to travel to work almost anywhere in the city. Also, households may adjust to long journey to work times by moving house to be closer to work. Finally, larger cities frequently offer a greater choice of transport mode since their public transportation facilities are usually superior.[14] In

Table 5.3

Indices of comparative living costs based on the city worker's family budget, 1971

(US Urban Average = 100)

Area	Total budget	Family Consumption							Personal income taxes	Population (000)
		Total	Food	Housing	Transportation	Clothing and personal care	Medical care	Other Family consumption		
Urban United States	100	100	100	100	100	100	100	100	100	–
Metropolitan areas	102	101	102	102	96	102	103	104	103	–
Non-metropolitan areas	93	94	93	92	120	93	85	81	85	–
Northeast										
Boston, Mass.	108	107	105	117	102	102	98	112	129	2,730
Buffalo, N.Y.	101	101	104	97	102	103	90	106	103	1,334
Hartford, Conn.	110	111	107	124	107	108	97	114	104	657
Lancaster, Pa.	98	97	103	94	93	98	89	94	112	320
New York,										
Northeastern N.J.	105	104	112	100	86	101	110	111	111	11,448
Philadelphia, Pa. N.J.	103	100	107	91	93	100	101	106	133	4,777
Pittsburgh, Pa.	98	96	101	92	97	100	85	99	115	2,384
Portland, Maine	103	104	103	112	95	99	95	113	96	140
Non-metropolitan areas	98	98	101	94	126	93	90	83	95	–
Northcentral										
Cedar Rapids, Iowa	97	97	93	100	86	108	90	102	106	161
Champaign-Urbana, Ill.	104	105	98	121	91	105	100	100	108	162
Chicago Ill.										
Northwestern Ind.	104	105	104	105	105	104	105	107	107	6,893
Cincinnati, Ohio-Ky.-Ind.	95	95	99	89	98	99	85	104	93	1,373
Cleveland, Ohio.	100	101	100	98	104	104	100	105	97	2,043
Dayton, Ohio.	96	97	98	95	93	98	90	106	91	842
Detroit, Mich.	98	98	102	92	95	102	101	102	96	4,164

City										
Green Bay, Wis.	97	96	94	98	87	108	88	96	114	157
Indianapolis, Ind.	100	101	99	103	101	99	101	109	97	1,100
Kansas City, Mo.-Kans.	100	100	101	96	103	106	97	102	104	1,241
Milwaukee, Wis.	101	99	94	105	92	105	94	102	124	1,393
Minneapolis-St. Paul, Minn.	100	99	97	102	95	103	94	103	114	1,805
St. Louis, Mo.-Ill.	100	100	104	96	110	101	92	99	103	2,331
Wichita. Kans.	95	95	96	97	85	98	94	96	87	386
Non-metropolitan areas	96	97	94	102	118	96	83	82	92	—
South										
Atlanta, Ga.	93	94	92	94	91	96	94	107	78	1,374
Austin, Tex.	88	90	90	84	87	96	93	100	68	290
Baltimore, Md.	104	102	95	111	99	101	109	104	125	2,045
Baton Rouge, La.	91	93	96	88	92	92	90	102	73	277
Dallas, Tex.	94	96	93	92	92	93	116	104	77	1,539
Durham, N.C.	97	97	91	103	86	97	108	102	77	189
Houston, Tex.	93	94	94	88	95	94	106	102	100	1,958
Nashville, Tenn.	91	93	90	93	93	100	88	103	75	536
Orlando, Fla.	94	96	88	106	89	90	102	103	73	427
Washington, D.C.-Md.-Va.	104	103	99	113	101	95	102	106	117	2,836
Non-metropolitan areas	87	88	88	84	117	88	81	81	70	—
West										
Bakersfield, Calif.	98	98	98	92	98	102	113	94	84	325
Denver, Colo.	95	96	96	90	97	102	96	96	85	1,223
Los Angeles,-Long Beach, Calif.	106	106	98	112	103	107	122	98	99	6,974
San Diego, Calif.	103	103	98	106	100	103	116	97	92	1,318
San Franciso-Oakland, Calif.	111	110	102	123	103	112	113	103	108	3,070
Seattle-Everett, Wash.	106	107	106	111	97	112	109	104	99	1,404
Non-metropolitan areas	100	99	95	101	123	105	91	79	108	—
Honolulu, Hawaii.	125	122	124	142	114	106	105	108	167	613
Anchorage, Alaska	153	149	124	202	169	119	155	95	227	48

Source: *Monthly Labor Review*, June 1972, p. 47. The budget used here is the lowest of three.
Population estimates for 1970 from *UN Demographic Yearbook*, 1970.

view of these doubts and the intractable problems of valuing travel time, it is probably on balance safer to exclude journey to work time from cost of living calculations.

Even adopting restricted definitions of the cost of living, the analytical problems are tricky enough.[15] For instance, after assuming away the usual cost of living index problems such as differences in expenditure patterns between income groups, there is still the problem that living costs may vary about as widely within a city as between cities, e.g. differentials between the central city and the suburbs, particularly for housing costs. An obvious instance of this is the widespread public discussion in the United States a few years ago about the higher food prices in ghetto shops relative to other parts of the city. It is probable that the deviations about the mean for intraurban living costs are much wider in the very large than in the smaller city, so that standard cost of living indices tend to overstate living costs in the larger city for the householder who can take the time and trouble to shop around. Another factor which may militate against larger cities is that expectations about living standards can be very important. For example, it may be possible to live in a big city as cheaply as in a small town but a person is less content to do so because he is influenced by the expediture patterns of others (Alonso and Fajans, 1970); this is a hypothesis which has a close degree of kinship with the relative income hypothesis in consumption theory.

One of the earliest observations on urban cost of living differences was made, as in so many other topics in regional and urban economics, by Lösch (1954, especially Table 38, p.487). He commented on the retail prices of particular commodities in American and Canadian cities in 1936. As is the case with subsequent studies, there are wide variations between cities but scantier evidence of systematic variation of these costs with city size. Neutze (1965) looked at Australian data for 1952 and found that most large cities were more expensive than small towns. However, the most striking factor was the higher price levels in isolated centres such as Broken Hill, Townsville, Kalgoorlie and Geraldton. The absence of medium-size cities in Australia, particularly at that time, inhibited firm conclusions. Newcastle, Geelong and Launceston were all cheaper than their respective capitals, but they were small and close to them.

Both these studies were based on analysis of retail prices rather than on the costs of a standardised family budget. The BLS data for the United States are superior in this respect, though its main drawback is its restricted scope. These data (Table 5.3 presents the updated lower budget cost of living index for 1971) have been used in several analyses of the association between costs of living and city size (Alonso and Fajans, 1970; Shefer, 1970; Hoch, 1972). Despite using the same data, there were some differences in interpretation. Shefer argued that there was no significant relationship between SMSA population size and the consumer expenditure necessary for a given standard of living.[16] Alonso and Fajans found evidence of a 'slight positive association', while Hoch found that population size was significant at the 5 per cent level. Shefer's conclusions may have been the result of inadequate tests (rank correlation techniques[17]), whereas the other two studies used regression analysis. The best summary of the data excluding Honolulu but including the non-metropolitan areas, expressing the cost of living index in fractional form and stratifying by region is shown in Table 5.4 (derived from Hoch, p. 311). This clearly confirms the observation made by all the researchers that regional differences were more significant than city size differences. In particular, living costs were markedly lower in the South (even in large cities such as Houston, Dallas and Atlanta[18]). One element in this could be climatic differences resulting in lower heating and clothing costs, and Alonso and Fajans found that climate was a significant variable for the medium budget. On the other hand, a glance at Table 5.3 shows that the widest spread in budget items occurs in housing[19] and taxation rather than clothing. Hoch's regression results showed that housing costs are positively associated[20] and transport costs are negatively associated with city size (Hoch, 1972, p. 316). The Southern differential is in large measure due to cheap housing, expecially owner-occupied housing, whereas transportation tended to be cheaper in the North-east than in the other regions.

Table 5.4

Cost of Living Index (1966) by Population Size and Region

Population Size (000)	Northeast	North Central	South	West
5	0·935	0·923	0·875	0·930
50	0·970	0·954	0·894	0·960
125	0·987	0·968	0·903	0·978
250	0·999	0·979	0·910	0·990
375	1·007	0·986	0·914	0·997
750	1·021	0·999	0·921	1·011
1000	1·027	1·004	0·925	1·016
2000	1·042	1·018	0·933	1·031
5000	1·064	1·037	0·945	1·052

The most clear-cut finding of these studies, however, was the high degree of correlation between the cost of living and income. This lends some support to Tolley's concept of the wage multiplier (1969), according to which wages tend to be pushed up still higher in initially high wage areas because of rising costs of local (nontraded) goods and services. The positive association between income and the cost of living also explains the close relationship between taxes, particularly Federal taxes, and living costs shown in Table 5.3. Despite this finding, and even taking into account the wide cost of living differences evident in the data of Tables 5.3 and 5.4, all the analysts confirm that cost of living differences are much narrower than money income differentials. Thus although the association between living costs and income reduces the apparent advantages of large cities revealed in money income data, the fact remains that after deflation of these money incomes households remain much better off in real income terms in large metropolitan areas. Thus, to argue that the quality of life is poorer in the great cities we would either have to adopt the subjective and untestable hypothesis that expectations rise faster than income or rely heavily on the negative net externalities argument, taking the view that the higher real wages merely reflect compensating payments for the discomforts of pollution, congestion, noise and the greater risks of exposure to crime.

Unemployment and city size

Large cities show up more favourably than small cities on most major economic variables directly affecting individual welfare such as level of income, its distribution and poverty indices. A possible exception to the rule is unemployment. Here the evidence is not at all clear, but certainly there are few indications to support the plausible hypothesis of an inverse relationship between unemployment and city size. Strangely enough, this important topic has been neglected. Two reasons are the shortage of data and the fact that where data exist they are difficult to interpret, either because of metropolitan area boundary changes or due to shifts in labour market perimeters over time. Also, in this case the US statistics are somewhat poorer than in other countries (such as the UK); accordingly, American economists have not examined SMSA unemployment very deeply while outside the United States economists have not sustained the same degree of interest in urban economic problems. For the United States the only reasonable estimates are the decennial estimates from the Census of Population; for intercensal years inadequate data are obtained from the CPS (Current Population Survey) programme. The CPS labour force data are based on a relatively small national sample which results in fairly substantial sampling errors even for the largest SMSAs (see Flaim, 1968). Although in Britain there are regular unemployment statistics available for employment exchange areas in addition to Census data, these are unwieldy to use for several reasons: the fact that they refer to registered not total unemployment; the difficulty of linking up the exchange boundaries with urban area boundaries; and the absence of information for 'standardisation' purposes except for Census areas. These factors make the Census data much easier to use, though time series analysis and examination of cyclical and seasonal impacts would have to be based on the DEP employment exchange statistics.

Of all the complex forces that may influence the relationship between city size and unemployment, there are three broad types of hypothesis that deserve a specific mention. These hypotheses are not mutually exclusive, and none of them point inevitably to a unidirectional city size–unemployment relationship. It depends upon the specific formulation of the hypothesis and upon the empirical results. The first hypothesis starts from the obvious fact that the size of the labour market will be a direct function of city size, and then suggests that there may be economies and diseconomies of scale associated with metropolitan labour markets. The major economy consists of a greater choice of varied employment opportunities, complementarities of skills, more vacancies, reduced duration of unemployment and hence lower unemployment rates. The obvious diseconomy is the possibility that at a certain large size the labour market begins to function inefficiently, possibly because of the difficulties of communication. This *may* imply that word-of-mouth communications are an important source of information diffusion about available jobs and that these decay rapidly with distance. Too little is known about the extent of these economies and diseconomies or where the critical size (if any) occur.

The second hypothesis is that city size is tied in with unemployment via industrial structure. Industrial structure effects could take many forms: diversification as a function of size, the attraction of certain types of industry to the business services and agglomeration economies concentrated in big cities, or a higher propensity for new industries to be introduced *first* into the larger cities (e.g. due to the concentration of innovations there). These factors all suggest an association between low unemployment rates and big cities, but a more general consideration is that a city's industry mix may have a direct effect on unemployment. The industry mix in a large city may be either favourable or unfavourable, and could turn out either way even between cities of the same size. Testing is made more difficult by the lack of a precise measure of industry mix.[21] An argument sometimes used is that the employment structure of large cities is heavily weighted with personal service industries which are characteristically low paid and with above-average unemployment rates, but there is insufficient evidence in support of this view. It is probably much easier to argue the contrary case: that on industry mix grounds large cities ought to have an advantage from the point of view of unemployment, at least in the sense

61

that a diversified employment structure cushions against the excessive unemployment sometimes experienced in highly specialised small towns.

A third hypothesis is that unemployment may be affected by supply of labour considerations that are sensitive to city size (the labour market and industrial structure hypotheses are based upon demand for labour arguments). For instance, fertility is inversely associated with city size so that in a low mobility economy unemployment should tend to be higher in small towns via the 'echo effects' of earlier high fertility. The stronger arguments, however, cut the other way. One possibility, difficult to test, is the 'drift' theory – a tendency for individuals or groups with a higher propensity to be unemployed to migrate (or 'drift') into larger cities, or even that the indigenous population as a product of the environment in which it lives (such as the large urban slum) is more prone to unemployment. This argument with its implicit emphasis on causal links between city size, high densities and social disorganisation spills over into the 'psychosocial stress' hypothesis.[22] Perhaps a more convincing, if less general, argument is that of a link between high immigration and high unemployment. Some large cities may be attractive to migrants, either because of non-economic factors such as amenities and life-style or because of long-term opportunities, even though it may be difficult for many migrants to find jobs in the short run. Also, in very special circumstances such as when migrants have been displaced from the land jobs may be difficult to obtain because the immigrants are badly educated or inadequately skilled.

As in most situations where supply and demand forces interact, serious identification problems arise. Consider for example the interpretation of the finding of the US CPS survey of metropolitan unemployment in 1967 which revealed that the highest unemployment rates among the 20 largest cities occurred in Los Angeles (5·6 per cent) and San Francisco (5·4 per cent). Two different explanations of this surprising fact have been offered. Flaim (1968, pp. 21–3) suggested that: 'Their high unemployment rates – despite above-average employment growth – must be attributed largely to the immigration factor. Apparently, many workers who move to California do not have a specific job waiting for them; instead, they go there because they like the area, and begin to look for work after they arrive'. Phillips (1972), on the other hand, offered a demand-based explanation: above-average white collar employment structures made these cities sensitive to nation-wide changes in the level of Federal spending (direct and indirect) on aerospace contracts and research. Although the Phillips argument is weakened by his methodology and by the inclusion of Washington in the affected cities (hardly plausible since Washington consistently had the lowest unemployment rate among the 20 cities), this does not mean that demand considerations were irrelevant. But even if data were available for econometric tests, separation out of the relative impacts of demand and supply factors would create insuperable theoretical and measurement problems.

The size-of-place analysis of US Census 1950 data by Duncan and Reiss (1956, p. 95) showed a clear tendency for unemployment rates to be highest in the million-plus urban areas both for whites and non-whites, with no clear-cut variation in size in smaller cities. An analysis of unemployment rates in the 20 largest US cities (all of them in the million-plus size class) in 1960 and 1967 (Flaim, 1968) revealed that these rates were dispersed around the US average, while between these cities there was no statistically significant association between population size and unemployment rates.[23] Phillips' argument is that the unemployment performance of big cities depends not upon their size but upon their degree of specialisation – whether in professional occupations such as the cases mentioned above or in blue collar occupations particularly in basic, nationally-sensitive industries (e.g. Detroit, Pittsburgh, Buffalo, Newark, St. Louis and Baltimore). Another general factor, in this case on the supply side, is race, but although black unemployment rates are consistently more than double the white rates the association between SMSA unemployment rates and the black labour force ratio is much weaker than this differential would suggest.

The most systematic study of the relationship between city size and unemployment is by Vipond (1974), and refers to the 155 cities and towns in Great Britain over 50,000 population using 1966 Census data. Male and female unemployment were analysed separately, and other variables included in the multiple regression analysis apart from city size were social class, age structure, activity rates, a crude measure of employment structure (the non-manufacturing employment ratio), commuting and two dummy variables – one representing whether the area in question was in a conurbation and the other whether the city was in a development area or not. In addition, the regression equations for female unemployment included an additional variable, the male unemployment residual, to reflect the possibility that unspecified factors influencing male unemployment may also affect female unemployment. The influence of all these variables was statistically significant, apart from the conurbation variable, employment structure (male unemployment only), commuting and age structure (female unemployment only).

As for the unemployment–city size relationship, two types of function were analysed. These were:

1 $U(\%) = f(\log_{10} \text{Pop})$ Logarithmic

2 $U(\%) = f[+ \text{Pop}.10^{-6} - (\text{Pop}.10^{-6})^2]$ Quadratic

The regression coefficients for the size variables are shown in Table 5.5. The results show that male and female unemployment rates behave differently. In the logarithmic function case, male unemployment increases consistently

with city size (a ten-fold increase in population is associated with an increase in the unemployment rate of 0·73 per cent), while female unemployment declines (a ten-fold population increase being associated with a decline in unemployment of 0·46 per cent). In addition, there is a *possibility* that a quadratic function yields a good fit, especially for female unemployment. The male unemployment data take the form of an inverted U with the maximum point at a population size of 4 million, while the female function is U-shaped with a minimum point at the half-million mark. However, the quadractic function only fits the male data because of the single observation on the downward slope of the inverted U (i.e. London itself), and it only explains the female unemployment–city size relationship if London is excluded. Thus the UK results may be distorted by the fact that unemployment rates are lower in London than in other major cities for both males and females. Leaving aside London as an aberration, the data clearly point to a rise in unemployment with city size for males, and a fall in unemployment for females up to the 500,000 population level and a rise thereafter.

The Vipond study is rather stronger on its analysis of the empirical relationships between city size and unemployment than on their explanation. For males it was suggested that, despite the failure of the crude employment structure variable, industrial structure might be the key to the tendency for unemployment to increase with city size, but this speculation must await the outcome of future research and, in particular, the development of more satisfactory industry-mix variables. A more satisfactory explanation was offered of the female results. First, as we move up the urban hierarchy

Table 5.5

Unemployment and City Size in Great Britain

	Male		Female	
	Quadratic	Logarithmic	Quadratic*	Logarithmic
Regression coefficients (t values)	+1·929 P (3·494) −0·232 P^2 (3·224)	+0·727 log P (3·126)	−3·332 P (2.348) +3·137 P^2 (2.033)	−0·459 log P (1·832)
	0·698	0·691	0·521	0·505

* Excludes Greater London
$t \geqslant 2·326$, significant at 0·01
$t \geqslant 1·645$, significant at 0.05.

the employment position for women improves because of several mutually reinforcing favourable factors: shifts in industrial structure, particularly an increasing proportion of service jobs; a greater variety and flexibility in the terms and conditions of employment, e.g. variability in hours of work, workplaces closer to schools and shops, etc., and other factors conducive to the employment of women from the point of view of dovetailing with their domestic functions; more provision of labour-saving and housewife-substituting services such as nurseries. Second, at some level (according to the UK data around the half-million city size) these scale economies are exhausted, perhaps because the industrial structure begins to change unfavourably or because of labour market diseconomies (women may rely more on word-of-mouth and informal contacts in finding jobs). A more probable explanation, however, is the need for longer journeys to work. This is a general effect of increasing city size, partly because of the geographical extension of urban boundaries, partly because of greater areal specialisation and widening spatial maladjustments between the locations of residences and workplaces. Longer journeys to work are more serious for women because their lower pay means that they can less afford the higher costs while their domestic commitments mean that they can less afford the travel time. All these forces may tend to increase female unemployment in the larger cities.

As yet, there is insufficient research on which to base a firm judgement about the relationship between unemployment and city size. With notable exceptions (London, New York, Chicago, Boston and Washington), male unemployment rates tend to deteriorate with increasing city size. For females there may well be substantial urban economies of scale with the possibility of a turning point in the larger size classes. However, it is clear – even on the evidence currently available – that the prospects of lower unemployment do not generally figure among the many economic and social advantages of big cities.

Inflation and city size

An interesting, if neglected, question is whether there is any relationship between price inflation and city size. In one sense, this amounts to introducing a dynamic aspect into analysis of a problem that has been explored in some depth with cross-sectional data – the relationships between city size and earnings, on the one hand, and living costs on the other. However, it has broader implications in that rising prices may have effects on consumer and business expectations and, more generally, on social welfare that are independent of whether prices rise faster than incomes or not. Election

Table 5.6

Consumer price increases by city size class, annually and by category,
United States, December 1966–December 1971

Size class	Number in sample	By year %					All items	1966–71 %				
		1967	1968	1969	1970	1971		Food	Housing	Apparel, upkeep	Transport	Health, recreation
3.5 million plus	3	2·8	4·9	6·4	6·2	3·7	26·3	22·5	29·4	23·0	25·4	28·4
1·4–3·5 million	7	2·9	5·1	6·2	5·4	3·4	25·2	20·6	28·2	25·4	22·5	27·2
250,000–1·4 million	17	3·1	4·5	6·5	5·0	3·4	24·6	19·9	29·3	24·1	18·7	26·5
50,000–250,000	10	3·1	4·6	5·6	4·9	3·2	23·4	19·5	27·0	24·2	17·4	26·4
2,500–50,000	17	2·9	4·3	5·4	5·3	2·9	22·6	19·4	25·8	23·1	17·5	24·2
United States		3·0	4·7	6·1	5·5	3·4	24·8	20·7	28·2	23·7	20·8	26·8

Source: *Monthly Labor Review*, August 1972.

promises, the stated goals of economic policy and the mass media have led us to believe that inflation is undesirable with the result that we do believe it. If prices were to rise faster in one size of city than in another this would be a black mark against that city size, regardless of whether the price rises were fully compensated for by higher earnings or not.

Until recently there were no data available for analysis of this question. Now, however, there is a limited quantity of information on consumer price indices in a sample of 56 American cities over the five year period 1966–71 (Bahr, Meiners and Nakayama, 1972). The basic data are summarised in Table 5.6. They show that prices rose more rapidly with increasing city size. Regression analysis indicates close similarity in the average quarterly percentage price changes within the range 1·14–1·33 per cent per quarter, with the rate of change increasing fairly steadily with city size. The differences in the rates of inflation from one city size class to another are statistically significant.[24] When components in the price index are separated out, a slightly different picture emerges. Clothing and general upkeep price increases did not vary systematically with city size, the price of housing increased at a similar rate in cities above the 50,000 population level (though it rose faster than the aggregate price level in all cities), while the spread of food price rises – though varying regularly with city size – was narrower than in prices as a whole. The widest city size spread occurred in transport costs, even though the rate of inflation was lower than for the aggregate price level.

It is difficult to draw firm conclusions from such a limited study over so brief a period. Also, the city size classes used in this inquiry are rather different from those used elsewhere in the book which prevents a direct comparison of results. Nevertheless, the available income data – though supporting the hypothesis that the *per capita* income and wage *levels* are much higher in big cities – do not reveal any consistent tendency for incomes to rise faster in larger cities (see Table 9.2, p. 116). Indeed, in the very long run – over several decades – there are some signs of *per capita* income convergence among cities of different size. If these price trends were to continue, they could represent a very gradual whittling away of the real income advantages of city size. Similarly, the adverse social welfare effects of rising prices appear to be stronger in the larger city size classes (on the reasonable assumption that these adverse effects are either a constant or increasing function of the rate of inflation). On the scanty evidence available hitherto, the social costs of faster inflation are a disadvantage of life in big cities.

Notes

[1] Fuchs (1967) is attracted to the disequilibrium hypothesis: A 'possible explanation is the existence of a disequilibrium in the supply of labour and capital. Surplus labour from agriculture may tend to move first to the small towns, and then later to the larger cities. Capital may be more readily available in the large cities. If there is disequilibrium, we should observe a tendency for labour to migrate from small to large cities, and for industry to move in the reverse direction.' This is, in effect, an interurban version of the Borts-Stein (1964) regional growth model.

[2] Evidence on how the distribution of personal income varies with city size is briefly discussed below.

[3] For Sweden see Royal Ministry for Foreign Affairs (1972a), p. 16; for Germany, Lösch (1954, p.456) and *Statistisches Jahrbuch Deutschen Gemeinden*; for Japan, K. Mera (1970); while for the United Kingdom the Department of Health and Social Security Earnings Survey is virtually the only source (urban data are unpublished).

[4] Another source is US Department of Labor, *Handbook of Labor Statistics* which provides pay estimates by very broad occupational categories. These data suggest substantial size-of-place differentials for clerical, skilled maintenance and unskilled plant workers in all regions apart from the North Central (for a summary see Hoover, 1971, p. 162).

[5] Rural–urban migration was probably the critical factor in this convergence.

[6] These orders of magnitude appear fairly consistent between countries. Alonso (1970b) suggests that there may be slight evidence for a turndown in cities larger than 3 million, though even in such a case the most likely explanation is that a sizeable proportion of the very rich in large cities lives outside the metropolitan boundary.

[7] The continued attraction of the largest cities for blacks might be explained in terms of following friends and relatives or of the gravitational pull of long-established and large black settlements.

[8] See also Bell (1970).

[9] This is what the sociologists call *relative deprivation*.

[10] Considered alone, the findings from the 1950 Census are dubious because of the large proportion of income recipients in the open-ended upper income range.

[11] At 1960 income levels, $ 10,000 and over is defined as high income and $ 3,000 and under as low income.

[12] I.e. $Q_3 - Q_1/Q_1 + Q_3$.

[13] See Foster and Richardson (1972): 'Apart from higher prices and differential commuting time, we might also wish to include in the definition of

real income such things as differential hours of work, the level of public facilities, the extent of pollution and the quality of the environment'.

14 The proportion of worktrips by public transport in the United States was only 9.3 per cent in cities in the 50–250,000 range but 34.1 per cent in cities larger than 3 million population (Schnore, 1963).

15 Another problem very difficult to handle is what to do about goods and services that require a high threshold population level to justify operation. These can be consumed only in large cities so that if the cost of living index is suficiently disaggregated they would figure in large city 'baskets' but not in those for the small town.

16 An exception was the low standard of living budget in Southern urban areas

17 The rank correlation coefficient between living costs and city size in 1971 equals 0·45 excluding Honolulu and Anchorage).

18 See Table 5.3.

19 Climate influences the cost of housing e.g. air conditioning, quality of insulating materials.

20 According to Hoover (1971) the main factors behind housing costs are city size, recent rapid urban growth and a rigorous climate.

21 Phillips (1972) claims to have devised a measure of industry mix by measuring the regression slope obtained from regressing local against national unemployment rates for 18 occupational groups, but all this yields is an *unweighted* average local/national unemployment ratio whereas the ratio of the city's overall unemployment rate to the national is *weighted* according to the relative size of each industry. Mathur (1970) used the coefficient of industrial specialisation as a surrogate for industry mix. Incidentally, Mathur found evidence of an association between favourable occupational mix (in the sense of an occupational distribution weighted in favour of higher paid occupations) and city size among SMSAs, though not among smaller urban areas.

22 See below, pp. 102–08.

23 In 1960 the rank correlation coefficient was +0·3783, and in 1967 +0·4112, both barely significant even at the 10 per cent level.

24 The *t* values ranged from 4·92 to 6·84 when rates of price increases between adjacent city size classes were compared; $t \geqslant 2·88$ is statistically significant at the 0·01 level.

6 Economic Structure

The economic structures of cities and towns can vary widely, between cities of the same size as well as between cities in separate size-classes. The question is whether economic structure varies systematically with city size, and whether – if size is a determinant – this is due to size *per se* or because size stands as a surrogate for other variables. Although the problem is a very complex one, it is worth investigating for several reasons. First, the impact that city size may have on industrial structure is intrinsically interesting and raises the issue of whether old-established theories in urban analysis such as economic base models and central place theory still have any relevance. Second, the existence of agglomeration economies may be a major force via which the impact of city size is felt so that the attraction of large cities for industries could be an element in assessing the economic advantages of cities equally as important as their attraction for migrants. Third, if certain industries were attracted to the larger cities while other industries tended to locate in smaller towns, this could provide some guidelines for action to link industrial planning to urban planning, or in a more ambitious context to integrate a location of industry policy with a national urban growth policy.

An analysis of this kind is not made easy by the data problems, and the difficulties of interpreting the data that are available. In the United Kingdom only employment and unemployment data exist at the urban level, apart from sporadic distribution data; the Census of Production is not broken down into urban areas though some approximate coverage might be derived from subregional data in cases where disclosure rules do not intervene. In the United States there is a wide variety of information at the SMSA level – employment, earnings, income, etc. – but in most sources the level of industry aggregation is very high, and really detailed analysis is feasible only with the periodic industrial census data. In any event, both the minimum list heading (UK) and the 3- and 4- digit (US) levels of the SIC are often still too highly aggregated, since the differences in the economic structure of cities are frequently very subtle, implying particular degrees of specialisation within the same industrial category.

Moreover, many of the variables are simultaneously determined, and this reduces confidence in interpretation of the evidence even in cases where there are no data problems. For example, city size may be in part a function of age of settlement, and age of settlement could reflect when the area was attractive for certain kinds of industry. These initial industries to a large extent would have moulded the subsequent growth of the city and the development of its industrial structure so that in attempting to evaluate the impact of current city size on the future structure we cannot ignore how current size is a function of the past structure. Size influences structure, and structure influences size, in ways which are complicated to unravel. The complications are increased by the fact that some of the key initial location decisions may have been random with respect to both region and size of city within the selected region.

Another difficulty of interpretation arises from the possibility that the forces attracting industries to large cities, i.e. agglomeration economies, may have a spatial range long enough to make it possible for an industry to choose a location in a small city and yet take advantage of the services and agglomeration economies offered in the nearby larger city. Bergsman, Greenston and Healy (1972) argue that the spatial influence of agglomeration economies really needs a distance–decay function to measure it. If we select the SMSA as the appropriate city size unit, and if we do not take explicit account of the location of other nearby cities, this implies the assumption that agglomerative forces do not vary with distance within the SMSA but fall to zero once the SMSA boundary is crossed.

A useful starting point is whether economic base theory and central place analysis (or the more general forms of hierarchy models) have any implications for size of place and economic structure comparisons. Economic base models stress the role of export activities in city structure and growth. An empirical finding, plausible on *a priori* grounds, is that the base ratio (i.e. gross exports ÷ output) declines with increasing city size. This suggests that a distinctive feature in comparing small towns and big cities is that exports figure much more prominently in the former than in the latter. This does not *inevitably* mean differences in industrial structure since what is supplied for export in the small town may be supplied for local consumption in the larger urban area. However, in most cases the high export ratio does have repercussions on economic structure. The corollary of export dependence for small towns is that they cannot be viable on the basis of the size of their local market alone since this market is too small to sustain most industries. Instead, their viability derives from one or more of several alternative sources of export earnings which, by definition, are not related to the size of the urban population. These include: provision of low-order services for an agricultural hinterland (the main function of very small agricultural service centres in rural regions); specialised manufacturing serving non-local markets; resort facilities and tourism. In cases such as these, the export activities may dominate the local economy.

Central place theory predicts that the smallest size-class of towns provides services to a rural hinterland while larger towns supply high order services both to hinterlands and to smaller urban centres. This means that larger towns specialise in 'higher-order' economic activities (i.e. defined as service industries with a large market threshold in terms of population and/or purchasing power) which are provided both for the intraurban population and are exported down the hierarchy to smaller centres. Also, since the large towns are also producers of the lower-order services, the model predicts that the *number* of industries and services rises with increasing city size; in other words, large urban areas are more diversified than smaller urban areas. Although there have been attempts to extend the hierarchy model framework to manufacturing (e.g. Tinbergen, 1961 and 1964; Bos, 1965), these have had only restricted success since market areas for many manufactured goods are much broader than the 'force field' of a single urban area, no matter how large. Thus, in some cases it is possible for a small town to specialise in a manufacturing activity that serves the whole nation.

The central place model primarily refers to specialisation in consumer services among urban centres of different size. Big cities also provide business services on a much larger scale (relative to population) than smaller urban areas. The market for these business services is not local population directly but local manufacturing and commercial firms. These services have developed because of the urban concentration of industrial activities in the past, and their presence is frequently a source of attraction for new firms. Thus, business services – a product of the past industrial structure – are a determinant of the current and future structure. In particular, they account for the fact that manufacturing – especially small-scale manufacturing – can be an important component in the economic structure of even the largest centres. Whereas some kinds of manufacturing, e.g. industries which are natural resource based or which use a large volume of moderate skill, low wage labour, locate primarily in small towns, other types of manufacturing, particularly the so-called 'external economy' industries, are heavily concentrated in the multi-million cities. This distinction, which is in reality a very sharp one and highly stratified by city size, obviously requires a greater degree of industrial disaggregation than primary, manufacturing, construction and services classifications.

The variety of determinants of location for different manufacturing industries suggests that city size and industrial structure may be linked via locational advantages and disadvantages which are themselves functionally related to city size (von Böventer, 1971; Smith, 1971; Evans, 1972). In particular, large cities may offer business services, access to sources of capital and highly skilled and specialised (but highly paid) labour. On the other hand, smaller urban areas have much lower land rental costs and lower wages. Since industries vary in the degree to which they use these inputs, and the cost of these inputs varies with city size, the optimal city size can vary widely from one industry to another. For instance, standardised textile

73

industries which are labour-intensive and occupy a large floor space will tend to be located in small towns while sectors such as insurance, banking, finance, and the headquarter offices of manufacturing with their demand for professional and managerial labour, need for information resources and face-to-face personal contact, specialised business services and business entertainment facilities will gravitate towards the large cities. Furthermore, within sectors finding their ideal location in a particular size of city these input characteristics will be accentuated by substitution of relatively cheap for dear inputs (e.g. space- and clerical labour-saving computer installations being substituted for routine office personnel and large offices in the very big city).

A similar perspective is to develop an even broader location framework for explaining how firms choose where to locate from among all possible locations. Such a framework might emphasise four key factors: market area analysis; economies of agglomeration; location of resource supplies; transport costs on raw materials and finished products. The first two are directly related to city size, the third may be random in its spatial incidence, while the fourth is relevant to city size primarily in the case of the location of service establishments where consumers travel to the source of supply. The relative importance of these determinants will determine the relative size of the city in which a firm locates, or indeed whether an urban location is chosen at all. Wingo (1972) argues that this type of analysis may be particularly valuable in respect to firms serving non-local markets (typically manufacturing firms in industries with high location quotients). Such an analysis would shed light on the competitive advantages of cities of varying size for different types of industry. The integration of city size variables with models of interregional trade, industrial location and urban hierarchies would be a useful approach to understanding the determinants of urban industrial structure.

Another strand of analysis is not so much to emphasise the differential advantages of cities of varying size throughout the urban hierarchy, but to stress the special advantages of large cities as a location for economic activities which result in their having economic structures that are more complex and more viable than those found in smaller urban centres. Many of these advantages could be defined as agglomeration economies, but our knowledge of agglomeration functions is so skimpy that we cannot identify precisely the city size classes where these economies become important. Leaving aside the attraction of the metropolis to households (externalities in consumption) and the possibility of scale economies and diseconomies in the public sector,[1] we are left with a wide range of business agglomeration economies. These include: labour market economies (more skills, a wider range of skills, training facilities, better organised placement services, greater elasticity of labour supply); common pools of technical and marketing facilities and business services; opportunities for face-to-face contact and other communication economies; greater adaptability and flexibility of fixed investments, particularly in structures; direct transportation links with other centres and scale economies in executive transport (i.e. airport services) and in warehousing, distributing and other terminal facilities; greater provision of educational facilities, hospitals and other types of social infrastructure that have a potentially favourable effect on labour and managerial productivity. The impact of each of these economies may vary widely between industries.

Of more general significance are the opportunities for specialisation offered by the large market. This implies potential for product specialisation[2] but it also means that technical externalities are a function of city size (Cameron, 1970, p. 30; *Strategic Plan for the South East*, 1970, p.72). An extension of this argument (associated with Wilbur Thompson) is that the large city provides a climate conducive to the development of newer industries. This emphasises the role of the metropolis as an innovation centre, the disproportionate concentration of scientific and technological talent, the presence of an infrastructure and environment favourable to growth, and the capacity of the big city (via supply of finance) to spawn small new firms.

How this transformation comes about remains nebulous, but if the argument is valid its results are clear. The industrial structure of large cities should, on average, be more heavily weighted with new industries than that of smaller cities. Also, new industries should first develop in the largest cities and subsequently 'filter down' into smaller, less skilled and lower wage areas. Information about the generation and diffusion of new firms and industries is too scanty to permit an effective test of this interesting hypothesis. Nevertheless, the indirect evidence is rather unconvincing. If the industrial structure of large metropolises were more heavily weighted with new industries, it might be expected that employment growth in the highest city size class would exceed that of other cities. In fact, a study of US urban performance in the 1950s suggested that the opposite was true (Stanback and Knight, 1970, p. 102). Moreover, some analysts have adopted the contrary position and argued that the metropolitan structure will be weighted down with older industries, less dynamic firms and lower skilled workers (Eversley, 1972b). Probably, this dichotomy of opinion merely illustrates the dangers of generalisation rather than suggests that one view is right and the other is wrong. Although large size does offer potential economies that are not feasible in smaller towns, it may nevertheless remain true that there can be no clear-cut, direct correspondence between city size and *type* of economic structure. The examples of Houston and Atlanta can be matched with the examples of Glasgow and Buffalo.

A striking empirical illustration of the relationship between large metro-politan size and economic structure is the role of external economies in attracting and concentrating certain types of economic activity in New York as demonstrated in the New York Metropolitan Region Study of the late 1950s (Vernon, 1960; Lichtenberg, 1960; Hoover and Vernon, 1959). Similar patterns of industrial, commercial and financial structure have been noticed in London (Martin, 1966; Economists Advisory Group, 1971). The evidence shows that there are several types of specialisation and external economy involved. First, there is the existence of facilities for manufacturing. Lichtenberg (1960) drew attention to 87 relatively small industries with a high degree of concentration in the New York metropolitan region (of these, in 14 industries more than 75 per cent of national employment was in New York, in 11 more industries more than 50 per cent and in a further 29 indus-tries more than 33 per cent[3]). These are primarily industries 'whose over-riding locational need is to be able to tap a pool of facilities – of space, of skills, of suppliers, or of freight services'. Firms in these industries are usually very small, single-plant establishments using labour-intensive methods, relying heavily on outside suppliers, marked by instability of out-put, uncertainty and carrying very low inventories. These are the classic 'external economy' industries, the small manufacturing firms that are attracted to the great metropolis because the facilities offered there could only be provided elsewhere *within* large firms. It is the existence of such industries which justifies Hoyt's argument that what most characterises the world's great cities is not their government employment, not their tourist amenities, their sights and their art treasures, not their concentration of financial and commercial expertise but their manufacturing activities. New York had 34,425 manufacturing establishments in 1967, more than two-thirds of which employed less than 20 people. A similar picture emerges from London, Paris, Tokyo, Chicago and other large cities.

Second, other types of external economy – communication economies, access to information resources, specialist expertise in commerce and finance, opportunities for face-to-face contact – lead to specialisation in the service sector in large cities. Such cities have a high concentration of banking, security and commodity brokers, communications industries, insurance firms, advertising, legal services, miscellaneous business services, headquarter offices of manufacturing firms, non-profit membership organisations, data processing and non-profit research organisations. These activities tend to build up through self-generating attraction of more establishments within the same sectors. The relative weight of the agglomerative forces are difficult to identify, but most of the metropolitan offices need to minimise the costs of personal contact. It is argued that specialisation in the business service and finance sector increases as we ascend the urban hierarchy, and that this

76

specialisation itself constitutes a major agglomeration economy for the large metropolis via its pull on other industries and on labour. There is little doubt that these activities are highly concentrated in New York and London. For example, one-third of the 500 largest US industrial corporations have their headquarters in New York City, and over one-half of the 500 largest British companies have headquarters in London. Similar or higher proportions of the management consultancies, life insurance offices, commodity brokers and similar activities are also located in these cities.

However, this heavy concentration is not as overwhelming or as static as these figures might suggest. Although the largest and most specialised of these activities are still found in the giant traditional commercial and financial centres, these industries are also developing elsewhere on an increasing scale. Employment in the business services sector is not only disproportionately high in the United States in many of the multi-million metropolises (New York, Chicago, San Franscisco, Boston) but also in some smaller cities with hinterland functions (Des Moines, Lincoln and Fargo). Over the SMSA size range, Bergsman et al. (1972) found that specialisation in business services increases significantly, but slowly, with city size. Cities with good communications (e.g. frequent airport services) and developed information centres (e.g. universities, institutes of higher education) may attract more of these business services than justified by size alone. On the other hand, holding city size constant, Bergsman found no relationship between business service specialisation and population growth or distance from the main 'business service exporting' cities. There are indications that the pull of the largest metropolises is declining to a degree, and that they are responding by becoming even more specialised, e.g. in international finance functions. Thus, in the United States large-medium centres such as Atlanta, Dallas and Denver have taken on more banking, advertising and consultancy functions. In the United Kingdom some of the main building society and insurance offices have decentralised out of London, though they have usually remained within the Outer Metropolitan Region.[4] The critical question is whether or not improved telecommunications and data processing technology will favour decentralisation or centralisation, or lead to a spatial separation of activities between big city core locations for the key decision-makers and other locations for the more routine activities. Opinions vary, and the empirical evidence is unclear.

This emphasis on the role of manufacturing and business services in the economic structure of large cities receives some support in the employment structure and size of place data of Table 6.1. The shares of both manufacturing[5] and business services increase with city size, and provide the most marked difference in the employment structure of varying size-classes. The other major but more obvious change is the decline in primary industries between non-metropolitan and metropolitan areas and up the urban hierarchy. A more surprising difference at first sight is the declining share of government employment with increasing city size, but this is probably due to the existence of small and medium-size State capitals and is peculiar to a Federal structure.[6] Shares in other employment categories are invariant with city size.

Table 6.1

Employment Structure and Size of Place, 1960

	Non-metropolitan counties	Metropolitan labour markets		
		Small	Medium	Large
Primary	20·7	7·1	3·4	1·0
Construction	6·3	6·0	6·1	4·8
Manufacturing	21·0	25·1	27·5	30·2
Utilities	1·3	1·4	1·4	1·3
Business services	10·5	13·4	16·4	18·7
Consumer services	31·5	34·8	32·8	31·7
Government	6·2	9·0	8·4	7·0
Others	2·6	3·1	4·1	5·3

Small=25–200,000; Medium=200–1,600,000; Large=>1,600,000
Source: Stanback and Knight, 1970, p. 81.

Unfortunately, though revealing in some respects, aggregate statistics of this kind mask many of the most striking differences in economic structure between urban areas of diverse size. For instance, within the manufacturing sector certain manufacturing industries are prone to locate in centres of a particular size while other industries may be found in all sizes of towns. Hoover (1971) made a sharp distinction between industries which locate predominately in large cities and those which prefer small cities and towns. In the former case, external economies of concentration are important; the latter may be resource-oriented, recreation-oriented or labour-oriented. One implication of this – to be explored below – is that small towns tend to be much more specialised than large cities. Another is that, apart from differences in interindustry structure, there will be significant differences in the *type* of industry located in cities of different size. In some cases (e.g. where industries are close together for localisation economy and other technical reasons) industries will have a wide choice of size ranges; the petroleum refining–chemicals complex is an obvious example. In other situations, industries will be attracted to particular sizes or types of city because a key locational determinant varies with city size. For instance, low wage industries in the United States (leather, textiles, etc.) are attracted to small, depressed metropolitan areas (the coal towns of Pennsylvania - Scranton, Wilkes-Barr – or the textile towns of New England – Fall River, Brockton), to smaller South Eastern cities (Greenville, Lynchburg) or to the poverty areas within great metropolises such as New York and Philadelphia. These locations imply clearly defined city sizes, but this is largely accidental since city size in this context stands merely as a surrogate for low wage area. Other industries may be attracted to large cities because these industries are heavily market-oriented, and in this case city size is merely a surrogate for the market. Yet other industries (manufacturers tied to port activities, quarries, grain products, etc.) will be attracted to natural resource locations, and here we would expect city size to be a random variable.

Hoover presents some data which classifies industries by the city size class in which they have the greatest concentration (as measured by the value of the location quotient), and examines the classifications in association with size of industry and the share of US employment in SMSAs (Hoover, 1971, pp. 157–8). The size classes selected are 500,000 plus; 100,000–500,000; 50,000–100,000; 10,000–50,000; 2,500–10,000; and all other places. The results are very interesting. The industries in the highest size-class are all small with a high degree of concentration in SMSAs; these are the type of industry that gravitates towards New York or (in the UK context) towards London. As we descend the urban hierarchy, the industries become larger as measured by national employment and less urbanised generally. Also, the degree of concentration in the favoured size-class declines. Notable examples include: tyres and photographic equipment in the 100,000–500,000 group; motor vehicles and ports, steel foundries and transformers in cities in the 50,000–100,000 range; internal combustion engines, electrical equipment and glassware in the 10,000–50,000 class; tractors and hosiery in the 2,500–10,000 class; and logging, beet sugar, clay and lime in even smaller places. Also, several important industries such as machine shops, nonferrous foundries, plastics, primary metals, paper and certain food products had location quotients within the 0·80–1·70 range in every city-size class. The most striking features of these results are the large numbers of industries with a favoured city-size class in the lower range, the high degree of flexibility in choice of location in terms of city size, and many key industries scattered indiscriminately among all city sizes. These results also receive support from the Urban Institute's findings (Bergsman *et al.*, 1972) which show that the top-ranking cities in terms of concentration of specific industrial clusters vary widely in size within each cluster. Using rather different methods, in particular, indices of urbanisation and Kendall's tau (which enables a comparison to be made between city size rank and specialisation in employment rank for each industry), Winsborough (1959) came to similar results, though fabricating industries tended to be located more strongly in larger towns than processing industries. Thus, the relationship between specialisation in specific industries and city size is much more blurred than *a priori* analysis might suggest.

Whereas central place theory provides an orderly framework for stratifying service industries by city size, no parallel principle exists for manufacturing industries. The spatial distribution of natural resources in the economy is very uneven so that the location of resource-oriented manufacturing reflects the random distribution of these resources. As for market-oriented manufacturing industries, even they do not exhibit regular location patterns with city size because most manufacturing firms serve non-local more than local markets. Regional specialisation in manufacturing is far more marked than city-size specialisation (Stanback and Knight, 1970) with the result that towns in an old-established manufacturing region tend to reflect the dominance of manufacturing in the regional economic structure regardless of their size. Furthermore, the differential growth in service employment and manufacturing employment in recent decades (the former growing much faster than the latter) has distorted manufacturing – city size relationships since among manufacturing towns and cities some will have moved from one size class to the next depending upon whether they were well placed for expanding their service functions or not.

An important implication of the tendency for many substantial manufacturing industries (with large individual plant size) to find a convenient location in small urban areas is that small towns will – to the extent that they are manufacturing towns – tend to be more specialised than larger cities. This must be the case since the larger the individual employment workplaces and the smaller the area in which they locate the less is the scope for the development of other industries. Similarly, we know that hierarchy models for service sectors imply that larger centres have more diversified service employment structures than small centres because they embrace all the lower-order service functions as well as the high-order functions not found in smaller towns. This can be most easily understood by the concept of 'minimal critical city size' which measures the lower local market threshold for particular types of activity, usually service functions[7] but also certain kinds of manufacturing. As cities grow in size they cross more and more market thresholds which justify the existence of additional higher-order industries. Unless the lower-order functions are then passed down to smaller urban areas (this happens in a few but not in most cases) the larger urban areas must become more diversified and less specialised than the small.[8] In addition, new functions develop in large cities which have little or nothing to do with central place functions, but merely reflect the opportunities offered by scale economies for functions to be transferred from firms and households to service establishments. This, too, will show up in a highly disaggregated diversification index, even though in this case the increase in diversification is largely spurious, since it merely represents a transfer of functions from a firm in an existing industry or from the household sector to a new industry without necessarily any increase in their *per capita* per-, formance.

Although the theoretical case for the view that large cities have more diversified employment structures than smaller cities appears clear-cut, the empirical evidence is much more ambiguous. A major explanation could be the level of aggregation of the data. An occasional reason could be that extreme functional specialisation may be promoted in a large city because of unique features (e.g. the centre of large-scale government activity such as Washington, D.C.) or because a strongly favourable socio-economic status mix (Duncan and Reiss, 1956; Mathur, 1970) attracts a limited number of high-quality labour sectors on a substantial scale. International comparisons by Gibbs and Martin (1962) showed a high correlation between industrial diversification and the percentage of total population within metropolitan areas, but this could easily be explained by industrial development being associated with dispersion of population into *more* centres rather than in larger centres. Ullman and Dacey's analysis (1960) of specialisation indices among metropolitan areas larger than 300,000 found some small areas at the top (e.g. Wilkes-Barr, Charleston (West Virginia), Akron and Youngstown) and big cities at the bottom (Kansas, San Francisco, Dallas, Denver and Seattle) but there were even larger cities fairly high in the rankings among 57 metropolitan areas (Washington (5), Detroit (6) and Pittsburgh (11)). Moreover, the cut-off point of 300,000 is too high to reveal striking city-size differences. A recent study by Clemente and Sturgis (1971) found a relationship between industrial diversification and population size, but much less strong than the theoretical arguments might suggest. Using the Gibbs-Martin industrial diversification measure (implying that the more evenly the labour force is distributed, the greater the degree of industrial diversification) on a 25 industry basis they found that in the United States 17 per cent of the variation in industrial diversification was due to population size, with a regional spread from 12·9 per cent in the North-East to 30·3 per cent in the West. One suggestion of why the diversification tendencies were not as strong as might have been expected was the possibility of growing functional interdependence in a system of cities, with more specialisation and greater division of labour between cities in the system.

The corollary of the relationship between a diversified industrial structure and city size is that large cities are potentially more stable than small

(Thompson's 'growth stability' hypothesis) and that large cities are more *alike* than small. Some support for the latter view was found by Czamanski (1964) in that the effects on location of urban-oriented industries (the main urban service sectors) tended to become more stable with increasing city size and less subject to variation among individual cities. Studies of functional classifications of cities also suggest the same point (Stanback and Knight, 1970; Duncan and Reiss, 1956; Armen, 1972) in that the type of city varies much more widely in the smaller size classes. For instance, specialised city types such as resort cities, university towns, resource-oriented towns, specialised manufacturing export towns, new towns, industrial estate towns, nodal service centres, administrative centres are much more common and varied than the structures of the great metropolitan areas. On the other hand, this is not to imply that the large cities are completely uniform. In the United States, there are wide differences between, say, New York or Chicago, on the one hand, and Washington or Los Angeles and, to take a pair of typically specialised manufacturing cities, Detroit and Pittsburgh. Similarly, in the United Kingdom there is a major difference in structure (apart from size effects) between London and Birmingham, Glasgow and Liverpool. On an international basis, however, the multi-million cities exercising cosmopolitan functions are more comparable in spite of the huge differences in the economic structure and levels of development of the countries concerned. All this suggests that it is much easier to generalise about the economic structures of large cities than those of small towns.

Notes

[1] Both these topics are discussed elsewhere, see pp. 45, 85–96.

[2] A large market also implies that some services can be provided either that are not available at all in smaller centres (primarily in the consumption externality field) or that are provided internally in firms (specialist business services supplied within the firm by the largest enterprises but where in a large city the demand warrants specialist firms supplying both large and small firms). The latter argument has been stressed heavily by Duncan (1959) in his explanation of why the economic structure of large cities can only be partly explained in terms of central place theory.

[3] The most concentrated industries were: hatters' fur; lapidary work; artists' materials; fur goods; dolls; Schiffli-machine embroideries; hat and cap materials; suspenders and garters; women's neckwear and scarves; hairwork; other embroideries; tucking and pleating; handbags; tobacco pipes; millinery; children's coats; belts; artificial flowers; women's clothing. Other typical industries include umbrellas, leather goods, gramophone

records, printing and publishing, other clothing industries, bookbinding, jewellery, rainwear, luggage, typesetting, china, toys, metal engraving, greeting cards, mirrors, advertising signs and art goods.

[4] In the 1960s the only expanding employment categories in Greater London remained professional and science, insurance, banking and finance and (with considerable fluctuations) public administration (Foster and Richardson, 1972).

[5] In the Soviet Union the positive correlation between manufacturing and city size is very strong. This reflects the importance of industrial planning in the State's central planning functions and the related tendency for services to account for a very much smaller proportion of employment and output than in Western countries. 'Government policy on industrial development... must always be borne in mind as part of the driving force behind the rapid urbanisation and as a factor in the distribution, size characteristics and economic functions of cities' (Harris, 1970, p. 27).

[6] On the other hand, certain types of Federal expenditure are heavily concentrated in the million-plus metropolitan areas. Concentration ratios (i.e. ratios of the share of expenditures to the population share of the size class) in these cities were 2·19 in mass transit, 1·86 for space research, 1·86 for water transportation, 1·49 for air transportation, 1·36 for defence contracts, 1·35 for postal service expenditures and 1·26 for health services and care (see Alonso, 1971b, Table I).

[7] For estimates of the critical city size for personal and business services see Duncan (1959, pp. 112, 115).

[8] On the other hand, they *specialise* in complex, high market threshold activities in the sense that such activities can be found only in the larger cities. We must not become confused by the greater *diversification* of a large city's employment structure and that city's *specialisation* in functions not carried out in smaller cities. In this sense, diversification and specialisation are complementary not contradictory. It is merely necessary to distinguish between specialisation in the overall employment structure and specialisation in an individual activity relative to other cities of different size. The development of specialist functions in large areas (Duncan, 1959), is, in fact, a diversification-inducing force.

7 Scale Economies in Local Government

Of the many aspects of urban size, the question of economies of scale in urban governments has received perhaps the most attention. Although much of the research has been concerned with the problem of returns to scale in individual urban public services, a much wider focus of interest has been the idea that there might be an optimal size for urban government units and, by extension, for cities themselves. It is wise to make a sharp distinction between these approaches. The evidence on economies of scale is, with a few exceptions, unconvincing, but there are still several analytical problems to be solved before a firm conclusion can be reached. The solution to the second approach is unequivocal; there can be no optimal size urban government just as there can be no unique optimal city size. The reasons for this view will soon be made clear.

In discussions of economies of scale in urban government, there are several distinct aspects that merit analysis. First, there is the question of economies of scale in the provision of urban services (either individually or as a whole). This appears to be the most important aspect as measured by the quantity of research output and the complexity of the issues raised. Second, we must give some attention to managerial economies and diseconomies in relation to the urban government as a whole. Third, it is necessary to recognise that an urban government size which is efficient from the point of view of public goods *provision* is not inevitably an appropriate size for financing these services. Fourth, non-economic factors may be important, particularly the fact that a suitable size of urban government may be determined, in part, by the desire for political participation. To cater for these desires may be worth some sacrifice in economic efficiency.

Estimates of an efficient size range for urban governments have varied widely: 50–100,000 (Hirsch, 1959 and 1968); 100–150,000 (Lomax, 1943); 100–200,000 (Clark, 1945); 30–250,000 (SVIMEZ, 1967); 100–250,000 (Royal Commission on Local Government in Greater London, 1960); 200–1,000,000 (Hoover, 1971); 250–1,000,000 (Royal Commission on Local Government in England, 1969); 500–1,000,000 (Duncan, 1956). Even these examples do not provide a comprehensive list of the varied estimates. There are many reasons why estimates should vary from place to place (both internationally and interregionally) and over time. For instance, the overall estimate depends upon the services selected for detailed study, and the urban government service 'mix' may differ according to community tastes, the institutional and ideological traditions of the country[1] and the number of hierarchical levels of government in the administration. Moreover, the logic of an overall estimate requires the assumption that the cost curves for individual services can be aggregated. This assumption is highly debatable: communities are very heterogeneous in their service needs even within the same city size class; weighting changes with scale and, much more critical, the *number* of services supplied increases with scale; there may be marked interdependencies in supply (Isard, 1960, pp. 527–33) ruling out simple additivity. A standard procedure for evading these problems is to assume a 'representative bundle of services of given quality in a standardised city', but this can be justified only at an abstract, theoretical level. A more appropriate focus is to examine the scale economies problem service by service. Even in this context, there are serious methodological difficulties such as how to separate out transfer payments from real resource costs or whether the data should refer to current, capital or total costs.

The most difficult methodological problem is how, within the restrictions set by available data, to approximate a long-run average cost curve with city size measured on the horizontal axis. Cameron (1970) mentions three types of study: cross-sectional analysis of expenditures *per capita* in relation to city population; examination of the *per capita* costs of providing a standard range of infrastructure assets in communities of varying size; estimation in real-world urban conditions of the public investment costs associated with a given increase in industrial activity in a sample of cities of varying size (Morse, *et al.*, 1968). The last method is useful as a component of a location study, but its marginalist focus and the possibility that the initial situation could be one of disequilibrium mean that it does not provide a scientific analysis of scale economies. The second approach suffers from all the drawbacks associated with standardisation of service mix pointed out above.

Much of the literature, particularly the early literature, has been concerned with how expenditures *per capita* vary with city size at the level of the individual service or group of services (Hirsch, 1959; Brazer, 1959; Lomax, 1943; Hughes, 1967; Scott and Feder, 1957; Walker, 1930; Hawley, 1951; Neutze, 1965; Bahl, 1969; Hirsch, 1960; Breton, 1965; Schmandt and Stephens, 1963; Shapiro, 1963). The results of these studies have not been fully consistent. However, there is evidence of high costs in very small urban units, a long flat horizontal bottom to the cost curve indicating a very wide range of efficient city sizes, and an exhaustion of economies below the quarter million mark, and for many services closer to the 100,000 level. Several studies revealed no relationship at all between population size and *per capita* expenditures on municipal functions (e.g. Brazer, Hughes). Of course, there are some notable exceptions, since there are significant economies of scale in air pollution control, water supply, electric power, urban transportation and, somewhat less convincingly, sewage plants, industrialised housebuilding, municipal administration, planning, and certain public health services, particularly hospitals.[2] One or two studies (e.g. Bahl) revealed a positive relationship between city size and *per capita* expenditures which could indicate diseconomies of size, though it might equally suggest more and/or better services.

This last point suggests that there is little advantage in discussing the results of this type of analysis in depth, since the methodology involves irremediable weaknesses. The volume of services provided, and even more critical their quality, may change with the size of unit. Thus, variations in expenditures *per capita* reflect changes in costs, the level of service and in quality. It consequently becomes necessary to achieve a more precise specification of the long-run average cost function, by devising measures that show the influence of scale on unit costs of homogeneous output. This gives rise to additional problems: the heterogeneity of urban services provided even within a single category of expenditure; ambiguities as to what constitutes output in public goods which are not exchanged in a proper market.[3]

There are several, not entirely satisfactory, solutions to these problems. One of the simplest procedures, adopted by Hirsch (1960), was to introduce proxies for the quality and quantity of services and to include these as additional regressors in an expenditures *per capita* equation. However, this method fails if these variables are themselves functionally related to population.

An extension of this kind of approach, though it is potentially applicable only to a limited range of services, is to include an effectiveness measure among the dependent variables. In their study of police protection, Popp and Sebold (1972) suggest the use of a total cost measure made up of two components: total expenditures and total unrecovered losses due to crime (i.e. the amount of compensation needed to achieve a zero-loss service for the entire population). The argument is that the end product of police services is the protection of lives and property, and that the measure suggested achieves some degree of homogeneity and avoids the use of input standards (an intermediate rather than a final measure of output). Expressed on a *per capita* basis, the total cost measure was regressed against population size (specified in quadratic form) and other economic and social characteristics of the city (population density; demographic characteristics e.g. age, sex, race; relative stability of the population; climate; and economic status variables such as unemployment, median income and incidence of poverty), and was tested on a cross-sectional basis for 161 SMSAs in 1967. The results showed that expenditure decreased up to 250,000 and then rose, while *per capita* losses increased up to 8·4 million. For the overall cost measure there were clear signs of decreasing returns to scale. Average costs increased steadily up to a city size of 2½ million, then jumped markedly in the 5 and 10 million size class; in a SMSA of 10 million the average costs of police protection were 65 per cent higher than in a comparable SMSA of 100,000.

Another common method of dealing with the homogeneity of output problem is to disaggregate an overall service category into a number of sub-functions and activities, which are regarded as more homogeneous. Schmandt and Stephens (1960) attempted to quantify output by constructing an index of activities, and measured quality in terms of the number of sub-services provided. But the index assigned equal weight to each activity, the quality of activities was assumed to be the same across cities, and the activities index was an intermediate rather than a final output measure since it did not directly represent service efficiency. They found evidence of a negative relationship between expenditures and service levels in some cases, while in others there was a high positive correlation between service output and population. These results indicated economies of scale, but their analysis was weakened by ignoring intercity geographical, social and economic differences which might affect service efficiency.[4] Gupta and Hutton (1968) also used a disaggregation approach in their English study, but data limitations prevented disaggregation to the extent needed to achieve homogeneous categories. For instance, in regard to health services they examined ambulance services (minimum LRAC=50,000), home nursing (no relationship, except when total number of units is substituted for population as the scale variable, in which case economies of scale exist) and administrative costs (minimum LRAC=1,388,000). Their results for local authority housing and highways were even less clear.

A related approach is to draw upon professional standards or experts to construct a quality index. This usually involves input criteria; for instance, in police services Hirsch suggested measures including variables such as the strength of the force, the quality of supporting equipment and so on. On similar lines, Will (1965) proposed measuring service requirements in terms of standard units of effort (SUE), such as a motorised police patrol, a refuse collection unit, a street sweeping unit, etc. The *per capita* costs of maintaining services measured in SUEs are then related to city population. The empirical analysis was perhaps confined to too narrow a sample (Baltimore was the largest of 38 sample cities), but a test on fire protection services concluded that 'there are significant economies of scale associated with the provision of municipal fire protection services, at standard levels of service, for central cities ranging from 50,000 to nearly one million in population' (Will, 1965, p.60).

These examples suggest that the output measurement problem for urban services has not yet been satisfactorily solved. If a solution were found, and the LRAC function was hypothesised to be U-shaped an appropriate empirical test would be to estimate an equation of the following form:

$$C_i = b_0 - b_1 P + b_2 P^2 + b_3 x_1 + \cdots + b_n x_{n-2} \qquad (7.1)$$

where C_i = average costs per unit of output of service i

P = city size measured in terms of population

$x_1, \ldots, x_{n-2}$ = variables reflecting social, economic and environmental characteristics of the city likely to influence the efficiency of service provision.

Available evidence indicates that even if acceptable tests of this kind could be carried out, the results would vary widely from service to service. If efficiency criteria in the supply of individual services do not point to either a single size of unit or a narrow range of sizes, the next question is whether inclusion of the other aspects of scale economies and diseconomies clarifies the results.

A factor that may favour a larger size unit is the possibility of managerial economies. Thus the Royal Commission on Local Government (1969) argued that only an authority serving a population in excess of 250,000 would be large enough for efficient management and to afford the technical skills, quality of staff and use of ancillary services and management tools needed for sound administration. However, it was accepted that this argument was difficult to establish statistically, and much of the research evidence placed before the Commission (e.g. Greater London Group, 1968) was based on interviews with local government officers themselves, whose opinions on efficient size might well reflect their own experiences and subjective reactions. There is some firmer evidence that administrative costs/total expenditure ratios decline with increasing city size (Neutze, 1965; Gupta and Hutton, 1968), but this throws very little light on efficiency. Nicholson and Topham (1972) carried out some tests on housing investment decisions by 82 County Boroughs, which involved dividing these into two equal groups (the 41 largest and the remainder) and examining whether or not the large authorities behaved more rationally (i.e. in terms of consistency with an investment function model) than the small. The results were not very good in a statistical sense (high multicollinearity, low R^2s, and many variables were insignificant), but they were also inconclusive in economic terms. Neither of the two hypotheses tested – that large authorities prepared their programmes in closer agreement with national policy objectives and that large authorities were more systematic or behaved differently from the small – received any clear support in their analysis. However, a major defect was the arbitrary cut-off point between large and small authorities (i.e. 107,000) implied by dividing the total sample into two equal groups, one designated large, the other small. There is no *a priori* justification for this procedure, and indeed all the general evidence available would indicate a much higher cut-off point.

The plausible argument in favour of managerial scale economies can be matched with equally plausible, but untested arguments on the other side. H. J. Barnett (in Perloff and Wingo, 1968, p. 231) argued that management was the indivisible factor of production which could explain eventually increasing costs and declining quality of public services in large cities. Kirwan (1972) points out that the establishment of the GLC in the 1960s has not resulted in any *demonstrable* scale economies, whereas there are clear signs of losses in terms of local political identity and participation. Hirsch (1968) suggests other related problems: efficiency requires geographical proximity of service units to service recipients[5]; the dangers of too much labour bargaining power resulting from very large concentrations of workers (urban government services are highly labour-intensive); size disadvantages associated with administration such as a top-heavy bureaucracy, the difficulties of co-ordination and communication, remoteness from the general public, and in some countries (e.g. the United States) the adverse consequences of political patronage in very large urban governments. The motivation for efficiency in production is weak among urban governments, and the monopoly power exerted by such governments may be a function of their size and the absence of nearby competitors for population and industry. On the other hand, Thompson (1968) has drawn attention to the benefits of a learning process in which city managers can profit from the experiences of managers in larger cities who are the first to have to cope with certain kinds of problem: 'If there is a downward-sloping learning curve in public management and the challenges of the field are a function of size, Chicago finds the path a little easier because New York has gone before, and Detroit profits from the pioneering of both' (1968, p.61). This is an area where opinions have developed much further than the supporting facts. On general grounds, however, it might be reasonable to argue that a unit serving 250,000 ought to be large enough to draw upon the specialist skills, make use of management aids and attract high quality staff, and that increasing size much beyond this level incurs higher risks of administrative scale diseconomies.

Much of the argument about administrative diseconomies and non-economic disadvantages of large size hinges around the benefits of active participation in the community in the decisions that affect them, particularly in regard to the provision of education, health and welfare, and to planning functions. This phenomenon is what Isard called *community participation potential*. It is difficult to assign a quantifiable value to the benefits of local identity, active political participation and involvement, but generally speaking these benefits may be substantial enough to favour small areas except where economic efficiency advantages of large size are very strong.[6]

The trouble arises in those fields of urban service activity (e.g. education, health and planning) where the desire for participation is strong but the economic advantages of size may be substantial. However, by appropriate consultative procedures and representation it is possible to generate a high degree of involvement even within a large authority, though the difficulties of achieving this no doubt become greater with increasing size. Another factor also favouring small authorities is the greater choice offered in terms of tax-service mixes to mobile consumer-voters (Tiebout, 1956); this can be especially important in the context of a large metropolitan area where an in-migrant may have considerable choice of area in which to live (for an analysis of public sector influences on residential location theory see Ellickson, 1971[7]).

The size of urban government unit which is efficient from the point of view of provision of urban services will, as we have seen, not necessarily coincide with the scale of area which permits a high degree of participation by the individual. Less frequently discussed, though no less important, is that the most efficient service area may not be an optimal size from the point of view of financing services. The financing criterion may tend to favour large areas since they have greater revenue-raising powers, they minimise the risk of intrametropolitan migration by firms and households to avoid high taxes, and they reduce areal spillovers in costs and benefits that can have a distorting impact on budget decisions. On the other hand, although big urban government units may reduce the need for heavy open cross-community subsidies, wide gaps may remain between benefits received and taxes paid by groups of individuals within the jurisdiction. This is inevitable because both the intrametropolitan spatial distribution of income (and hence potential tax yield) and public service needs vary regularly with distance from the CBD.

Many metropolitan fiscal problems stem from the wide gap between the demand for services and the ability to pay for them in different parts of the city, but especially in the central city. One feasible approach to the urban government size problem is to choose that size which attempts to attain tax-service balance over the fiscal area as a whole. This means ensuring that the government unit is large enough to obtain the tax revenue needed to pay for the public services that it provides, even though this will still mean an imbalance between the demand for services and the ability to pay for individual households and, if residences tend to be segregated by income, at the neighbourhood level.

At the theoretical level this approach may be illustrated with a simple model. In Figure 7.1 pp' is a population density gradient showing the relationship between population and distance from the city centre. The role of pp' is merely as a reference guideline. The function cc' represents total con-

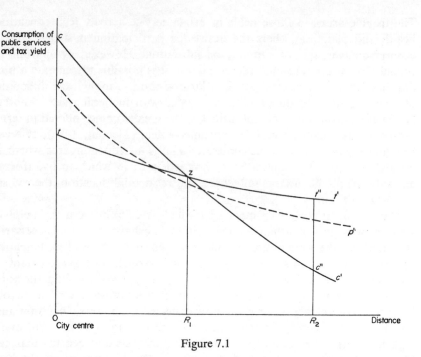

Figure 7.1

sumption of urban services with distance from the city centre. The slope of
cc' is greater than pp' throughout its length because the *per capita* demand
for urban social and welfare services will tend to be higher in the inner
city where the poor live than in the suburbs; also, the demand for many
other urban services (police and fire protection, traffic management, street
cleaning and lighting, etc.) will also be higher in the central city. The function
tt' – the tax yield function – represents the revenue obtained from the
population at each unit of distance from the city centre. The slope of tt' is
drawn as being less than that of pp'. There are two reasons for this: the
average *per capita* income-distance function slopes upwards reflecting the
empirical generalisation that the poor tend to live in the inner city close to
the centre whereas the wealthy tend to live further out; a progressive tax
structure would imply that the tax yield function slopes upward more
steeply than the *per capita* income function.[8] Upon these assumptions the
slope of the tax yield function depends on the population density gradient,
the spatial distribution of income and the progressiveness of the tax
structure. It is even possible that tt' might in fact slope upwards through
all or part of its length.[9] The actual shape and slope of both functions would
require empirical verification.

The imbalance between services and ability to pay close to and at a great distance from the city centre is obvious from Fig. 7.1. An urban government unit with a radius of OR_1 or less is the worst possible situation for financing purposes since in each distance zone residents consume more services than they can afford to pay for. The ideal size for tax-service balance is a unit of a radius OR_2, where area $ctz = c''t''z$. Of course, there is some flexibility in size, since the revenue gap in a slightly smaller city could be bridged with central government grants. Also, a radius greater than OR_2 would make the financing of services even easier. However, there are sound reasons for minimising the size of government unit provided that this is consistent with the efficient provision of services: the desirability of encouraging community involvement; the difficulty of administrating large spread-out areas; and, most important of all, the hostility of suburban residents towards financing services for the inner city. This hostility will intensify with distance, especially for services which are only consumed at or near the point of provision and in cases where the boundary of the urban authority extends beyond the dense community band. This conflict of interests will be strong even when the urban government's radius is OR_2, but if suburban residents make some use of the central city (e.g. for leisure and culture, shopping, work) it should be possible to 'sell' them the idea that they should contribute to central city service provision. In any event, the problems arising from *intra*-authority transfers are much less severe than those associated with *inter*-governmental transfers, the pressure for which would be increased in conditions of excessive political fragmentation.

Shifts in each of the variables, but particularly the suburbanisation of population and changes in the income structure of neighbourhoods in each distance zone, will alter the cc' and tt' functions (in part but not wholly as a reflection of changes in pp'). This, in turn, may shift the ideal radius (OR_2) needed to achieve tax–service balance, and clearly frequent adjustments to urban government boundaries will be ruled out by political infeasibility and administrative inconvenience. However, minor shifts in the cc' and tt' functions can be accommodated by policy adjustments to the tt' function, in particular by varying the progressiveness of the tax system. Also, most systems of urban government financing will include an element of outside funding, and variations in the level of central government grants can also correct for minor shifts. On the other hand, there are circumstances in which intrametropolitan migration and associated spatial changes in the social and economic structure can make prevailing urban government boundaries untenable from a tax–service balance point of view. Estimation of the cc' and tt' functions will be useful in such a case for both diagnosis and prescription.[10]

Since it is clear, as already suggested, that an efficient size for service financing is not necessarily efficient for service provision, it is necessary to inquire into the compatibility between the two concepts of efficient scale. In terms of Fig. 7.1, once the optimal radius from the point of view of tax–service balance has been derived, it will be useful to translate this into population size terms by integrating the population density gradient (pp') to the left of OR_2 and converting into areal terms. The result can then be compared with estimates of population thresholds for the efficient provision of particular services. A more complicated alternative is to disaggregate the cc' function into constituent services and via appropriate integration to estimate the overall consumption of a particular service as implied by the ideal radius.

Although investigation of economies of scale in urban public services is an important research topic, we should not expect the results to be of much direct value in discussions of whether or not there is an optimal city size. Scale economies, where they exist, vary widely for different services, and aggregation into an overall estimate of the minimum average cost population is dubious because of the fact that the service mix varies between cities and is, in any event, a function of size. Also, public sector scale questions cover much wider problems than those relating to current service provision or infrastructure costs: managerial and administrative economies and diseconomies, the costs and benefits of local participation and community identity, and an efficient size for revenue-raising and financing services. In any event, the variables that affect analysis of efficient city sizes are – as the scope of topics analysed in this book suggests – much wider than those associated with public sector scale economies. Most important of all, however, is that there is sufficient flexibility in the administrative structures needed for providing urban services to loosen the direct correspondence between city size and urban government service units; *one* city does not necessarily imply *one* urban government unit. Because scale economies exist in some services but not in others a multi-level system will usually provide services more efficiently than a single unit system. Also, a multi-level system offers scope not only for efficiency in public service costs but also to maximise managerial economies at one extreme and to create opportunities for local participation at the other. Since there are obvious limits to divisibility into hierarchy ranks, a two-or-three-level system is usually the preferred alternative. Apart from vertical integration, there are opportunities horizontally to consolidate or subdivide authorities in order to create efficient service units, and there is no reason why the size of the service unit should be the same as the size of the city. Even if scale economies in urban services are exhausted at low population levels while the netting out of external economies and diseconomies favour a large city size, it is not logical to argue that the public sector scale economies criterion strengthens the argument in favour of small urban areas. The analysis of scale economies in public goods may have policy implications, but at a lower level and of a different character from those connected with a national urban policy.

Notes

[1] Some services, e.g. medical services, may be supplied by the private sector in some countries and by the public sector in others.

[2] Many of these functions have to be undertaken on an areawide basis or not at all, while several are vertically integrated involving different levels of government unit.

[3] In the private sector a higher quality product will reveal itself in a higher price.

[4] Also, in the framework of their study a more appropriate variable would have been total expenditures per activity rather than *per capita* expenditures.

[5] This raises the question of whether geographical extent of area served or population density might not be better size indicators than population itself. Many studies (Brazer, Bahl, Hawley, Scott and Feder) have found evidence of a positive association between expenditures and population density, which might indicate higher costs of servicing densely populated areas, though is more likely to reflect the association of population density with other independent variables e.g. the need for more social welfare provision on behalf of people living in low-class (high density) residential areas.

[6] Since the degree of interest and concern by the community may be directly related to the expenditure powers of the authority, it does not necessarily follow that the smaller the unit the better.

[7] Ellickson has criticised existing theories of fiscal federalism for ignoring the question of why households decide to live within a particular jurisdiction (1971, p.334).

[8] The easiest way to justify these assumptions theoretically is to assume that local taxation takes the form of income taxes on residents. In practice, in the UK, the USA and many other countries the main form of local taxation is property taxes. Property tax revenue from non-residential properties in the central city and the possibly lower degree of progressivity in a property tax structure imply a tt' function steeper than under an income tax system.

[9] This requires the decline in population densities with distance to be more than offset by the upward-sloping *per capita* tax yield–distance function, obtained by adjusting the *per capita* income–distance function for progressiveness of the tax structure.

[10] The data problems in the way of empirical verification are difficult, especially for the cc' function. The basic data for the tt' function can be obtained with US data from population and income data available at the

Census tract level in the US Census of Population. The income ranges in the data are now probably precise enough for the detailed income distribution analysis needed to estimate progressive income-based tax yields. An alternative approach closer to the actual revenue-raising methods employed would be to use property tax assessments. Derivation of the cc' function is a massive research task. Some urban services have a locational dimension, others do not. In a few cases (e.g. schools where a rigid zoning system may be adopted) it may be relatively easy to estimate local consumption; in some others where the area served is larger (e.g. police and fire services), apportionment techniques will have to be adopted to allocate between sub-areas; in yet other cases (transport services, parks, etc.) quantifying the spatial incidence will be very difficult and considerable ingenuity will be needed to produce estimates (e.g. use of gravity models to determine who enjoys the services of public parks). Aggregating these results to the common monetary value demanded in Fig. 7.1. is no simple task in view of the output measurement problem and the difficulty of assigning prices to public goods.

8 Non-Economic Social Costs

Crime

The association between increased urbanisation and higher crime rates is a well-known fact, without necessarily implying a causal connexion.[1] There is no doubt that the incidence of crime has been increasing in recent years,[2] and particularly in the United States there is widespread concern about the concentration of crime in big cities. The limited investigation here will focus on the question of how crime rates vary with city size as an aid to testing the hypothesis that the higher risk of being a crime victim is one of the social costs of large cities. It is not intended to carry out a sophisticated statistical analysis because crime statistics are notorious for their poor

Table 8.1

Crime and detection rates by population size,
England and Wales, 1965

Size class	Number of areas	Crime rates, 1965*	Increase in crime rate, 1955–65 (%)	Detection rates, 1965 (%)	Major† crime rates, 1965
London	1	3,378	188	21·4	1,565
Large cities (>400,000)	6	3,327	137	42·0	1,365
Large towns (200–400,000)	11	3,333	198	41·0	867
Medium-size towns (100–200,000)	29	2,795	189	46·9	741
Small towns (<100,000)	27	2,544	143	50·7	584
County forces	50	1,747	110	45·7	510
England and Wales		2,374	140	39·2	788

* Number of crimes per 100,000 of population.
† Number of selected major crimes (offences against the person, breaking offences and robbery, larceny) per 100,000 population.
Source: F. H. McClintock and N. H. Avison (1968), pp. 72, 74, 81, 100.

Table 8.2

Crime rates by size and type of area, United States, 1969

Size or type of area	Number of cities and towns	Crime rate*	Violent crime rate	Property crime rate
250,000 or more	58	6,485	860	5,619
100,000–249,999	97	5,116	359	4,753
50,000–99,999	265	4,058	232	3,823
25,000–49,999	462	3,401	174	3,224
10,000–24,999	1,233	2,893	136	2,756
<10,000	2,202	2,327	109	2,218
Suburbs	2,341† ‡	2,904	163	2,738
Rural Areas	1,620†	1,266	103	1,156

* Not merely serious crimes, i.e. includes negligent manslaughter (such as negligent motor accident fatalities) and petty theft.

† Number of agencies.

‡ Agencies represented in suburban areas are also included in other city groups

Source: *Statistical Abstract of the United States*, 1971, Table 219, p. 142. Data based on *FBI Uniform Crime Reports*.

quality. Reported crimes are the tip of an unknown iceberg, particularly with respect to crimes of violence.

Accepting crime statistics as indicating relative orders of magnitude between city size classes, some of the basic data for England and Wales and the United States are assembled in Tables 8.1, 8.2 and 8.3. They show that in both countries there is some association between crime rates (used as a measure of the *per capita* incidence of crime) and city size, though with some qualifications. It may be simpler to consider the two countries in turn.

In England and Wales, overall crime rates are much the same in the top three size classes (i.e. in cities over the 200,000 population level).[3] They are much lower in the smaller towns, and almost half the big city rate in the county force areas which covered the rural as well as some of the urban areas.[4] The incidence of major crimes, on the other hand, shows a much stronger positive correlation with city size (the last column of Table 8.1). The evidence of a faster increase in crime rates in large urban areas is much less clear, though there is a firm inverse relationship between detection rates (i.e. the percentage of crimes cleared up) and city size. As for types of crime, the incidence of more serious crimes against property was much higher in

Table 8.3

Serious crime* rate by city, SMSAs, 1970

SMSA size class	Number of SMSAs	Average crime rate†
5 million plus	3	4358
3–5 million	3	4186
2–3 million	6	3376
1–2 million	21	3543
750,000–1 million	10	3369
500,000–750,000	22	2927
250,000–500,000	60	2700
SMSAs		3396
Other cities		1848
Rural areas		927
United States		2741

* There are seven categories of serious crime: murder and non-negligent manslaughter, forcible rape, robbery, aggravated assault, burglary, larceny ($50 upwards) and auto theft.
† For SMSA size classes average crime rate equals unweighted average of number of reported serious crimes per 100,000 population.
Source: Crime data from FBI, *Uniform Crime Reports for the United States*, 1970.

London and the large cities than elsewhere. Offences against persons were relatively more numerous in the county than in the urban police areas, and within urban areas the ratio of offences against the person to total crimes increases as the size of urban area decreases (mainly because of sex offences rather than crimes of violence). As for intraurban crime relationships, research by L. Wilkins and W. Scott has confirmed the connection between economically depressed neighbourhoods, low social class, social disorganisation and crime frequently observed in US studies, while tests of the 'ecological theory' of the growth of crime (i.e. that crime rates decline with distance from the city centre) by McClintock and Avison (1968, pp. 136–40) found some support for the theory in British data.

The American evidence on city size and crime rates is presented in Tables 8.2 and 8.3. These two tables are not directly comparable. The urban place data of Table 8.2 yield higher crime rates than the SMSA data of Table 8.3 because of the narrower geographical boundaries and the fact that there is a crime–distance function declining outwards from the city centre analogous to the population density gradient. Also, the crime rates of Table 8.2 are more comprehensive in that they include negligent manslaughter and petty larceny as opposed to the more restrictive 'serious crimes' used in the FBI crime index which form the basis of the data shown in Table 8.3. Nevertheless, the tables considered together indicate a positive association between crime rates and city size. The urban place statistics show a regular decline in crime rates with decreasing size, except for the fact that suburban crime rates are now higher than in smaller towns (<25,000). This reflects the tendency for suburban crime to become more prevalent. The big cities fare much worse in respect to violent crimes, but such crimes are a small proportion of the total. As for SMSA crime rates, it is interesting that there is little difference in average crime rates in cities between 750,000 and 3 million. Apart from within this range, crime rates are higher on average in the larger SMSAs. However, the averages mask wide inter-SMSA differences. In the top tier, for instance, crime rates in Chicago are only about 55 per cent of those prevailing in New York and Los Angeles; in the second size class the crime rate in Philadelphia is less than 40 per cent of that in San Francisco and Detroit. Also, there are sizable regional differences. Crime rates in Pennsylvania and New York State (apart from New York City) are very low, while crime rates in the Far West and in Florida are consistently high. Both tables stress the much lower incidence of crime in rural as opposed to urban areas – as far as serious crime is concerned, the rural crime rate is only a third of the national average. The differentials between type of area vary widely from one type of crime to another. The ratio of 'other cities' to 'rural areas' crime varies between 0·7 for murder to 2·5 for car theft, but the SMSA–rural ratio ranges from 17:1 for robbery and 8:1 for car theft down to 1·5:1 for murder.

There have been numerous studies (for instance, Schmid, 1960, and the President's Commission on Law Enforcement and Administration of Justice, 1967) that have demonstrated the concentration of crime in slum areas, and have revealed high correlations at the neighbourhood level between crime and delinquency rates, on the one hand, and such indicators as school truancy, infant mortality, tuberculosis, mental disorder, declining population, high proportions of families on relief, low rents, low owner occupancy rates, high percentages of blacks and foreign born among heads of households, low education and high rates of housing demolitions. These correlations are particularly marked for burglary, robbery and serious assault.[5] On the other hand, a recent multiple regression analysis over 161 SMSAs of the determinants of crime rates found that very few of the plausible independent variables (population, percentage of blacks, age structure, unemployment, income, poverty, industrial structure, degree of urbanisation, percentage of foreign born, migration, population density and climate) had a statistically significant effect (Popp and Sebold, 1972). Population size[6] was significant for total crime (measured in terms of uncompensated losses due to crime) and for each type of crime (number of crimes *per capita*). Population density was significant (negatively) for three types of crime (rape, assault and burglary) encouraged by the absence of crowds, while there was a positive association between a warm climate and assault, burglary, larceny and total crime losses. There was a negative association between migration rates and murder, and the only other variable which was statistically significant was the proportion of blacks, and then only for total crime losses and for murder. Perhaps surprisingly, income, unemployment and poverty all had no statistically significant effect and the signs varied from crime to crime.

Hoch (1972) argued that 'Because Negroes are not uniformly distributed by city size, but tend to locate in large cities, there is apt to be confounding of city size and racial effect', and that the city size effect would be overstated if racial variables were not isolated. The results quoted in the previous paragraph suggest that city size generally overwhelms race as a determinant of crime. However, race is of crucial importance in certain respects. The ratio of black to white crime is very high (particularly for murder, but also for assault and robbery), and a very high proportion of crime is *intra*racial (Chicago records indicated that more than 85 per cent of crimes by blacks involved black victims). If 70–80 per cent of major big city crime occurs in black neighbourhoods (Inbau and Carrington, 1971) and if street crime victimises the ghetto resident at least a hundred times more than the suburban resident (Packer, 1970), the implications are clear. Blacks must figure prominently both as victims and criminals. In Chicago a black man runs the risk of being a victim of crime six times greater than that of a white man, a black woman eight times greater than a white woman. The opinion polls reveal that over 30 per cent of all Americans do not feel safe about walking alone at night in their own neighbourhoods, but the proportion increases with city size and among blacks and the lower income groups. Blacks also figure disproportionately among arrests (in 1967, they accounted for 27 per cent of arrests but only 12 per cent of the population). Also, in a large proportion of cases the victims are known – though usually only slightly – to the criminals. How far the incidence of black crime reflects other factors correlated with race such as low socio-economic status or recent migration into the central city is beyond the scope of this investigation. However, it is clear that the social costs (as opposed to the economic costs) of higher crime rates in the larger cities bear more heavily upon blacks than upon whites. Since it has already been shown (see p. 50) that the income gains associated with increasing city size are much lower, and in some cases non-existent, for blacks, especially in big cities outside the South, the burden of the evidence suggests that if there are net benefits to households from big city living these benefits are not shared equally between the races. It may still be true that migration to Northern big cities has been the main channel of upward mobility for rural blacks, but betterment has not been achieved without cost.

The cost of crime in terms of losses due to crime, crime control and prevention, the administration of criminal justice, and correction and rehabilitation has increased very rapidly in recent years.[7] Although part of this is financed via the central government, a substantial proportion – particularly in the United States – is financed locally, while most of the losses due to crime are incurred where the crimes take place. Thus, the economic costs of crime are much heavier for big city residents: to mention merely one example, the *per capita* cost of municipal police department expenditures in the United States in cities larger than 500,000 was 44·8 dollars *per capita* in 1969, more than double the *per capita* cost in all cities smaller than 250,000.

In conclusion, the evidence is clear that the incidence of crime is higher in big cities than in smaller towns, and in urban than in rural areas. The social and economic costs of crime are greater for big city residents than for others. Yet, as usual, the aggregate picture can be misleading. There are wide regional and inter-city differentials in crime rates, and it is much less convincing to argue that more crime is the direct result of city size.[8] The burden of crime falls disproportionately on central city as opposed to suburban residents and on blacks and poor people; apart from higher taxes and perhaps an irrational feeling of insecurity, the risks of being a crime victim are not much higher for the middle class white in the big metropolis than in the smaller city. Also, the fear of crime can be serious even in a small town (Poveda, 1972). Even if we accept the overall evidence on city size – crime correlations as impressive, there are no implications for national urban policy. There is no case whatsoever for utopian social engineers who prescribe physical planning solutions to social problems.

Psycho-social stress and big cities

A widespread argument, buttressed by television, journalism and other mass media outlets, is that psychological stress, alienation, social disorganisation and higher propensities to be mentally ill are associated with big city life and constitute one of the major disadvantages of city size. The importance of these views is accentuated by the fact that the propositions are very hard to test, the available evidence is rather sparse, and yet there is some scientific support for at least some of the hypotheses. Since it is very difficult to balance costs due to increased stress against economic and monetary gains, there may

102

be some tendency to exaggerate these costs and assign to them an absolute, sacrosanct value. This topic cannot be ignored and it is vital to offer some brief observations here, even though the primary objective is the analysis of the *economics* of urban size.

Economists, planners and sociologists have not been averse to making incidental comments on this problem. Some have taken the view that big city life involves alienation, isolation and increased social and psychological stress (e.g. Osborn and Whittick, 1969). A more balanced assessment has been made by Alonso: 'It appears that the traditional dichotomy between alienating metropolis and the cohesive small city is a gross oversimplification, and that people can lead alienated or full lives in either place' (Alonso, 1970a, p. 46). In support, he cites three arguments: that each sociological study of big city alienation and relative deprivation can be matched with another study on the claustrophobia of small town life; that much of the hard evidence relates to animals, and it is dangerous to draw analogies about human behaviour; that a distinction must be drawn between the effects of population density and overcrowding. Others have found evidence that family life is stronger in small towns and that indices of family dislocation (such as divorce rates, illegitimate births, incidence of parentless children, etc.) increase with city size (Ogburn and Duncan, 1964; Duncan, 1956; Lillibridge, 1952; Duncan and Reiss, 1956). The link between family dislocation and increased psychosocial stress, however, though plausible is tenuous.

Even if evidence could be found which supported the 'psychological and social disadvantages of large size' case, how could these be weighed against the many *non-economic* advantages of cities and the continued pressure of big cities to grow? For instance, it might be argued that modern living involves a certain degree of stress and cannot be avoided, except by becoming a hermit. A case could even be made that some stress is good for most people, though it may be necessary to distinguish between 'tolerable' stress and stress inducing illness and disease. The many advantages of large cities are, however, beyond dispute. If cities are a source of stress, they are also the fount of civilisation: 'A city is that place where whatever is highest in the civilisation is being most actively, most vividly, most truly carried on' (J. R. Seeley, 1968). The *per capita* incidence of people in eminence groups (inventors, artists, writers, persons in *Who's Who*, leading scientists, etc.) increases markedly with city size. Large cities are the major locus of innovations, both technical and social. Moreover, there may well be stress problems arising at the other end of the urban scale, associated with the depopulation of small towns in rural areas, for instance. Even settlements supposed to be of 'ideal' size and specifically planned as pleasant social living environments may not be free from problems. For example, a study of a British new town

(Taylor and Chave, 1964, p. 70) found that, despite the existence of 300 organisations catering for every form of interest, almost half the adult population complained about the lack of entertainment. What they missed was *passive entertainment*, as opposed to leisure pursuits involving active participation, and this can only be supplied in varied form in a large city. Moreover, the new towns are not free from symptoms of social disorganisation, anomie or social manifestations of stress.

Another problem is the significance to be attached to locational preferences as indicated by survey responses. In the absence of direct evidence on psycho-social stress, could these responses indicate some degree of malaise about living in cities or towns of particular size independent of income and level of living advantages? For instance, a survey of young Swedes suggested that 90–95 per cent of those living in small towns or in rural areas would not wish to move to a large city, while two thirds of those living in large cities would prefer to move away (Gallup Poll, quoted by Carlestam and Levi, 1971). Similar results have been obtained from other countries such as the United States and France (Hansen, 1970; Girard and Bastide, 1960). A study of rural migrants who had settled in large cities (Price, 1969) indicated that substantial proportions (e.g. 46 per cent of the sample of Mexican–American males who had moved from South Texas to Chicago) would consider moving back even though all were financially better off and large numbers stated that they were happier (!). In this writer's view, locational preferences are very important determinants of the distribution of population (and hence of the size of cities), but answers to hypothetical questions of this kind have to be treated with considerable suspicion. It would be dangerous to infer anything about the stress of city life from these results, and it might also be risky to use evidence of this kind as a basis for national urban policy.

It has been suggested above that it would be difficult to derive policy conclusions even if we could accept as given the 'big city induces stress' case. This is because we know that big cities also confer substantial economic and social advantages (whether these are *net* is more debatable), and there are no common units of measurement to net out non-comparable and frequently non-quantifiable gains and losses. However, we do not have to accept the psycho-social stress case as being established. The conceptual problems are very complicated, and the evidence is far from clear.[9] Stress related to urban agglomeration could arise from several sources: 'side effects' of an urban society, such as high population density, technological supply deficiencies or to inadequate social organisation; deficiencies in the individual's living conditions affecting his physical and mental health, social contacts, education and so on, or to rapid environmental change inherent in urbanisation itself. There are other complications. The links between stress and urbanisation are reciprocal and complex, and do not necessarily manifest themselves immediately; Krapf (1964) suggested a possible time span of three generations as an incubation period for the socio-pathological effects of rapid social change to show. Moreover, the evidence for the relationship between *physical* environmental stimuli and disease is much better documented than that for *psycho-social* stimuli. Another difficulty is that the impact of the environment on stress is not necessarily objectively determined, nor – to take the opposite extreme – merely the result of a subjective response, but is also influenced by the value system and norms which may be specific to a particular society. What causes stress in London may be quite acceptable in New York or in Calcutta. Similarly, reactions may vary from one section of the population to another; for instance, upper socio-economic status groups might show signs of stress in response to quite trivial problems from a physical environment point of view.[10]

Carlestam and Levi (1971) have defined psycho-social stressors as stimuli suspected of causing disease which originate in social relationships or arrangements (i.e. in the environment) and affect the organism through the medium of higher nervous pressures. The strength of such stimuli may be modified (in either direction) by predisposing or protective intervening variables: 'the generalisation seems justified that rapid urbanisation and life in the overcrowded slums of the largest cities does in fact comprise an increase of predisposing and a decrease in protective intervening variables as compared to rural life' (Carlestam and Levi, p. 18).

Much of the argument about psycho-social stress in large cities revolves around the impact of high population density and overcrowding. Several, sometimes conflicting, hypotheses have been suggested here. Hamburg (1971) argued that the essence of big cities is that they *crowd strangers*[11] inducing a high level of irritability in public encounters and reactions associated with impersonality and anonymity. Some observers, such as Jane Jacobs (1962), have argued that overcrowding (persons per room) may have adverse effects, initially in the form of stress, ultimately as high death, disease and social disorganisation rates, but that high population densities (persons per acre) are not harmful. There is also some disagreement between the *structuralist* view of high population density, according to which it is an essential prerequisite for exploiting the division of labour, and the *behaviouralist* view which emphasises the strain and stresses arising from the frequent stimulation and interaction associated with dense living (Simmel, 1957). An important extension is Calhoun's hypothesis (1962) that there are two key states: the *economic climax* state, the density which maximises the division of labour, and the *social climax* state, the density which minimises the psychological and physiological stress from interaction. He further hypothesises that the economic climax tends to be greater than the social climax so that market forces result in densities of living that are too high from the point of view of minimising psycho-social stress. This hypothesis is interesting but speculative, and it relies too much on the concept of 'optimum density' which is almost as nebulous as that of 'optimal city size'.[12]

The evidence is even more contradictory than the alternative hypotheses. A test of Jacobs' thesis about the relative importance of high density and overcrowding by Schmitt (1966) on 42 census tracts in Honolulu (1950) examined the relationship between alternative density measures and health and disorganisation indices such as death rates, infant mortality, suicides, tuberculosis rates, venereal disease, admissions to mental hospitals, illegitimacy, juvenile delinquency and prison admissions. The association, overall, was 'moderately close', but the perhaps surprising finding was that population per net residential acre was much more closely related to health and social disorganisation measures than overcrowding or other density indicators. Winsborough (1970) in a study of Chicago examined how infant mortality, death rates, tuberculosis, public assistance and public assistance to juveniles varied with gross population density. However, he first corrected for the influence of socio-economic variables (such as socio-economic status, housing quality and migration) known to have an impact on social organisation. The positive association remained only in the case of infant mortality, and the association for three out of four of the other variables actually became negative! Another study of overcrowding in Hong Kong, where the median living area per person is only 4 square metres – only one quarter of the 'essential minimum' according to some analysts, e.g. Chombart de Lauwe quoted by Koupernik (1968) – found no relationship between density and measures of strain and stress, apart from parental supervision of children[13] (Mitchell, 1971).

Although there is evidence to support a relationship between overcrowding coupled with poor housing and the incidence of certain physical diseases, the direct studies of association with psycho-social stress are much more equivocal.[14] A very high proportion of the literature refers to the effects of increasing living densities among animals, frequently under laboratory conditions, and then extrapolating the results to the behaviour of humans. Calhoun's experiments on increasing living densities for rats are typical; the doubling of density levels providing moderate stress led to miscarriages, very high rates of infant mortality, sexual deviance and cannibalism among males, and either frenetic over-activity or pathological withdrawal. Other studies (Marler and Hamilton, 1966; Lindburg, 1969) have found a strong association between overcrowding and increased aggression, both in laboratory conditions and in natural habitats, particularly for primates. The extension of the argument to man is made very difficult, of course, by the fact that man is a cultural creature[15] with a considerable ability to modify his living environment.

Some studies (Zimbardo, 1969; Milgrim, 1970; Hamburg, 1971) have produced evidence that people in big cities are much more hostile and less friendly towards strangers than people in small towns. Epidemiological research has attempted to correlate the incidence of defined mental disorders with crowding and unfavourable social conditions. For instance, there is some evidence (Strotzka, 1964; Dohrenwend and Dohrenwend, 1972) that schizophrenia, neuroses and personality disorders are more common in large urban slums than, say, in rural areas or small towns where psychoses may be more common. However, this kind of evidence is difficult to interpret not only because diagnosis rates and access to treatment may be associated with city size but because of insufficient knowledge about causation. In particular, it is as yet impossible to determine whether the predisposition to personality disorder is due to the nature of social life in urban slums or whether the concentration of psychiatric cases there is due to downward social drift of people predisposed to become psychiatrically ill.

Of course, there may be an association between high living densities and unfavourable psychological reactions, falling short of disease, e.g. annoyance, hostility, dissatisfaction. This kind of reaction may be conditioned very much by the personality of the individual and by social factors, such as relative deprivation. On the other hand, crowded slum areas may give rise to favourable reactions (Fried and Gleicher, 1970). Also relevant here is how people react not to high densities and overcrowding as such but to the environmental consequences of density and congestion such as pollution and noise. The evidence obtained from surveys of the overall population, as opposed, say, to that based on the propaganda of environmental pressure groups and the mass media, is unclear. A survey in Nashville, Tennessee – a city with a serious pollution problem – revealed that only 2·5 per cent of respondents expressed any concern for air pollution and 85 per cent considered the city a healthy place to live (Smith *et al.*, 1964; it should be noted that this was carried out some years ago before the environmental issue became a major focus of national concern). As for studies of noise, it has been suggested that only one-quarter of the variability in reported annoyance can be explained by changes in the noise environment alone, with almost all the remaining variability due to differences in personal attitudes and experiences (Borsky, 1971). Of course, surveys of this kind are notoriously difficult to design and administer objectively, and there is much evidence pointing the other way. But the position is certainly not as clearcut as compaigners for pollution control would like us to believe.

A brief and superficial survey of these very complex questions by a nonspecialist cannot hope to come up with definite answers. Indeed, the present state of research in this area makes it clear that no such answers are yet possible. However, this inconclusiveness is very important. A predisposition

107

to psycho-social stress and even mental illness may indeed be associated with life in big cities, but the evidence supporting this hypothesis is still very flimsy and there are some inconvenient results which back the negative case. If, and when, the hypothesis is firmly established, we would still have to balance these psycho-social costs against the many benefits of the metropolis, social and cultural as well as narrowly economic. It would be wrong, in the present state of knowledge at least, to use the psycho-social stress arguments as providing a case for a smaller 'desirable' size of settlement as a guideline for a national urban policy.[16]

A question not examined here in any detail is whether there is any relationship between the incidence of physical illness and city size. A very accessible source of data is mortality rate statistics (for the United Kingdom see Registrar-General, *Statistical Review*, Part 1, annual). These show that there are some causes of death that vary positively with city size[17] (lung cancer, pneumonia, bronchitis) and others where the association is negative (e.g. influenza and, to a lesser extent, cerebrovascular diseases). The aggregate death rate varies little, if at all, with city size, though death rates are lower in rural as opposed to urban areas, especially for males.

Notes

[1] However, several causal hypotheses may be advanced, e.g. that urbanisation reduces the possibilities of social control, particularly informal control; that crime is a function of 'relative deprivation' which is stronger in cities; that there are significant differences in the personality traits of urban and rural man; that crime is related to indices of social disorganisation; and so on. See the essays in Glaser (1970).

[2] In the United States the overall increase in serious crime was 144 per cent, 1960–70, particularly noticeable in larceny and robbery, and in England and Wales total indictable crimes increased by 140 per cent, 1955–65, and much higher than this rate for robbery, malicious damage and malicious woundings. More recently, the growth in crime in England and Wales has slackened; indictable crimes increased by less than 14 per cent, 1969–72, though crimes of violence increased by 37 per cent.

[3] There are, however, wide intercity differences. The crime rate in Newcastle (the worst case) was more than two-and-a-half times higher than in Bristol (the best city in the largest 18).

[4] These data refer to police areas prior to reorganisation and consolidation of police forces. The amalgamation of 124 into 46 forces makes it virtually impossible to undertake meaningful urban size analysis with more recent data.

108

5 The proportion of total business premises burgled in 1967–8 was 14 per cent in the country at large, but 28 per cent in the ghettos.

6 Crimes increase exponentially with city size, apart from total losses, murder and rape where an inverted-U quadratic function fits best, though with maximum points at the several million mark.

7 In the United States, the total cost of lawlessness, according to one estimate (Inbau and Carrington, 1971), exceeds 51 billion dollars. Public crime control cost 7.34 billion dollars in 1969 and employed 800,000 employees. An earlier estimate of the economic cost of crime (1965) was 21 billion dollars (President's Commission on Law Enforcement and Administration of Justice, 1967).

8 The relationship between crime and population density is also complex. As pointed out above, many types of crime are inversely correlated with population density, and many of the most spread-out cities – such as Los Angeles – have very high crime rates.

9 The survey by Carlestam and Levi (1971) was very helpful in writing this section. Also useful were Simmel (1957), Calhoun (1962), Schmitt (1966) and Winsborough (1970).

10 The old, the very young and the handicapped may be particularly vulnerable to environmental influences.

11 In a suburb of a big city it is possible, within 10 minutes, to meet approximately 11,000 persons walking or driving. In a medium-sized city like Newark, one may encounter some 20,000 people, and on central Manhattan some 220,000 people' (Carlestam and Levi, pp. 47–8).

12 See below, pp. 132–5.

13 Thirty nine per cent of the Hong Kong respondents shared their dwelling unit (typically one room) with non-kinsmen; 28 per cent slept three or more to a bed and 13 per cent slept four or more to a bed.

14 There is evidence of an association between crowding and fatigue, sleep deficiencies and intrafamily friction.

15 In the light of recent research, however, man is not the *only* tool-maker.

16 None of the studies carried out have been sufficiently sensitive to variations in city size to throw any light on the relative merits or demerits of cities in different size classes from the psycho-social stress point of view. Many have been concerned merely with the effects of urbanisation in general or in making comparisons between metropolitan slums and rural areas.

17 Certain other causes of death, e.g. infant mortality, suicide, also vary directly with city size. At first sight, the suicide statistics appear to give some support to the psycho-social stress arguments. However, deaths from suicide are a minute proportion of total deaths (two-thirds of one per cent), and suicide-prone people may tend to be drawn towards the larger cities (the personality vs. environment dilemma once again).

9 Market Tests of City Size

An obvious, though possibly naive, response to the argument that big cities are social 'bads' is to ask how cities managed to become large in the first place. Presumably, households and firms moved to (or stayed in) large cities because it was beneficial and profitable for them to do so. To challenge the implications of this view, there are two major counterarguments. First, it can be argued that what benefits the individual does not necessarily benefit society as a whole. Thus, although each migrant may have gained personally from moving into the metropolis, the fact that his decision was based on a distorted set of relative prices or that his decision imposes external diseconomies on other city residents may bring about a divergence between marginal private cost and marginal social cost. Second, some observers may adopt the position that although rapid growth in big cities has been desirable and beneficial in the past both to individuals and society, this is no longer true today. The effects of social and economic change associated with urbanisation in recent decades, such as the almost universal spread of automobile ownership and the environmental impacts of high rates of urbanised industrialisation, have brought about a situation – so the argument runs – where the quality of life in the large metropolises is ruined by traffic congestion, pollution and social disorganisation. The first counterargument has been discussed, and indeed recurs intermittently throughout the book. The second argument implies that the net advantages of big city life have now been reduced. If this is so, we would expect this to manifest itself in a declining attractiveness of big cities to migrants, lower rates of population growth and inferior economic performance.

If assumptions appropriate to a competitive economy are made, such as no bars to occupational or geographic mobility, perfect knowledge and no major external economies or diseconomies, it is feasible to judge the relative efficiency of different city sizes by subjecting them to a test of market performance. A nation's cities and towns may be conceived of as being stratified into a set of city size classes, each of which is in direct competition with the others for households and firms. Since there is a high correlation between the net movement of people and firms, it may be hypothesised that the size class which increases its population fastest is the most efficient from a societal point of view. It may also be useful to supplement this prediction with analysis of urban indicators, total and *per capita* income growth and other measures of economic performance. This market test model is analogous to the 'survivor' technique used in measuring economies of scale at the firm level, according to which the size class of firms which expands its market share most is treated as being closest to the optimum size of firm. The 'survivor' technique is subject to many weaknesses, for instance, the possibility that variations in managerial efficiency between firms standardised for size may be wider than variations in average costs with scale, but the analogous market test model of city size is used for a much more restricted purpose. That is, the aim is not to employ the method to identify the most efficient city size but merely to test the hypothesis that the disadvantages of large cities are *now* overwhelming enough for them to be reflected in a much poorer competitive performance than that of smaller cities.

Before testing the market performance hypothesis, it is useful to place the big city phenomenon into a world-wide perspective. If large cities are such a grossly inefficient and undesirable form of spatial organisation for living, it would be necessary to explain away the huge and increasing role of big cities in the modern urbanisation process. About one half of the world's urban population lives in cities of 500,000 population or more. Using a higher cut-off point there were only 13 cities of one million or more in 1900; by 1950 there were 83 and by 1970 the count had reached 149.[1] At the latter date there were 41 of these cities larger than $2\frac{1}{2}$ million, of which a dozen were in the five million-plus class. Large cities are found in all parts of the world, developed and developing. The one major exception is Africa, south of the North African coastline and north of South Africa, which is much less urbanised, though even in Africa cities above the 100,000 level are growing at more than four times the rate of the total population and about twice as fast as the urban population. In some developing areas, e.g. Latin America and South East Asia, big cities have played a much more dominating role in urbanisation than in Europe and the United States. In Latin America, for instance, there are ten cities in the million-plus class, and in more than two-thirds of Latin American countries more than 50 per cent of the urban population is in one metropolitan area. In some developed countries (the United Kingdom, Australia, USA and Japan) over a third of the population lives in million-plus cities. In most cases the rates of growth of the million-plus cities have been impressive, and only in very few instances have they grown more slowly than the urban population in general.[2]

The continued growth of these major metropolises seems inherent in the urbanisation process itself.[3] Despite the differences in the forces behind urbanisation and in the economic structure of big cities between developing and developed countries, despite the differences in economic systems and in regional development planning between western and socialist societies,[4] and despite the huge cross-cultural variations in the tempo and nature of social change, the big city phenomenon is virtually universal. Although critics may drum up arguments to justify the hypothesis that big cities give

112

rise to net social costs (congestion and pollution in advanced countries, 'parasitism' in the less developed countries), it is difficult to understand why so many countries should be pursuing a non-optimal spatial development path. One reason may be that they have little choice; many of these countries have been concerned about the increasing concentration of the population in their largest cities, but hitherto attempts to check the process have been unsuccessful. On the other hand, unless we are prepared to argue that people were forced by economic necessity to move into the large cities, the inexorable process of metropolitanisation has been consistent with individual preferences and the improvement of living standards. Since so many migrants have been involved, the net social costs case has to rest on the argument that though the big city resident gained as an individual when he moved to the city he now suffers because of the migration decisions of his successors, and yet is unable to leave the metropolis either because he is 'locked in' or because of the lack of job opportunities elsewhere. There are too many 'ifs' and 'buts' in this reasoning to make it convincing.

The market performance hypothesis will be examined with American data. The quality of US demographic and urban growth statistics, the closer approximation of their SMSA boundaries to reasonable definitions of metropolitan areas and the large number of spatially dispersed cities of varying size in a geographically vast country, all these factors make an analysis of interurban competition much more clear-cut than in other countries.[5] However, Davis's (1969) study of world urbanisation trends in the 1950s and 1960s showed that the world's twenty largest cities almost unanimously[6] experienced substantial growth. All these cities were larger than $4\frac{1}{2}$ million in 1970, yet their average annual growth rate was 3·6 per cent in the 1950s and 3.1 per cent in the 1960s.

There is some scattered evidence in previous studies of the United States that throws light on the growth performance of different city size classes. Lampard (in Perloff and Wingo, 1968, p. 107) showed that urbanisation continued steadily in the United States over the period 1790–1960, and the share of population in the smaller size classes increased more or less continuously, but the population shares accounted for by cities in both the million-plus and the 250,000-plus size classes reached a peak in 1930 and fell a little thereafter. Analysis of US population changes in the 1950s shows that population in cities in the 500,000–1 million range increased by 36 per cent, whereas in all other size classes the increase clustered between 23 and 36 per cent. This finding was supported by Stanback and Knight's study of metropolitan labour markets (1970); they demonstrated that the medium-size labour markets (defined as $200 \leqslant 1,600$ thousand) experienced the largest net gains in employment, while the largest labour markets on average grew the most slowly in net terms. Evidence on population shares and numbers

113

of urban places by size class for 1950, 1960 and 1970 is given in Table 9.1. These data show that the share of total population in million-plus urban places fell over the twenty year period, with the most marked increases in population shares experienced in the 10,000–100,000 groups (15·6 per cent in 1950 rising to 27·5 per cent by 1970). However, it would be very mis-leading to interpret this as support for the hypothesis that the 10,000 to 100,000 urban places are the most efficient on the basis of market perfor-mance tests. Much of the increase in population shares is explained by the increased *number* of towns in these groups (1,156–1,767), and the structure of the national urban hierarchy inevitably means that new entrants to any city size class will be clustered in the lower rather than the upper ranks of the hierarchy. Moreover, the urban place definition is a much less satisfactory classification of city sizes than that based on SMSA boundaries, since the changing spatial structure of a large metropolitan area – representing its

Table 9.1

Population Shares and Numbers of Urban and Rural Places
by Size Class, 1950, 1960 and 1970

	1950		1960		1970	
	Share in total population (%)	Number of places	Share in total population (%)	Number of places	Share in total population (%)	Number of places
Urban	64·0	4,741	69·9	6,041	73·5	7,061
1,000,000 +	11·5	5	9·8	5	9·2	6
500,000–1,000,000	6·1	13	6·2	16	6·4	20
250,000–500,000	5·5	23	6·0	30	5·1	30
100,000–250,000	6·3	65	6·5	81	7·0	100
50,000–100,000	5·9	126	7·7	201	8·2	240
25,000–50,000	5·8	252	8·3	432	8·8	519
10,000–25,000	7·9	778	9·8	1,134	10·5	1,384
5,000–10,000	5·4	1,176	5·5	1,394	6·4	1,840
2,500–5,000	4·3	1,846	4·2	2,152	4·0	2,296
Places under 2,500	0·4	457	0·4	596	0·4	626
Unincorporated parts of urbanised areas	4·9	–	5·5	–	7·5	–
Rural	36·0	13,807	30·1	13,749	26·5	13,707
1,000–2,500	4·3	4,158	3·6	4,151	3·3	4,193
< 1,000	2·7	9,649	2·2	9,598	1·9	9,514
Other rural	29·0	–	24·3	–	21·3	–

Source: *US Census of Population, 1970*, as given in the *Statistical Abstract of the United States*, Table 16, p. 17.

successful adaptation to larger size – would be misinterpreted in terms of Table 9.1 as a population shift from larger to smaller urban places.

Alonso and Medrich's (1972) analysis of SGCs (spontaneous growth centres, i.e. cities that are growing without the benefits of special assistance, or at least without the benefit of conscious or explicit policy), showed that these could occur anywhere in the urban size hierarchy. Although the faster growth rates were experienced by the SGCs lower down the urban hierarchy,[7] the average performance within SMSA size classes in the first half of the 1960s was much better for cities in the 1–2 million range than for any other group, both in regard to total population change and net migration. In another study of the same period, Alonso (1970a) noticed that nine metropolitan areas – all of them in the million-plus size class – accounted for 81 per cent of all net migration. The pattern becomes somewhat more confusing when the overall picture is disaggregated, e.g. by region or by race. For instance, the aggregate data for the 1960s clearly suggests that the 500,000– 1 million SMSAs experienced the highest population growth rate, but a regional breakdown shows that this is true only in the West while population growth rates in the South were strongly associated positively with city size (Hoch, 1972). Similarly, the black population has consistently grown most rapidly in the largest cities in recent decades.

The average performance of a size class may also be misleading. A major – though not unexpected – finding of the Alonso and Medrich study was that the spread in performance widened in the smaller city sizes. The distribution of growth rates for larger cities is skewed to the right, i.e. either fast or steady growth. This is consistent with Thompson's 'growth stability' thesis: that large size (suggested as $\geqslant 250,000$) ensures continued growth at a near-average rate, if not better. Smaller cities, on the other hand, may include both the fastest growers and many that actually lose population. These small cities may be treated as unstable, either growing very fast into large cities or losing ground. This draws attention to problems inherent in this kind of analysis. The performance of a given size class depends upon the choice of base year; for instance, a base of 1880 or 1900 would bias the results in favour of smaller size classes. Similarly, on statistical grounds, a smaller absolute size is more likely to be associated with a greater percentage growth rate simply because the denominator is small. This may be one reason for Madden's finding (1958) that the growth rates of American cities, with very few exceptions, exhibited retardation trends over time as their age and absolute size increased. These drawbacks are minimised in the analysis that follows by taking the most recent period for which statistics are available (up to 1970)[8] and restricting its scope to cities greater than 100,000.

A limitation of most of the studies mentioned is that they concentrate solely on population growth. This is important from the point of view of measuring the relative attractiveness to households of cities in the urban system (there is a strong relationship between net migration and population change), but it is only one aspect of a city's competitive power. It would be useful, for example, to have information on the net movement of firms to measure the relative pull of cities of varying sizes for industry. Also, within the framework of a neo-classical interurban growth model, provided that cities do not offer increasing returns to labour, high rates of in-migration will tend to be associated with a dampening of *per capita* income growth so that the net advantage of city residence may be reduced as a consequence of rapid population growth. Similarly, high rates of in-migration may worsen the urban distribution of income.[9] Moreover, even apart from interurban movements of population and industry, some light may be shed on the relative efficiency of city sizes by analysis of economic indicators, such as income and output measures.

Table 9.2

Average increases* in population, total income and *per capita* income by size class of SMSA, US

SMSAs Size class†	Number in size class	Population increase 1960–70	Total personal income increase 1959–70	Per capita income increase 1959–70
		(%)		
5 million plus	3	11·1	98	74
3–5 million	2	10·4	100	79
2–3 million	5	13·5	107	78
1–2 million	14	18·9	113	75
750,000–1 million	9	23·9	121	74
500,000–750,000	23	21·7	122	80
250,000–500,000	55	12·1	104	78
100,000–250,000	85	15·8	110	78

* Average=unweighted mean of percentage change of each member within the size class.
† Size classes are drawn up on the basis of 1960 population.
Sources: Population data from *US Census of Population*
Income data from 'Metropolitan Area Income in 1970', *Survey of Current Business*, 52 (1972), No. 5, 27–44.

Evidence on these points is presented in Table 9.2. All city size classes shared in population growth in the 1960s, though undoubtedly the 500,000–1,000,000 size range fared best. As far as total income growth is concerned, however, the spread is much narrower though the 3 million-plus cities grew more slowly than the rest. The *per capita* income growth comparisons, on the other hand, make it clear that no city size class stands above the rest, partly due to the inverse correlation between population change and *per capita* income change. Furthermore, in none of the three series is there a regular relationship with city size. On the basis of the evidence given in Table 9.2, it is difficult to argue that larger cities suffer a major disadvantage in interurban competition. Indeed, as shown in the companion Table 9.3, regional differentials are much wider than the city size differentials. The distinction between the north east and central regions, on the one hand, and the south and west regions on the other is much wider than that between large and small cities.

Table 9.3

Increase in population, total and *per capita* income
in SMSAs by region

Region	Number* of SMSAs	Population† increase, 1960–70	(%) Total personal income increase 1959–70	*Per capita* income increase 1959–70
New England	12	9·2	108	83
Mid East	28	8·1	102	78
Great Lakes	44	12·7	96	72
Plains	14	10·2	100	73
South East	49	16·6	134	89
South West	21	14·5	131	80
Rocky Mountains	6	25·7	120	68
Far West	21	36·0	119	70

* SMSAs over 100,000 in 1960.
† Unweighted mean of SMSA percentage changes in each region.
Sources: Population data from *US Census of Population*
Income data from 'Metropolitan Area Income in 1970', *Survey of Current Business*, 52 (1972), No. 5, 27–44.

The finding that the larger city size classes fare little worse, and in some respects rather better, than other city sizes[10] makes it difficult for those who argue that big cities are bad. To salvage the pessimists' position three arguments are possible. First, the aggregate indices could mask unfavourable distributional effects concentrated in the larger cities. As pointed out elsewhere,[11] the evidence on income distribution and poverty indices in relation to city size refutes this speculation. Second, although the individual migrants who move into the larger cities increase their own welfare, it is arguable that the negative net externalities of urban scale may reduce the quality of life for big city residents without necessarily being large enough to offset the internal benefits in terms of higher incomes. Even if smaller cities offer lower incomes they may offer higher levels of welfare if these are combined with positive net externalities. This argument will not be discussed in detail at this point. However, there are major difficulties. The evidence on the variation of externalities with city size is patchy and incomplete, and presents insuperable weighting problems. Most of the literature has overemphasised the diseconomies. Evaluation of external economies has been much more rudimentary, and some of these economies, such as the systemic functions of national and regional metropolises in the spatial diffusion of economic growth and the consumption externalities of big cities, are very hard to quantify. Also, many negative externalities are in fact monetised (the compensating payments thesis). Although external to the firm, industry or household, they are often internal to the city economy as a whole. To the extent that these diseconomies are reflected in higher incomes, they are taken into account in the migration decisions of households, and hence in the market performance tests.

The third argument is that the market performance tests are deficient because neither households nor firms pay the 'proper' prices for services and costs associated with in-migration, i.e. the prices and costs that allocate resources efficiently. For instance, migrants are charged only the average costs for urban services and for transportation, yet in both cases marginal costs may rise with city size. The general validity of this argument depends upon the correctness of three assumptions: that in each case (congestion, pollution, urban service costs) marginal costs increase with city size[12]; that the divergence from optimality is merely the result of incorrect pricing, so that if households and firms had to pay the marginal social costs of their decisions a competitive optimum would be achieved; and that the existence of marginal social benefits may either be ignored or assumed invariant with city size. The burden of proof lies with those who challenge the inconclusiveness of the market tests.

Notes

[1] Estimates from the United Nations, *Demographic Yearbook*. A count of this kind can never be exact because of differences in Census years and international variations in the quality of population statistics.

[2] For useful statistics on the structure of urbanisation see Breese (1969).

[3] 'Big cities can become numerous and increase in size only where the urban population is already large. Part of the increase in big-city population is drawn from the surpassing of size-limits and the absorption of previously smaller cities and towns. In addition, individual big cities tend to grow in rough proportion with the general increase in urban population. It seems possible to consider that some average relationship might persist between levels of urbanisation, general growth in population, and the emergence and growth of big cities', (United Nations, 1969).

[4] The Soviet Union and China are well-represented among the million-plus cities, though the share of the total population in these cities is quite small in both cases.

[5] Testing would be very difficult in the United Kingdom because of boundary changes, the absence of metropolitan area as opposed to local authority statistics, and overlapping commuting boundaries in a small, highly urbanised and densely populated country.

[6] The exceptions were London (0·5 per cent per annum, 1950–70) and Moscow (1·0 per cent). The fastest growers were Peking, Sao Paulo, Seoul and Djakarta. On the other hand, large cities (>1·5 million) grew more slowly, 32 per cent between 1960 and 1970, than smaller cities (100,000–1·5 million) which grew by 39 per cent, 1960–70 (unweighted averages). See Davis (1972), especially Chapter V.

[7] On a longer-run view (i.e. since 1900), Alonso and Medrich found strong evidence of an 'overall shift towards larger urban sizes' among SGCs.

[8] On the pessimists' view that conditions in large cities are progressively deteriorating, tests on the most recent period are the most critical in any event.

[9] 'Poor people are drawn to rich communities. Thus, measuring overall averages, growth does not necessarily make a locality richer, only bigger' (Perloff and Wingo, 1968, p. 7).

[10] Many observers have argued that the 250,000–500,000 size range is best. This is not supported by the data of Table 9.2.

[11] See pp. 51–4. On the other hand, the benefits of urban growth may accrue disproportionately to real estate owners and shareholders in commercial, financial and industrial enterprises.

[12] This is reasonable on *a priori* grounds, but may not be universally true.

10 Optimal City Size and Density

The optimal city size myth

An earlier analysis (pp. 11–14) has indicated a possible diagrammatical approach to the theory of optimal city size. Even the presentation of this simple analysis gave rise to certain difficulties: the need to make a great many assumptions that weaken the value of its predictions; the generation of multiple optima depending on the focus and viewpoint of the analyst; doubts as to whether the quest for an optimal city size is a meaningful inquiry either in theory or for policy. The optimal city size literature appears to be snowballing despite these objections. It is appropriate, therefore, to expand some of the critical arguments[1] in an attempt to demonstrate that the search for a *unique* optimal city size is futile and for an optimal size appropriate to each city unnecessary. This discussion is an essential prelude to any analysis of national urban policy since its outcome will help to determine the objectives and scope of such a policy.

In one of the earliest papers on optimal city size (though *not* about the economic optimum), Duncan (1956) made a distinction between two elements: the *factual*, concerned with the more or less objective problem of establishing empirical relationships between the size of cities and variations in selected welfare indicators; and the *normative* concerned with placing a positive or negative valuation on the magnitude of these indicators, i.e. with the problem of weighting and aggregation. Elsewhere in this book there are many attempts to deal with the factual element, showing how such phenomena as incomes, unemployment, living costs, poverty, pollution, congestion costs, crime, economic structure, public service costs, production and consumption externalities and other factors vary with city size. Doubts have been expressed about the usefulness of the normative approach since the costs and benefits of each individual phenomenon neither indicate a preferred city size nor affect firms and households (as a whole or when divided by income, class or occupation) in the same way. Also, the net benefits or costs depend upon the viewpoint of the analyst, whether he is judging the impact of city size on the individual resident or immigrant, the urban community as a whole or from a regional or national welfare standpoint. Moreover, the attempt to assign weights to the welfare indicators and to aggregate them into an overall monetary or utility measure founders on the fact that monetary (or any other kind of quantifiable) valuations cannot easily be placed, if at all, on the indicators in question. Even if monetary weights could be produced, aggregation into an overall net benefit or cost measure assumes independence whereas many of the variables are closely interdependent (Isard, 1960, pp. 527–33). There are sound reasons for being suspicious of those who offer judgements, particularly those with policy inferences, about cities of a certain size being 'excessive' or 'too small'. Their observations are not based on scientific sifting of evidence, but on value judgements, implicit but untestable weighting systems, and arbitrary selection of a limited set of criteria.[2]

These arguments must destroy the concept of *the unique* optimal city size though they still leave open the possibility that there might be *an* optimal city size for a given entity (a production unit of a particular type, an individual of a particular occupational group in a household with a specific set of tastes and preferences) under certain defined conditions and according to a narrow range of specified criteria. To have a range of optimal city sizes of different size makes much more sense for several reasons: a city size distribution or hierarchy is a stubborn empirical fact; since the cost of inputs and agglomeration economies vary with city size, production establishments will differ in their preferences for locating in or near cities of particular sizes according to their input mix and their need for agglomeration economies; all households do not share the same tastes for life styles, and hence a variety of city sizes widens choice and offers opportunities for improving welfare[3]; the systemic functions of an urban hierarchy have important implications for national and regional development.

The dilemma of optimal city size protagonists is that in order to obtain a determinate solution they are forced to take either a restrictive view of the problem which means that the scope of their analysis is inadequate and incomplete or they make their focus more comprehensive in which case their task becomes impossible. The most limited approach is to examine how the costs of urban government services vary with city size,[4] to draw up a U-shaped cost curve relating urban service costs to population and to assume that the optimal city size occurs at the bottom point of this curve. Apart from its obvious theoretical inadequacies, estimates of the bottom point have varied widely over the range 50,000 to 1 million! It is possible that the urban cost curve has a long flat bottom, and it is scarcely surprising that estimates should vary between countries and over time as cost conditions and the urban service mix change. In any event, the whole procedure is dubious. The service mix varies according to community preferences even among cities of similar size, weighting of services in the bundle changes with scale and the *number* of services increases with city size. Many of the studies have failed to measure changes in unit costs of homogeneous output.[5]

Other costs, apart from public service costs, are important. Costs in the private sector have received less attention but it is known that living costs are influenced (though not very significantly) by city size as are producers' costs, particularly wage and rental costs.[6] The evidence is strong that income *per capita* increases with city size, while the incidence of poverty declines and the distribution of income (probably) becomes more equitable.[7] In the fields of industry, commerce and finance, productivity increases with city size in at least some sectors according to their reliance on agglomeration economies. All this suggests the need for a benefit as well as a cost appraisal of the influence of city size. This has the virtue that it avoids the worst excesses of the cost minimisation approach, but it remains unsatisfactory.

What the analyst usually does is to assume that all the costs and benefits of a given city size can be aggregated into a single net measure and that a net benefit function can be specified which enables us to identify the urban sizes that correspond to maximum net benefits, zero net benefits[8] and so on. Moreover, it is common to assume that the average cost and the average benefit functions have a particular shape. For example, Brown (1972), Barr (1972) and Klaassen (1972) all assume that average benefits increase with city size but at a diminishing rate (if $B[P]$ is the benefit–city size function, $B'[P]>0$ and $B''[P]<0$); thus, the benefit curve flattens out at a large city size. Average costs are also assumed to increase with city size but at an increasing rate $(C'[P]>0$ and $C''[P]>0)$. To derive the average net benefit curve $C[P]$ is subtracted vertically from $B[P]$ yielding an inverted-U function. The slope of this function which declines with city size and becomes negative at some point after the turndown in average net benefits is the marginal net benefit curve. This analysis yields three possible city size optima: maximum average net benefits < zero marginal net benefit (the most appropriate social optimum) < zero average net benefit.[9]

The trouble with this analysis is that there is no firm empirical evidence for assuming that the average benefit and cost functions have this shape. Klaassen (1965, pp. 27–31, and 1972) was able to justify these assumptions by confining the benefits to *per capita* income[10] and the costs to 'operating costs'; Brown (1972, pp. 164–7) draws the functions as implied above but admits the lack of evidence.[11] Klaassen ignores, or at least underplays, non-monetised externalities in his preoccupation with income generation.[12] Yet non-monetary costs and benefits need to be included in the cost and benefit functions since they undoubtedly influence the location decisions of firms and households that determine city size. Negative externalities such as traffic and other kinds of congestion, long journeys to work, noise, pollution, psycho-social stress, risks of being a victim of crime may be strongly related to scale. Conversely, positive externalities such as agglomeration economies for business, varied employment and educational opportunities for workers, and consumption externalities such as amenities, leisure, cultural and sports facilities, and entertainment opportunities may

122

also be important. Monetary valuations for most of these phenomena can scarcely be guessed at, never mind measured precisely enough for inclusion in the cost and benefit curves. Yet I suspect that a major explanation of why the cost and benefit functions are so frequently assumed to have the shape suggested above is that some of the non-quantifiable social costs have been implicitly taken into account in deciding upon the shape of the average cost function but that the positive externalities have been excluded. If this suspicion is correct, the wide concern about 'excessive' city size may stem, to a large extent, from preoccupation with the more visible, and *possibly* measurable, negative externalities while neglecting the hazy and less newsworthy, but no less important, positive externalities.

Judgements of what constitutes an optimal city size vary according to the perspective of those making the judgement. The resident, the new immigrant, the business firm, the city planner, the local politician, the regional policy maker, the national policy maker – each will have a different view. Sometimes, their respective views are inconsistent. For instance, despite the fact that the residents' optimum usually means a smaller city size than the social optimum, most cities want to grow at the same time as national governments are trying to stem their growth. The most obvious source of inconsistency, however, is the possible divergence in the optimum for households and that for firms. As shown by von Böventer (1970 and 1971) and Evans (1972), since both agglomeration economies and input costs are a function of city size, whether a firm chooses to locate in a smaller or a bigger city depends upon the exact nature of these functions and on the firm's need for agglomeration economies and on its input mix. The optimal city size is that which maximises the difference between agglomeration economies and input costs. Since both the importance of agglomeration economies and the input mix vary from one firm to another particularly across industries, so will the optimal city size. The determinants of optimal city size for households, on the other hand, are quite different. They include income and employment opportunities, externalities in consumption, the cost of living, public service and social costs. There is no *a priori* reason why matching between the optima for firms and those for households should occur. The location decisions of firms determine changes in the demand for labour while the location decisions of households determine changes in supply. Mismatching of these city sizes is therefore likely to be revealed as disequilibrium in the labour market. The question arises as to whether this disequilibrium is self-correcting. Brown (1972, p.11) has argued that this is indeed the case: 'If population and industry are drawn in different directions, the price mechanism ought to come to the rescue. The area sought by entrepreneurs and shunned by residents will become one of dearer labour, so that the divergent movements will be checked and eventually only a net flow of both industry and labour either in or out, produced by the resultant of the two initial preferences, will remain.' Although wages are the variable common to the city size decisions of both households and firms, this solution calls for a little too much faith in the efficacy of the price mechanism. On the other hand, disequilibrium in individual city sizes may be quite acceptable in a dynamic framework and not incompatible with equilibrium in the *distribution* of city sizes in the system as a whole.

There is a close degree of kinship between the concepts of optimal city size and optimum national population. No serious economist would use the optimum population concept nowadays, and it is paradoxical that urban economists, supposedly extending the frontiers of a new field, should find themselves chasing, if only in an analogous form, such an ancient will-o'-the-wisp. The gross defects of the theory of the optimum population are well known: the dependence on marginal productivity theory and the law of diminishing returns, the assumption of a closed economy, the use of a static model in a subject that cries out for growth dynamics, and the use of population as an index of economic well-being. The first is sometimes excusable for analytical and pedagogic convenience, though neo-classical models have serious drawbacks for urban analysis. Second, the 'openness' of city economies accentuates the theory's irrelevance for urban economics. Functional interdependence among cities and the systemic functions of the metropolis seriously undermine the value of an optimal city size concept. Third, a static framework is totally inappropriate since the optimum population concept has been discussed in the context of economic development. But the notion of optimal city size is not immediately consistent with the framework of a *growing* system of cities. It is true that the two things can be made compatible, but the results do not make very good sense. For instance, we could treat urban policy as a kind of bottling plant where each city represents a bottle of a standard size and where the policy maker's job is to fill each bottle to the brim in turn then move on and fill the next. This might be a practicable urban strategy but it is most unlikely to lead to an efficient system of cities. A modification of this approach is for urban policy makers to hold up population expansion when the so-called optimum is reached and then to shift attention to increasing *per capita* income. In an expanding economy this will be difficult without interurban migration controls since cities experiencing rapid increases in *per capita* income will also be attractive to potential migrants. Moreover, in a dynamic setting a large city may be functioning efficiently even if the gap $(AB-AC)$ is not maximised or even if $MC > MB$. This is because in the broader framework of a system of cities the efficiency of a large centre may be related to how well it performs its nationwide functions as a distributor of innovational activity, new ideas and managerial expertise down the city hierarchy.

124

The fourth objection to the optimum population concept is possibly most serious of all. Optimum city size is invariably discussed in terms of city population. It is unclear whether this is because the level of population is considered to be the most suitable index for determining the optimum (on the grounds that agglomeration economies and diseconomies can be functionally related in a more or less precise way to population size), or whether population is used as a surrogate for other size variables for which we lack data. Reliance on population data may be forced upon us by the poverty of urban social accounts but much of the literature gives the impression that the choice is deliberate. In fact, although useful for some purposes, e.g. determining the minimum threshold 'market' for health and educational facilities, some types of retail trade and public transport systems, population is a poor size proxy in many other respects. Particularly in medium or small cities, the same population could imply very different total urban incomes and widely dissimilar mixes and scale of public and private services. Moreover, for many business firms the agglomeration economies derived from locating in a centre of given size may have little connection with its population level but instead may be related to the number of competing firms, the availability of specialised business services and so on. Of course, for other firms (e.g. either those in consumer industries or those with specialised labour requirements) the population size of the centre may be the chief determinant of market potential and labour market economies.

A further difficulty is that a city's population is an ambiguous measure depending very much on the arbitrariness of geographical and political boundaries. Intertemporal, cross-spatial and cross-cultural comparisons require standardisation in urban delimitation. There are several solutions: aggregation of population within a given radius from the CBD; counting the population within a city region where the boundaries of the region are fixed by where the population falls to rural density levels; using a population potential index. Of course, the boundary problem arises with the adoption of other size variables too.[13]

If population is a relevant indicator, there is some value in the argument that density is a more relevant variable than size. The justification for this is the theoretical point that in urban economics there is a presumption that the spatial distribution of a phenomenon is more important that its aggregate level and the empirical finding that many diseconomies are more a function of density than city size. Many analysts (Wingo, 1972; Mills, 1972; Brown, 1972; Harris and Ullman, 1945) have recognised that spatial structure may be a more critical determinant of urban efficiency than city size.[14] This supports the argument that discussions of optimality in the urban economy that abstract from space are misplaced and inadequate.[15]

125

Other criteria have been suggested for determining optimal city size. For instance, it is sometimes argued that urban development and infrastructure construction costs are lower in medium-sized towns which offer the economies of scale and accessibility to building material sources frequently not found in small centres yet do not suffer from the high costs of development in large cities. But the latter is primarily due to high land costs which as a transfer payment rather than a resource cost do not necessarily mean high real costs unless economising on land in selecting factor coefficients involves higher costs, e.g. because of inelasticities in the supply of other factors. Moreover, the discounted stream of urban development costs is such a small fraction of the total economic product of the city and differences in streams among cities of different size much smaller still, that urban construction costs form much too narrow a criterion.

Another factor, stressed by Thompson (1965) and Barnett (1968) is the emergence of managerial diseconomies when the running of a city becomes a large-scale operation.[16] In specific cases large cities may be run inefficiently because of a scarcity of high quality urban management personnel, but such diseconomies are not inevitable. In the United Kingdom at least, impressionistic evidence points the other way: the small authorities are more likely to be inefficiently run, primarily because successful urban management calls for highly skilled specialised staff that can be justified and afforded only by large authorities. Furthermore, to what extent are managerial diseconomies in business due to the physical impossibility of handling problems above a certain scale or to the inefficiencies of monopoly power? The latter scarcely apply in the urban context since the major cities of the system are in competition with each other to attract business firms and migrants. As Baumol (1967) pointed out, no modern city can let its tax rates or quality of urban services get too far out of line with its competitors. Moreover, within each city-size class efficiency is normally distributed among cities much as it is among firms of a given size in a particular industry. I suspect that the 'efficiency gap' between cities within a given size class may be about as wide as between cities of extremely different size.

Optimal city size discussions stress the importance of agglomeration economies, among which the benefits of a large centralised labour market figure prominently. But if there were a precise scale for an efficient city labour market, this could still mean substantial variation in city population sizes because of intercity differentials in labour participation rates. Moreover, the notion of an optimal scale is probably as dubious in regard to labour markets as to cities themselves. An efficient scale will vary according to the industrial composition of the area, the skills required, turnover rates in individual industries and many other considerations. In general, however, the odds favour large labour markets, especially if they are spatially concentrated. They offer more chance of locational compatibility, i.e. that the aggregate demand for labour at the city's workplaces will match the total supply within travelling distance (see Goldner, 1955), and large size ensures threshold pool levels even for highly specialised types of labour.

A recent development in the optimal city size literature deals with the question of competitive equilibrium and efficient resource allocation in the individual city (for representative examples of this work see Solow and Vickrey, 1971; Mirrlees, 1972; Barr, 1972; Edel, 1972; Livesey, 1973). The models vary in their assumptions, structure, emphasis and predictions but all of them (with the partial exception of Edel) are not so much concerned with the problem of determining an optimal city size in the population numbers sense but with a much more restricted problem. What determines the optimal allocation of urban land between residences and other uses (primarily transportation) and what are the conditions of a competitive locational equilibrium that stabilise the distribution of residential population and the rent gradient over the city as a whole? This is a partial equilibrium problem which requires the exogenous specification of key variables (such as average lot size per inhabitant), assumes a well-behaved population density gradient and ignores the problem of efficiency in goods production (Richardson, 1973b). It is true that given the limiting assumptions, the predetermined variables and the partial equilibrium focus, satisfaction of the optimality conditions implies a certain population size, which might on some definitions be described as an 'optimal city size'. But this does not mean very much. It simply refers to the theoretical urban population that is associated with the attainment of certain narrow optimal allocative conditions and is not related in any direct way to the city size that maximises the welfare of its citizens, or of immigrants, or of society as a whole.

If any link can be forged between this narrow approach and the broader problem of optimal city size it must be via urban rents. Mirrlees (1972) suggested that the optimal town size occurs at that level of population (labour force) where the difference between the marginal and average product of labour is exactly absorbed by urban rents (strictly speaking, the excess of urban over rural rents).[17] Similarly, Barr (1972) argued that if there is competition for urban sites city size will expand to where benefits equal costs, at which point there are no gains from urban participation. Land rents adjust to eliminate locational gains, and introducing complications into the model (such as public good preferences, a taste for city living, zoning ordinances and planning controls) make no difference to this essential fact, but express themselves as shifts in benefit and/or cost curves. 'Whatever the benefits derived from agglomeration, land rents through the bidding of space will rise to eliminate them. Capital gains may accrue to some landowners, but these could be taxed away. Competition will push city size and rents until there are no net benefits to be gained by any household. This state does conform to our conditions of optimal city size' (Barr, 1972, p. 94). In this way urban rents are the equilibrating factor which equalises the net benefits of urban and rural living and stabilises the city population at the so-called 'optimal' level.

This feature was seized upon by Edel (1972), enabling him to convert an abstract theory into an operational mode of analysis. The optimal city size that maximises the total benefits provided by the city is that population level that equates marginal costs and benefits. At this city size total rents are also maximised as are land values (which represent the capitalised value of rents). Urban rents and land values capture, *inter alia*, congestion costs and agglomeration economies. Empirically, we may determine optimal city size by specifying the function relating land values to city size. In fact, Edel identifies two possible city size optima.[18] First, there is the city size where total land values (rents) are maximised, i.e. where $MB=MC$. This is the optimum from the aggregate economy's point of view, assuming perfect elasticity in the supply of population. Second, from the point of view of city residents *as a whole* the optimum occurs at a smaller city size where land values *per capita* are maximised.[19] This is the city size where rent *per capita* is maximised; rent *per capita* (AR) is defined as $(AB–AC)(1–\beta)$ where $\beta=$ proportion of benefits remaining to the individual. The value of β can be eroded away by competition in the land market. The residents' optimum is not an equilibrium, however, since there are still net benefits to be eliminated by competition for urban space from new city immigrants. Equilibrium is obtained when β declines to zero, i.e. when $MB=MC$ and total rents are maximised. This is not, of course, the city size that equates AB and AC, but rather where the whole excess of AB over AC is absorbed by urban rent. The dual argument that the costs and benefits of urban size are monetised in the land market and that competitive bidding for urban space by immigrants ultimately equates marginal costs and benefits is interesting and suggestive, but it does not provide a satisfactory answer to the optimal city size problem. It treats the city as an isolated production and consumption unit rather than as part of a wider spatial system with non-local functions and it ignores monopolistic elements in the urban land market. Also, it fails to meet many of the criticisms levied against the optimal city size concept in the preceding pages.

These arguments lead us to reject the value of the optimal city size concept, even in a simplified comparative statics framework. When we transfer the concept into a dynamic setting, its value depreciates even further. One reason for this is that urban growth dynamics require us to look at the individual city against the background of the wider system of which it forms a part, and in this wider framework it becomes clear that different cities perform different functions (purely local, regional, national or cosmopolitan), and some cities perform all four. If we accept the implications of multifunctional cities, there is no possibility of a unique optimum since optimality makes sense only in the context of efficient achievement of objectives, and these objectives vary according to the type and functions of the individual city (Shindman, 1959). Because of multiple functions and intercity specialisation, cities will differ in the local orientation of their industries and activities so that the local population threshold will be relevant in some cases but not in others. The efficient ranges of place size will be determined by the functions which each type of place has to perform. If the hierarchical structure implied by differentiation in function extends to the national system of cities, there would appear to be a basic inconsistency between the optimal city size concept and an efficient national urban hierarchy. This conflict, though obvious, has been neglected in the literature.

Can the concept of optimal city size be made compatible with the existence of a national urban hierarchy? The answer to this question depends on what is meant by optimal city size. As we have seen, von Böventer's concept of different optima for different firms is consistent with the hierarchy of city sizes. Second, instead of a single optimal city size it may be more meaningful to conceive of an optimal size for each rank order in the urban hierarchy. Third, if the looser concept of an efficient range of city sizes is interpreted very widely, a wide range may cover a large proportion of the city sizes in the hierarchy. Fourth, with increasing decentralisation from major cities into urban subcentres around the metropolises it becomes arbitrary whether we speak of one city or a family of linked cities. Since large cities of a prescribed size may imply conglomerations of smaller urban centres of variable size, it is possible depending on the definitions of urban areas adopted to envisage an optimal metropolitan area size which simultaneously embraces a hierarchy of city sizes. Finally, if optimal urban scale is measured not in terms of absolute size but of population density, the potential inconsistency may be resolved since average densities may vary less than absolute city sizes and the concept of optimal density (if it exists) is culturally and institutionally determined.[20]

It is well known that a hierarchy of urban centres is the efficient way of organising production and distribution within a region, i.e. the central place system. Similarly, the national urban hierarchy performs a number of important functions in the national economy which may make it an efficient medium for the distribution of the total population even if some individual cities in the size distribution are outside the efficient range from the point of view of the cities when considered alone.

The national hierarchy of leading cities is an instrument for achieving national growth. First, the urban hierarchy is an efficient vehicle for transmitting new technology, managerial expertise, new industries and general economic functions from the centre of the economy to the periphery. This permits social and economic change to 'leap-frog' over distance and avoid the slower gradual diffusion over space from the central city. This transmission function is aided by the fact that many modern forms of business organisation (in commerce, finance and industry) are themselves hierarchical with head offices and centres of decision making in the metropolitan centres and their decision trees spread out spatially down the urban hierarchy. Given the large scale and multiple establishments characteristic of modern business, a hierarchy of cities makes it easier to distribute the hierarchical structure and functions of business organisation over the economy as a whole.

Second, a hierarchy of cities permits specialisation, division of labour and differentiation in economic function. Market size requirements, infrastructure needs and agglomeration economies differ between firms in the same industry (many industries have a size distribution of firms similar in form to the distribution of city sizes) and between industries. A hierarchy of cities offers firms a wider choice in location and enables them to operate more efficiently (von Böventer, 1970).

Third, the hierarchical structure of cities dominant within their own regions enables each city to function in a manner appropriate to the size and character of its hinterland region. The leading city in a peripheral region, for instance, clearly plays an important role in the development of that region (the growth centre strategy).[21] Since regions vary in area, population and level of economic development it is inevitable that their leading cities will also vary in size.

The most appropriate size for a given city depends not only on its functions vis-à-vis other cities but also on its location relative to other cities in the system (von Böventer, 1970 and 1971; Alonso, 1971a). It may be possible for a small city to be viable if it is sufficiently close to a larger city to benefit from the latter's agglomeration economies (this raises the interesting but complex research question of the range of agglomeration economies; see p.72). A bigger city, on the other hand, is much more likely to be further away, since an element of monopolistic power over space (the hinterland effect) may have been necessary for its growth. Thus, city size optima depend very much on the distribution of cities in space. The problem becomes very complicated in relatively small countries and where suburbanisation has led to the growth of smaller towns and cities at some distance from but still interconnected with the large metropolises. The notion of an optimal city size becomes even more blurred in such situations because it is unclear what is meant by a city as compared with an economy characterised by a system of free-standing cities. A polinucleated megalopolitan structure may be a

130

very efficient form of spatial organisation, because it represents a successful adaptation to modern urban conditions and offers scope for shared agglomeration economies and functional specialisation, but it casts doubt on the relevance of models of optimal city size.

A minimum critical size for a city may be more sensible than an optimal size (Hoover, 1969 and 1971; Hansen, 1972). The rationale for this is based on two arguments: the concept of a threshold population level needed to create the demand for all major services; a critical size beyond which growth becomes self-sustaining.[22] There is no *a priori* reason why these two minima should coincide. Also, cities below the minimum may be quite efficient if conceived as part of a wider system, e.g. if they perform low order functions, or are locations for key national industries that require isolated sites because of high pollution rates. Criteria used to determine efficient minima include evaluation of critical demand thresholds for business services and items of consumption including amenities, engineering cost functions for urban services and comparisons of the growth performance of city size classes. Hansen (1972) found that growth spurts occurred in SMSAs soon after they reached the 200,000 level,[23] while an earlier study (Netherlands Economic Institute, 1961) of West Germany showed that cities above 275,000 experienced higher growth rates with a smaller variance than smaller cities. Although the evidence is not entirely conclusive, much of it supports the view that 200–250,000 is the minimum population for a relatively compact city to provide a comprehensive range of services (Thompson, 1965a, 1965b and 1972; Neutze, 1965; Clark, 1945; Alonso, 1970; Berry, 1968; Redcliffe-Maud, 1969; Hansen, 1970 and 1972; Cameron, 1970; Klaassen, 1972; Fox and Kumar, 1965).[24] For some services (particularly in the distribution and public sector fields), however, a much smaller size of 100,000 or less may be sufficient, while for other specialised services (public transit systems, specialist hospitals and certain cultural facilities) a population of at least one million is necessary.

To sum up, the search for an optimal city size is almost as idle as the quest for the philosopher's stone. Optimality in the urban economy may have meaning if it relates size to form and structure, but the crude measures of size in the literature have lacked a spatial dimension. There is more sense in the concept of minimum critical city size, but the threshold varies according to the city's functions and the service mix selected by its residents. Similarly, there may be value in the idea of an efficient (max–min) range of sizes within each functional class of cities. It is even possible that there is an upper bound to city size beyond which increasing obstacles to growth are encountered. But these modifications destroy the concept of a unique optimum. This is reassuring for the dynamic analysis of city systems since these always assume a hierarchical distribution.[25]

Population density

If the concept of an optimal city size is not very meaningful, is there anything to be said in favour of an optimal population density? The concern for spatial variables which motivates regional and urban economists to disaggregate the macroeconomy into regions and cities may also suggest that the intracity spatial distribution of population (i.e. population densities) is a more interesting phenomenon than city size itself. There is some evidence in support of this view. Many external diseconomies (pollution, traffic congestion, psycho-social stress) appear to be more a function of population density (especially central city density) than city size. The provision of certain public services becomes costly at very low densities (Treuner, 1970), while low densities imply a spatially large urban area and hence, if employment remains fairly centralised, long journeys to work. It is possible, though the evidence remains sketchy, that holding city size constant there is a U-shaped function relating urban costs to population density. Costs are heavy at high average population densities because of congestion effects and at very low densities because of long trip journeys and high transport, distribution and servicing costs. Medium densities may, on the other hand, be associated with lower urban costs. Since density is intimately related to urban structure, the implication of a hypothesis of this kind is that efficiency in spatial structure is a more significant determinant of whether a city is close to optimality than aggregate size. Too much of the urban size literature ignores or underplays intraurban space.

However, it remains doubtful whether there is much mileage in the concept of an optimal population density. Smith (1970) has given some attention to such a concept arguing that the demand curve for land per person is very inelastic and that large and radical changes in transportation costs or revolutionary shifts in household space preferences would be needed to alter densities by very much. He argues that optimal density is a cultural not a technological concept, and the value system underlying it derives from urban experience. The argument is interesting but unconvincing. The one piece of evidence supporting it is that average population densities are a function of the age of the city (hence in the United States densities in eastern and southern cities are much higher than in the west; see Hoch, 1972), so that the decline in densities over time could reflect a transformation in socio-cultural standard analogous to the upward drift in the concept of the subsistence standard of living and definition of poverty. On this view, lower density life styles are a product of social change over long historical periods rather than the more sudden consequence of advances in transportation technology.

On the other hand, if the optimal density concept were socio-culturally determined, we would expect – since households everywhere within a country are subject to the same broad set of social influences and forces – residential densities to vary very little both between cities and within cities. The reverse is true. There are wide intercity variations in average densities that cannot be explained in terms of either city size differences or the legacy of an inherited past spatial structure. Even more significant, the variations in densities within cities indicate a wide range of spatial preferences among households. Since the optimal density must bear some relationship to the average density from the point of view of operational analysis, the concept does not appear to have much value simply because average density itself does not make much sense. Just as the frequency distribution of cities casts considerable doubt on the validity of an optimal city size, so the spatial distribution of urban population densities throws suspicion on the usefulness of the optimal density concept. It is significant that the standard method of measuring urban population densities is not via an average density measure but by using the density gradient concept according to which the population density at any distance from the city centre, r, can be expressed in terms of two parameters – the city centre gross residential density (D_0) and the density gradient (D_1),

$$D_r = D_0 e^{-D_1 r} \qquad (10.1)$$

where $D_r =$ gross residential population density at distance r and e is the Napierian logarithmic base (2·718). Thus, population density is a negative exponential function of radial distance.[26] On the same lines the relationship between city size and the density parameters extrapolating the density gradient to zero densities is given by the equation[27]

$$P = 2\pi D_0 D_1^{-2} \qquad (10.2)$$

Although the simplifications behind eqn. (10.2) are crude, it nevertheless illustrates two important relationships: that city size is positively associated with central city densities; that city size is inversely related to the density gradient. Equation (10.1) cannot be expected to hold precisely once account is taken of real-world aspects of the urban spatial structure: the presence of non-residential uses and variation in their incidence with distance; irregularities in the density function due, for instance, to the presence of secondary foci of population and activity outside the CBD (sub-centring); and the threshold level to which urban population densities fall (rural density which is much higher than zero). Data on the values of D_0 and D_1 have been estimated for 46 United States cities in 1950 (Muth, 1969), 30 United States cities in 1960 (Barr, 1970), US cities for a variety of years (Mills, 1972c) and for a range of world cities at various points of time (Clark, 1967). For the first two cases, Hoch (1972) has examined the relationship between urbanised area population (city size) and the density parameters explicitly. He regressed the logarithm of the density parameters on the logarithm of urban population

Table 10.1

Relationship between density parameters and city size, United States 1950 and 1960

Year	Density parameter	Constant	Regional dummy variables		City size exponent	R^2
			North East	West		
1950	D_0	6·03	1·71†	0·73	0·208*	0·26
1960	D_0	2·89	1·92*	0·63	0·236	0·21
1950	D_1	4·54	1·49*	0·90	−0·424†	0·34
1960	D_1	11·8	1·41	0·69	−0·616†	0·34

* Significant at 0·10 level
† Significant at 0·05 level
Source: Hoch, 1972

(expressed in thousands) using regional dummy variables (since North Eastern experience is known to differ from that of the West), and the results (in antilog form) are shown in Table 10.1.

Despite the restricted scope of the samples, and the modest levels of statistical significance,[28] these results are consistent with *a priori* expectation and the implications of the density gradient model. Central densities increase with city size but less than proportionately (the elasticity of D_0 with respect to P is significantly different from, and less than, unity). The density gradient declines with city size,[29] and the statistical relationship is significantly better than that for D_0 (whether measured by the t statistic or by the R^2). This is consistent with the well-known observation that central gross residential population densities can be grossly distorted by non-residential land uses and by peculiarities in the structure of the CBD. The results are consistent between 1950 and 1960 in spite of extensive suburbanisation during the decade. Muth (1969) had some difficulty in supplying a deductive explanation for the negative relationship between D_1 and P on the grounds that city size is positively linked to traffic congestion and land rents so that high marginal transport costs ought to induce close-in living while high rents (and house prices) ought to lead to higher density living. His eventual explanation was that because the elasticity of substitution of land for other factors in the housing industry was less than unity housing output (and hence residential population) increases more rapidly in the outer part of the city, thereby flattening the density gradient as city size expands. The regional effects (the results in Table 10.1 suggest that only the North East dummy variable had a significant impact) are compatible with the hypothesis that age of the city affects both central densities and the slope of the gradient, presumably because of the lack of adaptability in the inherited transportation infrastructure and street layout. In an international setting, there are wide differences in the values of D_0 between developed and developing countries that transcend city size differences; for instance, D_0 values are high in India and South East Asia (Clark, 1967). Similarly, in the developed world both central densities and the gradient have declined over time, due primarily to suburbanisation and the replacement of residences by business and commerce in and near the CBD.[30] The behaviour of D_0 over time (during which urban populations have increased) and its cross-sectional relationship with city size is, therefore, dissimilar.

What are the implications of this analysis? First, the concept of optimal density is not very useful because of wide intraurban and intercity differentials. Urban densities make an important contribution to explaining many urban phenomena, but the search for optimality is elusive. People vary widely in their choice of living densities, and density measures for industrial cities are difficult to compare because of topography, differential non-residential use and other elements of urban spatial structure. Second, larger cities have higher central densities (D_0) and flatter density gradients (D_1). Loosely interpreted, this finding may have welfare implications. To the extent that congestion, pollution, psycho-social stress, social disorganisation and other evils are associated with high densities this helps to explain the prevalence of the 'central city problem' in large metropolises. Conversely, the flatter density gradient may imply higher levels of individual welfare (more consumption of space, cleaner air, more open space, etc.).[31] In this sense, the variation of the two density parameters with city size may be a symptom of the increasing central city–suburban distributional problems of big cities.[32]

Notes

[1] Some of the arguments here derive from my earlier paper on optimal city size (Richardson, 1972).

[2] This obvious point has not deterred policy makers, politicians and social scientists from making normative judgements about city size. Yet the deficiencies of these judgements had already been recognised by Duncan (1956, p. 385): 'The optimum size of cities is quite different from the standpoint of certain criteria from what it is on the basis of others. It is found that even an apparently unitary criterion, e.g. health, way give conflicting indications of the optimum. There is no immediately obvious way in which these various optima may be objectively equilibrated, compromised, weighted

or balanced to yield an unequivocal figure for *the* optimum population for a city. Any numerical choice of a figure for the optimum population is involved in subjective value preferences and impressionistic weighting systems. Most theorists proposing a size or size range as the optimum adopt this procedure, or the alternative one of confining attention to a few of the many criteria of optimum city size that have been proposed in the literature.'

[3] As pointed out by Leven (1969), this argument is analogous to the case for product differentiation in conditions of monopolistic competition.

[4] This first step, trying to identify economies and diseconomies of scale in urban government services, is in itself a legitimate exercise. See pp. 85–9.

[5] For a review of some of the studies see pp. 86–8.

[6] See pp. 54–60.

[7] See pp. 51–4.

[8] The zero net benefit case is that city size where the net benefits of urban living have fallen to the level that equalises the welfare of the citizen and the country dweller.

[9] For a more general diagrammatical analysis, again yielding several optima, see pp. 11–14.

[10] Even the evidence on how per capita incomes vary with city size, particularly in the multi-million size class, is very uncertain.

[11] In regard to benefits 'all the advantages will pretty certainly grow at a decreasing rate, after a point at least' (Brown, p. 164); as for costs 'This shape, however, is highly speculative, and the only thing one can be reasonably sure of is that the curve rises throughout the whole of the range' (*ibid.*, p. 165).

[12] In effect, he adopts a neo-classical outlook where the objective is to maximise the contribution to GNP of all cities considered together which implies that population should be distributed among the available cities so that marginal disposable income in each is equal.

[13] For a brief discussion of the urban boundary definition problem see above, pp. 5–7.

[14] See Mills (1972b, p. 122): 'To the extent that urban markets distort resource allocation, I believe that distortion merely affects the structure rather than the size of metropolitan areas... public policy should be concerned to improve market incentives rather than to control city size.'

[15] For further analysis of the possible importance of population density, see pp. 132–5.

[16] For more comments on this question, see pp. 89–90.

[17] In addition, he introduces the possibility of a correction factor – a commuter tax or subsidy – to take account of environmental externalities.

[18] As shown above (pp. 11–14, 122), there are other possibilities.

[19] Edel would deny that this market solution is a true social optimum

since the net benefits of urban agglomeration may be distributed regressively in favour of landowners, real estate owners, and other high income minority groups.

[20] For doubts about the value of optimal densities see pp. 132–3, 135.

[21] See below, pp. 181–4.

[22] 'The issue here is not one of optimum size but rather of the minimum size required to provide the range of services needed by people and firms and the impact of size on growth potentials' (Hansen, 1972, p. 117).

[23] A qualification to this finding is the analysis of Alonso and Medrich (1972) who found that SGC (spontaneous growth centres) could be found throughout the size hierarchy. For more analysis of variations in growth rates between city size classes see pp. 113–17.

[24] Thompson (1972) argues that middle-size cities of over 200,000 have 'the advantage of remaining relatively whole governmentally while becoming moderately stable economically'.

[25] This statement uses hierarchical in the loose sense, that is, implying a frequency distribution of city sizes in which the number of cities in each size class increases as city size declines.

[26] Recent research has suggested modifications to this function particularly to account for a 'crater' effect observable in central city densities. These complications need not be considered here.

[27] This simple model ignores the pre-emption of central sites for non-residential uses in addition to its other unrealistic assumptions.

[28] In the 1950 equation for D_0, population becomes significant at the 0·05 level if the dummy variable for the West is deleted.

[29] Muth's (1969) cross-sectional tests showed that out of a large number of plausible independent variables city size was the most important determinant of the density gradient.

[30] Of course, employment has also been suburbanised in recent decades to varying degrees (see Mills, 1972c, Chapter 3).

[31] Whether the flat density gradient generates significant social costs (higher urban infrastructure costs, greater disutility due to travelling, etc.) is a more open question.

[32] This argument may still be valid despite the evidence that the overall SMSA distribution of income tends to be more equal in the bigger cities (see pp. 51–4).

11 Theory of the Distribution of City Sizes

Introduction

How to explain the size distribution of cities is one of the most fascinating intellectual problems in urban analysis. There are several reasons for this: the topic is relevant to all societies, regardless of their level of development, location or cultural background; it has attracted the attention of many social scientists – economists, geographers, sociologists and statisticians – and no one discipline has the monopoly of wisdom; despite past research, there is no widely acceptable theory and the problem remains a mystery. Tinbergen (1968, p. 65) has argued that 'No scientific explanation worthy of that name has been advanced so far'. The models examined in this chapter suggest that this opinion is too harsh, but the theoretical challenges of the problem remain immense. First, Champernowne's (1953, p. 319) comments on the theory of income distribution apply with even more force to city size distributions: the forces 'are so varied and complex, and interact and fluctuate so continuously, that any theoretical model must either be unrealistically simplified or hopelessly complicated'. Second, it is difficult to sort out 'good' theories from 'bad' via empirical testing. The statistical functions of city size (see the next section) are so similar that the differences between them are insufficiently sensitive for any single function to dominate as the 'best' general relationship. It is impossible to favour one theory or another on the basis of its predictions, since any one of the observed statistical relationships is compatible with several theories while many of the individual theories are consistent with more than one of the standard empirical distributions. The future for empirical testing lies in the evaluation of the underlying individual hypotheses and assumptions that underpin each model rather than in comparing predicted and actual city size distributions.

The objective of this chapter is to survey a wide range of theories: to assess the standard explanations, to revive a few neglected contributions, to review some very recent suggestions and to offer one or two new ideas. The aim is not to search for the one superior theory since some of the theories are complementary, nor to present any empirical evidence, but rather to comment on the current state of the theory, to promote interest in the problem and to offer some guidelines for future research. First, however, we must clear the ground by making some general observations on statistical relationships of city size distributions.

Lognormal, Pareto and rank-size distributions

All city size distributions are strongly positively skewed to the right, i.e. there are many small but only a few very large cities with a tendency for the number of cities in each size class to decline as city size increases. This rules out normal distributions. The three main candidates then become the lognormal distribution, the Pareto distribution and the rank-size rule. As we shall see, all three have close similarities. If the frequency distribution of city sizes is hump-shaped and positively skewed the lognormal distribution may yield a good fit, i.e.

$$N = \log P \qquad (11.1)$$

where N=cumulative percentage of cities and P=city size. The lognormal distribution attempts to represent the whole range of city sizes, and this differentiates it from the Pareto distribution which deals only with the upper tail (city sizes above a defined level, $\bar{P}$). However, the lognormal can be translated into Pareto distribution terms by either arbitrarily imposing a threshold city size or estimating it from the data using a three-parameter distribution (Aitchison and Brown, 1957).

The Pareto distribution is given by

$$N(\bar{P}) = AP^{-\alpha} \qquad (11.2)$$

where $N(\bar{P})$=cumulative percentage of cities above the threshold level, $\bar{P}$

A, α =constants.

This can be expressed as

$$\log N(\bar{P}) = \log A - \alpha \log P \qquad (11.3)$$

which is similar to eqn. (11.1). If the data yield a good fit the city size distribution can be represented by a straight line with a slope of $-\alpha$.

The rank-size distribution is given by

$$R \cdot P^q = K \qquad (11.4)$$

where R=city rank

q, K=constants.

Rearranging, we obtain

$$R = KP^{-q} \qquad (11.5)$$

which is identical to the Pareto distribution except that rank of city is used instead of cumulative percentage of number of cities. A special case of the rank-size distribution is obtained where $q=1$. This is the so-called rank-size rule

$$R \cdot P = K = P_1 \qquad (11.6)$$

where P_1=size of the largest city. Thus the product of city size and its rank is a constant, equal to the size of the leading city in the system. A frequent reason for the failure of this special case to hold is that $K \neq P_1$ (this inequality also has repercussions on the value of q), usually because P_1 is overdeveloped relative to the rest of the urban system. The tendency for the largest city to be 'excessively' big with stunting effects on cities of nearby rank is the primate distribution case.[1]

The three distributions are so similar that it is difficult to choose between them. If we were concentrating on the upper tail there might be a preference for the Pareto or rank-size distributions, especially if data limitations impose a minimum urban place threshold as defined by census data, or if a minimum critical size for a viable urban service centre is determined on theoretical grounds. The Pareto may also be preferred if the upper tail is highly skewed. On the other hand, if very disaggregated data are available and if the analyst is concerned with the whole range of city sizes, the lognormal may be more appealing. Distortions due to the minimum threshold and/or primacy may be handled by using the three-and/or four-parameter lognormal form. Yet despite the greater generality of the lognormal and its flexibility from a statistical point of view, most of the literature has concentrated on Pareto and rank-size distributions, especially the latter. Christaller (1966, p.59 and n.19) described the rank-size rule as 'a most incredible law' which was 'not much more than playing with numbers'. This criticism is directed solely against the rule itself (i.e. the special case $q=1$). Despite satisfactory fits in some cases,[2] there is no reason for restricting analysis to the $q=1$ case. The rank-size distribution may instead be interpreted as a very general model according to the value of the exponent. If $q=1$ implies the rank-size rule, $q>1$ represents metropolitan dominance while $q<1$ stands for an urban system in which intermediate cities (such as regional capitals) are relatively large. The limiting cases, unknown in practice, are $q=\infty$ (only one city) and $q=0$ (all cities of the same size). This interpretation gives some support for Parr's view (1970) that the rank-size distribution has 'greater validity' than other models. Zipf (1949, p. 423) suggested that if the rank-frequency distribution were to include the *whole* population the curve would bend downward below the 2,500 population mark, and that this could be interpreted economically 'as an indication of a deficiency of smaller communities' and socially 'as the demarcation between the traditional classes, *urban* and *rural*'. This is analogous to the minimum threshold requirement of the Pareto distribution.

Hierarchy models

Hierarchy models have received most emphasis in the literature. Whereas the earliest studies on city size distributions merely concentrated on trying to account for the shape and nature of the observed statistical functions, the central place model was the first deductive theory of the distribution of cities. No-one has pruned the structure of the model to a minimum set

141

of assumptions more successfully than Beckmann (see next section). However, other hierarchy models are feasible. The Tinbergen model (see 'A more general urban hierarchy model') is more general in the sense that it can apply to manufacturing as well as service industries, though additional assumptions are needed to derive a determinate solution. It is also possible to construct a city size distribution model in which administrative functions substitute for service functions (see 'Administrative hierarchy models').

A central place model

Beckmann (1958 and 1968; Beckmann and McPherson, 1970) developed the key model relating central place and market area hierarchies to the distribution of city sizes, though the analysis stems directly from the Christaller–Lösch tradition. Cities of different size perform different functions because it is more efficient for some goods and services to be produced in small cities and others in larger centres. A city's prime economic functions are assumed to be to service its hinterland which, except for the smallest urban centre, encompasses smaller cities. Goods and services are ranked into higher and lower orders depending upon the demand *threshold* (i.e. the minimum viable level, in population and/or income, required to support the service) and the *range* (the outer limits of the market area) of each good. The threshold and the range, reflecting economies of scale and transport costs, act as lower and upper bounds, stratifying cities into a hierarchy and determining the number and size of urban places in each level.

Starting from a homogeneous plain over which resources are uniformly distributed, Beckmann makes two crucial assumptions. First, city size is proportional to the population the city serves:

$$p_m = kP_m \qquad (11.7)$$

where p_m=population of city of order m, P_m=population served by this city and k=proportionality factor.

This assumption implies simplistic production functions in which labour is the only input and the ratio of inputs to output is constant above the threshold level. Second, cities of each order have a fixed number (s) of satellite cities of the next lowest order,

$$P_m = p_m + sP_{m-1} \qquad (11.8)$$

The smallest urban centre serves a basic rural population (r_1) and itself; from this fact the population served by this centre may be derived

$$p_1 = r_1/1 - k \qquad (11.9)$$

Via substitution and rearrangement we obtain

$$p_m = \frac{ks^{m-1}r_1}{(1-k)^m} \qquad (11.10)$$

City size increases exponentially with the level of the city in the hierarchy.[3]

142

The basic parameters of the model are r_1 (the rural population served by the smallest town), k (the ratio of city size to population served) and s (the number of satellites per city).

The model predicts that all cities of the same rank are of equal size, and this conflicts with observation. However, if we treat the city size multiplier, $s/1-k$, as a random variable, the product after several multiplications will tend to lognormality. This transforms the discrete step-wise hierarchy into a more continuous distribution. Other modifications having a similar effect include the introduction of non-central place functions such as manufacturing, variations in production costs between cities, variable population densities and spatial differences in the impact of technology.

Many objections have been levied against the model. However, these have been misdirected since the main object of attack has been the model's simplifying assumptions. The objections can usually be accommodated without affecting the theory's basic structure. For instance, some observers (e.g. Mills, 1972a) have commented on the paradox of a theory of city size distribution built upon the foundations of a rural population (r_1). However, though the model needs a minimum base this could easily be an urban nucleus representing the minimum efficient size for urban functions. Others have argued that the assumption that cities only export down the hierarchy is wrong, but this can be dealt with via allowing k to be a variable rather than a constant; the same relaxation allows local demand to vary with city size (Dacey, 1966). The number of satellite cities (s) can also be permitted to vary between levels. These modifications make the mathematics more cumbersome, but do not destroy the rationale of the hierarchy model. Rather, by making it more flexible they transform it into a more general theory with a wider range of predictions compatible with more empirical examples.

Beckmann's version purges the hierarchy model of spatial elements. This has two defects. First, it ignores the fact that the relative size of cities is affected by distance between them. Deviations from the theoretical interurban distance may not account for major changes in ranks, but they distort the regularity of the hierarchy. Second, it ignores intraurban space. High commuting costs and density functions such as congestion and pollution are diseconomies of urban scale that may limit city size independent of hierarchical effects.[4]

A more general urban hierarchy model

Tinbergen (1968) developed a hierarchy model of city size distributions, similar in some ways to the classical (Beckmann) model, but described in terms of income and initially assuming that each city exports only its highest order good. Also, the model is more easily applied to manufacturing industry since it does not depend on central place functions.

He assumes a closed economy of regular shape evenly covered with farms except in cities. There are H industries ($h=0, 1, \ldots, H$), where h is called the rank of the industry (for agriculture $h=0$). Each industry consists of firms of optimal size (defined by scale economies). Demand for product h is satisfied by n_h firms[5] and its total demand is $a_h Y$ where Y=national income and a_h=demand ratio for h. It is assumed that there is only one firm in the highest ranked industry ($n_H=1$), and that the number of firms in each industry varies with its rank ($n_1 > n_2 > n_3 \ldots > n_H$). All income is spent, i.e. $\sum a_h = 1$. Rural income Y_0 is given by $a_0 Y$.

[h] To obtain predictions about the size distribution of cities other assumptions are made that are also testable hypotheses. There are only M orders of centre ($m=1, \ldots, M$). In any centre of rank m only the industries appear for which $h \leqslant m$. The number of firms in each industry in each centre is just sufficient to satisfy local demand for the industries of a rank lower than the centre's rank. The industry of rank h in centre of rank m satisfies both local demand and the demand for that product in lower rank centres, and exports down the hierarchy are equally distributed among all m centres. The total income earned (Y^m) in all centres of a given rank can be derived from

$$Y = \sum_m Y^m = Y_0 + \sum_m \sum_h Y_h^m = \frac{a_0 Y}{1 - \sum_h a_h} \qquad (11.11)$$

since total income can be calculated at any stage as we ascend the hierarchy, e.g.:

$$Y_0 + Y^1 + Y^2 = \frac{a_0 Y}{1 - (a_1 + a_2)}$$

We may derive the number of centres of each rank (n^m) if we assume that there is always *only* one firm of the highest rank in each centre. This is given by the relationship

$$n^m = n_h \frac{a_0}{1 - \sum_h a_h} \qquad (11.12)$$

Equations (11.11) and (11.12) determine the size distribution of cities. This simple hierarchy model can be extended by introducing complications such as foreign trade, intermediate products, various transportation assumptions, uniquely located industries and more complex interurban trade flow patterns (Bos, 1965).

The hierarchical structuring of administrative functions presents an alternative to central place models as a hierarchical theory of the distribution of city sizes. Although such an explanation is useful only as a special case, it may be valuable for interpreting the city size distributions observed in socialist economies. Service activities are so imperfectly developed in such countries (the share of service industries in employment is about two-and-a-half times greater in the USA than in the USSR) that central place models are unconvincing. In the Soviet economy highly developed administrative functions may substitute for underdeveloped service functions (Harris, 1970).

Christaller (1966) and Lösch (1954, p. 132) both emphasised the importance of administrative functions as a mechanism for stratifying the urban hierarchy, stressing 'the administrative principle' where a city of a given rank controls 7 cities – including itself – of the next lower rank. The nesting of seven case is unnecessarily restrictive. A plausible city size distribution can be generated from two key assumptions: a constant number of cities under direct control of the next highest order city; a constant ratio of the populations of the controlled area to the control centre as we ascend the hierarchy.[6] Modifications to these assumptions can be made as in the central place hierarchy model; for instance, the number of controlled centres can be treated as a parameter. Even so, the higher the *average* number of controlled centres the more skewed the distribution of city sizes will be. Also spatial considerations, as reflected in transport and communication costs, are no less important in determining the efficiency of an administrative hierarchy as that of a central place hierarchy.[7]

Hierarchical structures of this kind are not necessarily limited to public administration. In the private sector there are size hierarchies of firms and size hierarchies of establishments within firms. Although these are not necessarily distributed among cities with size of firm directly correlated with city size,[8] Edel (1972) has argued that such a correlation may be very important in explaining the upper tail of the city size distribution. He draws attention to the fact that the largest cities invariably tend to be 'corporate cities', i.e. cities that are locations for the headquarters of large business corporations.

Stochastic models

Since the size of a city is the net outcome of a multiplicity of forces the individual contributions to which are difficult to identify, there is a temptation to resort to stochastic models which treat urban growth determinants as proportional to city size (see sections 'The law of proportionate effect' and 'A market opportunities model') or the city size distribution as the probabilistically derived steady-state equilibrium (see 'Entropy maximisation').[9] Also, two of the models analysed in later sections ('A growth theory model' and 'A simultaneously multiplicative theory') contain substantial stochastic elements. Whereas the case in favour of including random variables in the theory of the distribution of city sizes is strong, it is implausible to exclude altogether systematic factors (such as central place concepts or agglomeration economies).

The law of proportionate effect

Simon argued that the distribution of city sizes could be regarded as the steady-state equilibrium of a stochastic process, and approximately described by the Pareto distribution, eqn. (11.2) above. The particular stochastic process is *the law of proportionate effect* which implies that city growth is proportional to city size. Not every city needs to grow proportionately, provided that the probabilities of proportionate growth are spread symmetrically. Even if the initial distribution of city sizes were a normal distribution, subjecting that distribution to a stochastic process by applying a transitional probability matrix may, after n operations, generate a steady-state Pareto distribution.

Simon suggested demographic forces as a possible explanation of why the law of proportionate effect might apply, e.g. if population growth was solely due to natural increase, and net growth was proportional to present population (either within each city or, less restrictively, within each size class). It is also possible to allow for migration if the net population change of individual cities *within any region* is proportional to city size. Another possibility is where rural–urban migration is determined by the 'friends and relatives' effect (Greenwood, 1970) provided that the probability of having a friend in a city is proportionate to its size.[10] The model can also allow for new cities crossing the minimum size threshold ($\bar{P}$) provided that the probability of this remains constant (or that new cities account for a constant fraction of total urban population growth); on the other hand, declines can be accommodated only if offset by the growth of another city in the same size class. Also, non-demographic factors could have a role in this model if their random influence on city size were proportionate to city size. The main drawback of the model is its total reliance on random and neglect of systematic factors. For example, the existence of diseconomies of urban scale (Mills, 1972a) could be a systematic influence that distorts its predictions.[11]

146

A market opportunities model

Following upon Simon's work Ward (1963) also used the law of proportionate effect. However, he focuses directly on migration rather than natural increase and his model is based more on economic than statistical theory. It is assumed that *all* changes in city sizes are due to migration, that employment opportunities are the main stimulus to migration, that these opportunities arise because of expansion in the market or technical change, that in the long run the latter can be subsumed under market expansion factors, and that all opportunities can be aggregated (ignoring the differential effects of technical change, demand- and product-mix effects and so on). The model is made endogenous by treating city population as a measure of market size so that market-expansion opportunities can be assumed to depend on city size. The probability of these opportunities occurring is proportionate to the size of the market (i.e. city size). This is the law of proportionate effect once again. To justify a Paretian distribution, Ward hypothesises that below a certain size of city the probability of opportunities developing is very low, partly because small towns are neglected in the search processes of entrepreneurs and migrants, partly because of economic efficiency thresholds for opportunity creation (e.g. supply of public services, labour marked thresholds, etc.). It is possible to relax some of the model's restrictive assumptions, for example, by disaggregating opportunities to allow for industrial structure differentials among cities and by taking account of the fact that some cities have special locational advantages such as access to a unique natural resource. These introduce more realism without distorting the final result. A limitation of the model is that its emphasis on market opportunities could make it a culture-bound explanation applicable to market-oriented societies but much less plausible as an explanation of the similar empirical distributions of city sizes found in socialist and centrally planned economies.

Entropy maximisation

Berry (1961, p. 587) argued that 'when many forces act in many ways with none predominant a lognormal size distribution is found'. This emphasis on a multiplicity of forces strengthens the case for treating city size distributions as the outcome of a stochastic process.[12] Curry (1964) developed an entropy maximisation model which provides an alternative stochastic model to Simon's law of proportionate effect. The attractiveness of entropy models is increased for those who believe in the value of a general systems approach (e.g. Berry, 1964; Olsson, 1967).

Entropy (derived from the second law of thermodynamics) is a measure of the degree of equalisation reached within a system, and is maximised when the system reaches equilibrium. The steady-state equilibrium is the most probable state. Given P individuals; the number of ways in which N cities can be distributed among size bands is given by

$$\frac{N!}{\prod_{i=0}^{P} p_i!} \qquad (0 \leqslant i \leqslant P) \qquad (11.13)$$

where p_i = city size class of i individuals.

In a large system entropy (E) may be defined as

$$E = N \log N - \sum p_i \log p_i \qquad (11.14)$$

This is maximised when

$$p_i = (N/n)\, e^{-(i/n)} \qquad (11.15)$$

where n = average city size (P/N).

This may be rewritten as

$$p_i = p_1 \left[1 - e^{-(i/n)} \right] \qquad (11.16)$$

where p_1 = the primate city.

This is similar to the rank-size rule. A city size distribution obeying the rank-size rule is the most probable distribution and represents the steady-state equilibrium in which entropy has been maximised.

The model achieves the most probable distribution of a random arrangement of a given number of people in a given number of cities. Randomness avoids too much concentration in large cities and ensures that population is spread (if unequally) among all cities. However, there is no reason why the most probable distribution should be either the observed or the optimal distribution (Richardson, 1972). As with other stochastic models, the chief drawback of the entropy-maximising model is the absence of a role for systematic forces. However, it is possible to introduce structuring and order into the framework of an entropy model (Berry, 1964; Fano, 1969) by resorting to central place notions and to information theory.

Quasi-economic models

The models in this section all rely upon deductive economic theory, though surprisingly two of them were not developed by economists.

A growth theory model

Davis and Swanson (1972) have recently developed a model that integrates growth theory with a stochastic process in order to generate a lognormal city size distribution. The model assumes Cobb-Douglas production functions. Each city is assumed to be constrained in its investment by local savings, assumed to be a constant fraction of output. Equilibrium in product markets is obtained via equality of savings and investment (i.e. no unintended savings or investment). The distribution of city sizes is changed over time by the differential growth of city labour forces (constant labour force participation rates are assumed). Each city enjoys a perfectly elastic supply of labour since workers can be drawn in from the hinterland by higher urban wages. Income is distributed according to the marginal products of factors.

The key to the model is an efficiency progress function, $\varepsilon(t)$, in which technical progress is assumed disembodied and Hicks-neutral. It is specified as follows:

$$\varepsilon(t) = \exp(\rho t + z) \tag{11.17}$$

where ρ=a parameter, t=time and z=a random variable. This equation makes $\varepsilon(t)$ also a random variable and its distribution over all cities can be described in two-parameter lognormal form. The economic reasoning here is that technical progress can either complement or detract from other attributes of each city such as natural resource endowment, amenities (e.g. climate), supply of entrepreneurs and so on. It is assumed that, on average, technical progress is complementary, but its random incidence may make for deviation in an individual city.

The simplifying assumptions of the growth theory enable the relative growth rates of city labour forces to be expressed as a function of the efficiency progress function

$$l(t) = \rho\beta + sc^{1-\beta}[\varepsilon(t)]^{\beta} \tag{11.18}$$

where $l(t)$=distribution of city labour force growth rates, s=propensity to save in each city, $\beta = \alpha^{-1}$ where α=capital's share in output and $c = w(1-\alpha)^{-1}$ where w=constant real wage. The variable $l(t)$ is a three-parameter lognormal variable with the threshold parameter equal to $\rho\beta$.[13] The results still hold even when some of the restrictive assumptions are relaxed. For instance, we could allow rural wages to increase, the capital stock to depreciate and interurban capital flows to take place (provided they are linear homogeneous functions of output in the receiving cities). The virtue of this model is that it draws upon deductive economic theory to predict a lognormal distribution of city sizes consistent with empirical observation.

A neo-classical equilibrium model

Nicolas Rashevsky (1943, 1947, 1951), a mathematical biologist, developed a theory of the distribution of city sizes based on the economic concept of neo-classical equilibrium. Migrants migrate between cities in pursuit of higher income, and if marginal productivity assumptions are made equilibrium is achieved when productivity per head (δ) is equalised between cities:

$$\delta_1 = \delta_2 = \delta_i = \bar{\delta} \tag{11.19}$$

149

Rashevsky suggests that the generalised production function takes the form

$$\delta_i = f(p_i, P_i) \qquad (11.20)$$

where P_i = total number of people inhabiting all cities of size p_i. The total number of cities

$$N = \sum \frac{P_i}{p_i} \qquad (11.21)$$

To solve the city size distribution problem the productivity function eqn. (11.20) needs to be specified. Rashevsky took a simple form whereby urban productivity was expressed as a function of city size and of population distribution characteristics of the system as a whole (total national population, population of the size class and the total number of cities). This simple model yielded an equilibrium distribution of city sizes satisfying eqn. (21).

Apart from doubts about the appropriateness of neo-classical migration models, the key question is whether such a model generates a distribution of city sizes consistent with those observed in the real world. Since such a distribution is not generated directly, something else must be added to the model. The most obvious solutions are: (1) to argue that urban production functions are lognormally distributed, either via an analogy between business firms and cities or, more plausibly, because several influences behind the urban production function combine together multiplicatively (as in the model developed on pp. 155–6); or (2) within a multisector framework to distribute industries among cities hierarchically (e.g. as in Tinbergen's model, pp. 143–4).

An economies of scale–transport costs model

Zipf (1949) is justly famous for his empirical research on rank-size relationships, but his theoretical contribution has been neglected or misunderstood.[14] Zipf's analysis is based on a set of theoretical forces governing social organisation in general. These 'mainsprings of human behaviour' are the *Principle of Least Effort* and its major manifestations the *Force of Unification* and the *Force of Diversification*. Another force – the *Force of Innovation* – is also important and shows itself as the *Economy of Specialisation*. Although these concepts are elevated in Zipf's theories to the status of natural laws, and vary slightly in meaning according to their context, they have direct analogies in economics. The principle of least effort is, in effect, a dynamic interpretation of cost minimisation which (under certain assumptions) is equivalent to utility maximisation. The force of unification refers to economies of agglomeration, while the force of diversification relates to the minimisation of transport costs. The effect of the force of unification would be to concentrate all population, production and consumption in one big city. The effect of the force of diversification would be to split total population into a very

150

large number of small, widely scattered and autarchic communities. The actual distribution of city sizes reflects the relative impact of the two forces.[15] This is equivalent to the familiar hypothesis that the relative strength of concentration and dispersion in the space economy is explained by the comparative strengths of economies of scale and the need to save transport costs. The force of innovation introduces a dynamic element into the model. This reinforces the force of unification since scale economies make it cheaper for new goods and industries to be first introduced in large population centres. Their attraction as production centres is associated with increased attractiveness as consumption centres (e.g. they offer a more diversified supply of consumer goods).

Isard's criticism (1956, p. 60) that Zipf fails to establish a link between the empirical findings and his theory is a little harsh. When properly interpreted, his basic forces do shed light on the distribution of urban population among cities. However, the level of his analysis is so general that it would require considerable amplification to show why the net operation of his mutually offsetting forces generates a Pareto distribution of city sizes. For this reason, his empirical analysis has won wider acclaim than the theoretical framework that underpins it.

Cities as coalitions and clubs

Evans (1972) has suggested an interesting theory of city size distribution that builds upon the economic theory of clubs. The idea is that business firms (and/or individuals[16]) are faced with alternative sizes of city. Each city can be treated as a coalition of firms (and/or individuals) offering a certain mix of costs and benefits. Each firm (or individuals) tries to join the coalition, membership of which maximises its own profits (or net benefits). Applying the theory of clubs, it can be shown that under certain assumptions a stable hierarchy of city sizes results from this process. These assumptions include the variation of market opportunities and input costs with city size.

The defect of the model is that, as it stands, there is no mechanism for generating the kind of city size distribution observed empirically. Evans argued that the number of cities in a given size class will decrease as cities (coalitions) increase in size. This depends upon the number and size of firms (or households) seeking locations in cities of a particular size. Thus, there will be a large number of very small cities only if a much larger number of firms (or households) find their ideal locations in cities of this size. It is easy to substantiate this condition *ex post*, but there is no assumption in the model to ensure it theoretically. However, there is an easy solution in the households model.[17] The number of coalitions of size p_i will be determined by the total population, P_i, seeking to join a coalition of that size.

If we assume that the population wanting to join each size class is equal $(P_1=P_2=P_3=\ldots=P_i=\bar{P})$,[18] a plausible city size distribution results. The number of cities at each hierarchical level $(1, 2,\ldots, i)$ will be equal to $\bar{P}/p_1$, $\bar{P}/p_2,\ldots, \bar{P}/p_i$, respectively. Thus, the number of cities increases as city size declines.

Allometric growth and general systems theory

The law of allometric growth has occasionally been used to explain city size distributions. Frequently used in animal biology,[19] the law is used to describe the relationship between dimensions of individual organs and those of the whole body. This can be expressed as

$$y = bx^\alpha \qquad (11.22)$$

where y stands for the relative growth of an organ and x stands for the entire body.

It is doubtful whether this has much concrete value for city size distribution theory. Beckmann (1958, pp. 247–8) demonstrated the similarity between the allometric equation and the Pareto distribution when we identify the capital city with an organ and the total urban population with the organism. But this merely implies that the statistical functions are similar.[20] Beckmann (1968, pp. 120–1) later attempted to show a theoretical link. He argued that the diffusion of production establishments in new industries from large cities to small in a dynamic central place model implies that the growth will be associated with decentralisation of production, increased competition and the growth of intermediate cities. Beckmann suggests that this process can be described as allometric growth because the relative size of a city increases with the overall size of the economy but at a different rate. However, the process could be better described via an economic model of growth diffusion without introducing the allometry concept.

Interpreted broadly, allometric growth easily merges into general systems theory. The concept of the system of cities as a general system has been advanced in some quarters (e.g. Berry, 1964), but the results are unconvincing, apart from the self-evident fact that the size and growth of an individual city cannot be satisfactorily explained independent of the wider urban system. Wilson (1969, p. 179) has put his finger on a major defect in analysing city size distributions in terms of general systems theory – the fact that not *one* system but several sub-systems are involved.

New suggestions

Although Markov chain models have been suggested as providing a useful approach to city size distribution theory, their potential has not been developed. An attempt is made here to use a Markovian framework to analyse interurban migration and capital flows as determinants of city sizes. The second proposal draws upon the multiplicative form of the Central Limit, Theorem, a concept which has been used before to explain the personal income distribution but never before suggested in a city size distribution context. These ideas are not introduced with any pretensions that they provide superior explanations to the earlier models, though they illustrate the fact that there is still scope for further theoretical work in the analysis of this complex phenomenon.

Markov chain models

Fano (1969) has criticised Curry's entropy maximisation approach for its excessive randomness and for its neglect of functional interconnections between cities and the fact that the urban system is indeed as system. Instead, there should be structural and ordering factors influencing the distribution of city sizes. There may be randomness, but it is a constrained randomness. A Markov model may be useful in this context[21] because it is 'essentially a model of evolution providing for selection within systems and ultimate structuring of systems as wholes' (Fano, p. 32). An unconstrained Markov process with all transitions from one city size class to another equally probable at each step yields a solution equivalent to the maximum entropy case, but with a different result – each size class having the same probability of containing an equal number of cities. To introduce an element of order we impose constraints by allowing different transitions to have different probabilities. For instance, growth takes so much time that cities cannot 'leap-frog' size classes, competition for limited high-order metropolitan functions constrains the number of cities that can move into the higher size classes and, conversely, the durability of urban capital prevents cities from declining very fast. If upper and lower bounds are imposed on size class jumping by making the transitional probabilities (p_{ij}) inversely proportional to the difference between the size classes $(i-j)$, the equilibrium city size distribution becomes a Pareto distribution.[22]

An elaboration of this approach would be to make it less abstract and to deal directly with the dynamics of population change or the process of interurban capital flows. This merely requires adapting interregional Markov models of migration (Rogers, 1966) and capital flows (Richardson, 1973a) to an interurban context. In the migration model a distribution of city sizes will be generated directly whereas the capital flows model needs an additional assumption such as

$$w_i = f(k_i) \qquad (11.23)$$

where w_i=population of city i and k_i=capital stock of city i.

Roger's migration model involves expressing the interurban migration flow matrix[23] in coefficient form in order to derive a transitional probability matrix, P. Death can be treated as the absorbing state in an absorbing Markov chain model, and if the initial vector of city size populations is w^0, we may write

$$\bar{w}^0 = w^0 Q \qquad (11.24)$$

where $\bar{w}^0 < w^0$ because of deaths during the transition period and Q is the non-absorbing sub-matrix.[24]

If we now add a vector of births b we obtain

$$w^1 = \bar{w}^0 + b = w^0 Q + b \qquad (11.25)$$

Repeating the process n times yields

$$w^n = w^0 Q^n + b(I + Q + \cdots + Q^{n-1}) \qquad (11.26)$$

However, since $Q < 1$, as n increases $Q^n \to 0$ while $(I + Q + \cdots + Q^{n-1}) \to (I-Q)^{-1}$ we may write

$$w^e = \lim_{n \to \infty} w^n = b(I-Q)^{-1} \qquad (11.27)$$

Over a long period of time, the initial population distribution fades out and the equilibrium distribution of city sizes becomes a function of births, deaths and migration.

In the capital flows model the Q matrix is the transitional probability matrix for interurban capital flows while the absorbing matrix ($\hat{R}$) is a diagonal matrix of intraurban absorption directly into investment (i.e. $T = (I-Q)^{-1}.\hat{R}$).[25] I have shown elsewhere (Richardson, 1973a) that the distribution of urban capital stocks at time period n is given by

$$k^n = k^0 (I+Z)^n \qquad (11.28)$$

where k^0=initial distribution of urban capital stocks, and

$$Z = \hat{A}\hat{V}^{-1}(I-Q)^{-1}\hat{R} \qquad (11.29)$$

where $\hat{A}$=diagonal matrix of urban propensities to save
and $\hat{V}^{-1}$=inverse of the diagonal matrix ($\hat{V}$) of urban capital–output ratios.

Taking a specific form of eqn. (11.23) the distribution of city sizes at period n can be expressed as a function of the distribution of urban capital stocks:

$$w^n = \hat{G}k^n = \hat{G}k^0 (I+Z)^n \qquad (11.30)$$

where $\hat{G}$=diagonal matrix of population-capital stock ratios.

The $\hat{G}$ matrix reflects the fact that city populations require urban infra-structure (housing, roads, schools and hospitals, investment in buildings and plant to provide jobs) to sustain them. The $\hat{G}$ coefficients can be allowed to vary systematically. For example, they may first increase and later decrease as we ascend the hierarchy to reflect economies and ultimately diseconomies of scale. Moreover, the $\hat{G}$ matrix could change over time to reflect technical progress and other changes in efficiency. Finally, it should be noted that the city size distribution of this model is not necessarily an equilibrium distribution because the closed economy growth process (income →savings→capital→income) does not move towards a steady state except in a special case.

Both models are of a general nature in the sense that they may generate several alternative city size distributions depending on the assumptions made about the structure of the transitional probability matrix. For example, sufficiently strong polarisation tendencies ($p_{i1} > p_{i2} > p_{i3}$, etc., where cities are ranked by size 1, 2, 3,...) can lead to a primate distribution in which people and capital are sucked into the largest city. Alternatively, the coefficients could reflect a filtering process in which labour and capital flow to cities of similar size (i.e. adjacent size classes) rather than to much larger or much smaller cities. This would imply the Pareto distribution yet again. Moreover, the city size distribution can change radically over time as a result of changes in the Q matrix. This would be useful in formulating a developmental model of city size distributions (e.g. from primacy to lognormality). The value of the Markov chain models is that with constrained transitional probabilities they offer a simple method of combining random and systematic (ordering) influences on the distribution of city sizes.

A simultaneously multiplicative theory

Simon's stochastic model was conceived as a dynamic process through time. There is no reason why a similar analysis cannot be applied to several independent factors combining multiplicatively at a given moment of time. This idea has been applied to income distribution theory by Roy (1950), but its potential for the explanation of city size distributions has been ignored. The statistical theory supporting the idea is the Central Limit Theorem. If a random variable, y, is the sum of independent random variables, the distribution of y approaches the normal distribution as the number of component variables increases, provided that no single variable dominates the others. Thus, if $y = \sum_{i=1}^{n} x_i$ then y approaches the normal distribution as $n \rightarrow \infty$. A corollary is that if $y = \prod_{i=1}^{n} x_i$ then, given the same assumptions, y will approach a lognormal distribution. The distribution of y will be skew and leptokurtic – characteristics typical of the city size distribution – even if the individual variable distributions are all symmetrical. Also, skewness increases with the number of variables, their coefficients of variation and

155

the degree of correlation between the variables (Haldane, 1942).

How appropriate is this statistical theory as a basis for a theory of city size distribution? First, the advantages of an urban centre may arise from several sources (for instance, natural resource endowment, transportation advantages, the supply of entrepreneurs, high local savings, age of settlement, topography, amenities, degree of nodality), and these may explain why some cities become bigger than others. Second, multiplicative effects simply mean that any one factor exercises its effect proportionately to city size rather than by the same absolute amount. There is substantial empirical support for the view that impacts are proportionate rather than absolute (Duncan and Reiss, 1956). Third, it is possible that some aggregate variable such as the 'growth potential of a city' could be a multiplicative function of a number of underlying factors, several of which are likely to be inter-correlated and therefore mutually reinforcing. Fourth, a major advantage of this approach is that it may be possible to test the theory directly by comparing the distribution of city sizes with the distribution of the product of key variables that influence size.

A problem as compared with Simon's model is that this theory assumes that the variables influence size at one point of time rather than over time. Since the size of an individual city at any moment of time reflects the combined influence of both current and past factors, and some of the latter are cumulative in their impact, the use of what is in effect a cross-sectional model is a substantial liability. However, this defect need not be critical. Some of the potential variables, e.g. age of settlement, industrial diversification, reflect factors that are built up over time. Other variables, e.g. mileage distance from other cities, are invariant with time. Perhaps most important of all, just as the size distribution of cities is itself stable over time it is possible that the distribution of the size-inducing determinants is itself also stable.

Concluding remarks

It is improbable that any one of the above models would be universally acceptable. There are so many influences interacting to mould the relative size of cities that it would be too difficult to include them all within a single model. Strands and elements drawn from different models may be appealing as partial explanations. Certainly, the search for a monocausal explanation is a chimera, and the choice of one model rather than another must be based on a judgement as to whether the selected model concentrates on key phenomena. Most of the models in this chapter are satisfactory in the sense that they generate size distributions of cities that are consistent with those found in the real world. Since at least a dozen distinct theories were discussed, the appeal of one rather than another is likely to be based on the analyst's preference for stochastic or systematic models, economic or statistical theories, hierarchy or non-hierarchy models and so on.

If the theory is in an unsatisfactory state, the fault lies in the nature and complexity of the subject rather than in the poverty of the theories already developed. However, a few conclusions may be drawn as pointers for future research. First, a satisfactory explanation probably needs to draw on both systematic and random factors and the weaknesses of some of the theories stem from exclusive reliance on one rather than the other. The Markov chain models represent one reasonable attempt to deal with this problem, while Beckmann's suggestion of introducing random elements into a central place hierarchy model is another. One method of achieving the latter is to treat the size of manufacturing towns as random influences and the size of nodal service centres as systematic elements. The point is that manufacturing cities and towns may be of any size, and therefore have no systematic effect on the size distribution.[26]

Second, of all possible systematic influences on the distribution of city sizes economic conditions may be the most important. The existence of cities *per se* may be justified on social, political and cultural grounds, but these criteria would not seem to demand cities of *different* size. The most plausible systematic explanations of why there is a *distribution* of city sizes are based on economic theory. For example, the number of highest order (national and supranational) functions is so limited that there is no scope for more than one or two cities to grow to the highest rank. In the interurban competition for big size there are few winners because there are so few prizes. Similarly, a tendency in some countries for the tail of the Pareto distribution to curve downwards could still be explained via the law of proportionate effect if the chances of growth to a higher size class decline with increasing city size. Such a tendency might be accounted for in terms of congestion costs, urban land constraints and other economic restrictions on urban growth rates.

Third, as we have seen, some models of city size distributions have drawn upon ideas used in theories of the distribution of incomes and firm sizes (Champernowne, Lydall, Simon, Roy). There remains scope for further parallel research on these lines.

Finally, a neglected question is the relationship between urbanisation and the distribution of city sizes. For example, in an interesting early empirical study Madden (1958) showed that US cities experienced retardation trends in their growth rates as they grew older. If city growth rates are a function of the age of the city, we might expect the size distribution of cities to be affected by such variables as the age of the economy since industrial take-off, the rate of population growth, the average age of cities and the pattern and rate of geographical expansion. Since the more obvious explanations of retardation trends are based on city rivalry within a growing urban system (competition for migrants and industry) and the time and space paths of technical progress (Pred, 1966), the relative growth rates of cities – and ultimately the distribution of city sizes – depend upon the stage of development at which new cities appear, the sequence in which they appear and how they cluster in time. In general terms, this is a manifestation of the fact that the size of any city at any point of time depends upon the size and location of all other cities, not only at that point in time but also historically. More particularly, it is feasible to devise a model based on the hypothesis that the size distribution of cities is a function of the age distribution of cities. This type of model could be of supplementary value in accounting for the variations in observed city size distributions from one country to another.

Notes

[1] The theory of primacy is another story, if a fascinating one. For some insights see Jefferson (1939), El Shaks (1965), Morse (1962), Mehta (1964), Linsky (1965), Harris (1971) and Mera (1973). See also below, pp. 166–70.

[2] The most widely tested successful fit is with United States data (Zipf, 1949; Duncan and Reiss, 1956; Madden, 1956a; Mills, 1972a).

[3] The ratio $p_m/p_{m-1}=s/1-k$. Since $s>1$ and $0 \leqslant k \leqslant 1$, it follows that $(s/1-k)>1$. Thus, city size increases geometrically with m.

[4] This argument suggests the desirability of allowing for both interurban and intraurban phenomena within the same general model. Weiss (1961) and Berry (1964) make two modest steps in this direction.

[5] Of course, $n_h = Y_h/\bar{Y}_h$ where $\bar{Y}_h =$ optimal output of firm in industry h.

[6] Lydall (1968) adopted a very similar model to explain the personal income distribution based on the assumption that large organisations – which dominate the upper tail of the income distribution – are organised on a hierarchical principle.

[7] Both Christaller and Tinbergen (1968) suggest that a nesting of four is most efficient from a communications point of view.

[8] The size distribution of firms between cities varies in the Tinbergen model for a different reason – the distribution of industries (each composed of firms of optimal size) among cities.

[9] Vining (1955) suggested that the rank-size distribution is a time-dependent stochastic process according to which the distribution of city sizes maintains a high degree of stability (a kind of statistical equilibrium) despite a great

deal of individual flux, e.g. changes in city populations, rank-jumping, births and deaths of towns.

[10] For an alternative explanation see Ward, 1963 ('A market opportunities model', p. 147).

[11] Analogously, when the law of proportionate effect is used to explain the skewness of the size distribution of firms it is necessary to assume constant long-run average cost functions.

[12] However, note the disparaging comment by Higgs (1970, p. 253): 'Explanations hinging upon unnamed "forces" which are "many and act randomly" are not theories at all but rationalisations for the lack of a theory.'

[13] Alternatively, $[l(t)-\rho\beta]$ can be treated as a two-parameter lognormal variable.

[14] His theory of the distribution of city sizes can be expressed in economic terms. Zipf (1949, p. 13) himself pointed out that his main organising principle – the principle of least effort – has a very close relationship to classical economics. In the brief exposition which follows I paraphrase Zipf freely.

[15] The special case where the two forces exactly balance each other is the rank-size rule where $q=1$ (or the Pareto distribution where $\alpha=1$).

[16] This extends Tiebout's (1965) model in which individuals move between cities to associate with people having similar preferences for public goods and services and for tax-expenditure mix.

[17] Additional complications arise from the need to achieve compatibility between the number of households wanting to join a city of a prescribed size and the number and size of firms choosing a location in cities of this size (von Böventer, 1970). One method of reconciliation is in the labour market via the supply of and demand for labour functions and the response of households and firms to changes in wages.

[18] This assumption is equivalent to the EHP (equal hierarchical population) assumption discussed by Parr (1970) in his typology of central place hierarchies.

[19] The biological analogy, despite its popularity with some city size distribution theorists, is not a necessary component of allometric explanations of city sizes.

[20] The stability of the α parameter in eqn. (11.22) above implies some kind of equilibrium between the growth of the whole body and individual organs, even though they do not grow at the same rate. Similarly, a stable Pareto exponent may imply the maintenance of equilibrium in city size distributions even though individual cities jump ranks.

[21] Fano's argument was anticipated by Olsson (1967) a few years earlier.

[22] Champernowne's (1953) model of income distribution is very similar.

²³ Rural–urban migration can be dealt with by adding one row and column to represent the rural sector.

²⁴ Obtained by partitioning the P matrix in the usual way

$$P = \left(\begin{array}{c|c} Q & R \\ \hline 0 & I \end{array} \right)$$

The absorbing state is excluded because it is implicit in the fact that the rows of Q do not sum to unity.

²⁵ The matrix T expresses the probabilities of inputs (savings) getting from each transient to each absorbing state after circulating through the transient states as indicated by the matrix Q.

²⁶ Of course, it is possible to give manufacturing a systematic influence by locating industries of a given rank in cities of given sizes as in the Tinbergen model.

12 City Size Distributions: Empirical Aspects

Empirical analysis of rank-size (Pareto) distributions

The advantage of the statistical distributions of city sizes is that they enable the relative size distribution of urban centres to be described in terms of a single parameter. Using the Pareto (rank-size) distribution, Table 12.1 presents the estimates of q for a large number of countries for years close to 1950. Some of the estimates use the legal boundaries of urban areas; others (marked*) adopt broader, metropolitan area definitions. The latter yield, on average, much lower q's with values closer to unity. Although not confirming the rank-size rule, most of the observations fall within the 0·90 to 1·20 range. As with all Pareto functions good fits are not obtained in the lower size range, and the estimates in Table 12.1 involve varying cut-off points, depending on the availability of data or empirically-determined departures from linearity, but primarily around the 2,000–2,500 mark. Another modification frequently needed to obtain a reasonable fit is to correct for the fact that the rank-size distributions, since it deals with integers, is more discontinuous than the Pareto distribution proper. A better fit of eqn. (11.2)[1] when $N(\bar{P})=1$ may be obtained not by taking P_1 but a population intermediate between the largest and the second-ranked city, i.e. $\sqrt{P_1 P_2}$.

It was suggested above (p.141) that the rank-size distribution is a very general model of city size distributions capable of describing many different patterns depending on the value of q. Occasionally, interpretations stronger than mere descriptions have been placed on the parameter. For example, the value of q changes very little in a country over time. Allen (1954, p. 187) argued that this was 'strongly at odds with the commonly held impression that in modern, western societies larger towns have been persistently growing relatively to the smaller towns'. A more suggestive interpretation is that the stability of q, in spite of many changes in individual ranks, is indicative of the constancy of the forces influencing city sizes over time. Thus, a constant q may represent some kind of equilibrium in city size distributions. This may make sense in terms of a *statistical* equilibrium,[2] but its meaning in the context of a social or economic equilibrium is unclear.[3] On the other hand, the stability of q should not be exaggerated. In the very long run the value of q may tend to decline; for instance, over the course of the nineteenth century it fell markedly in several countries for which data are

161

Table 12.1
Pareto coefficients for city size distributions

Europe		Other continents	
Country	q	Country	q
United Kingdom	0·98*	Canada	0·98
Czechoslovakia	1·30	United States	1·05 (1950)
Ireland	1·15*		0·96 (1960)*
Denmark	0·89	Costa Rica	0·70
France	1·23	Cuba	0.94*
Germany	1·13	Dominican Republic	0·79
Hungary	1·32	El Salvador	1·16
Iceland	0·91*	Haiti	1·01
Finland	1·21	Mexico	1·34*
Italy	1·41	Nicaragua	0·95
Belgium	1·41	Puerto Rico	1·02*
Holland	0·94*	Argentina	0·91
Luxembourg	1·11	Brazil	1·12*
Norway	0·85*	Chile	0·91
Poland	1·09	Ecuador	1·05
Portugal	1·43	Venezuela	1.00
Spain	1.17	New Zealand	0·74
Sweden	0·99*	Australia (under 65,000)	0·95
Yugoslavia	1.03	Australia (over 65,000)	0·62
USSR (under 720,000)	1·00	Hawaii	0·95*
Switzerland		Algeria	0·88
(under 200,000)	0·61	Egypt	1·77
		South Africa	0·85
		Turkey	1·27
		Iraq	0·93
		Israel	0·79
		Japan	1·16
		Malaya	0·88
		Pakistan	0·98
		China	1·24
		India (under 500,000)	1·29
		India (over 500,000)	0·83

Those marked * are based on broad (metropolitan area) definition of urban areas
Sources: Allen (1954), Clark (1967), Harris (1970) for USSR.

available (e.g. Germany, Spain, Japan). Singer (1936) went so far as to argue that the parameter could be regarded 'as a precise and unambiguous measure of urbanisation.' His grounds were that the smaller is q, the greater the proportion of large cities in a given number of urban centres and the greater the relative importance of urban land values and location rents. Certainly, we would expect rapid urbanisation to be associated with a decline in q because of the rise of intermediate size cities. But to use q as a measure of urbanisation places too much strain on a single parameter.

In many cases, the use of a single linear slope may require fitting the city size distribution to a Procrustean bed. The results for Australia, India, the USSR and Switzerland are indicative of the better fits obtained by dividing the cities into two groups of size classes. Extreme primate distributions also yield poor fits unless the primate city is either modified by a correction factor or even excluded altogether. Another irregular size distribution is described by Clark (1967) as an 'oligarchy', i.e. the domination of an urban system by a few very large cities (Australia, Brazil, India and Japan are the main examples quoted) with the size of the first-ranked city held in check. Oligarchies imply a break in slope, where the city size at the break indicates a disfavoured size. He also coins the concept 'counter-primacy' (e.g. USA, USSR, Belgium, Holland and Switzerland) to describe city size distributions where the largest centres have been controlled (either naturally or by policy) and where metropolitan areas of a particular size (around the million population level in the USA and the USSR) tend to predominate. Clark (1967, p. 322) goes as far as to suggest 'that this size suggests what may prove to be the economically optimum size for metropolitan areas in the future'. This is highly speculative, but perhaps is suggestive as a size distribution static equivalent to the market tests of city size (see above pp. 111–19). Finally, Clark points to the existence in some countries of definite 'steps' in the rank-size curve, indicating strong competition for the first (second or third) rank between a pair of triad of cities. Apart from the absence of a satisfactory theoretical explanation of this phenomenon, its main relevance here is as a potential distortion to the rank-size distribution.

While these deviations from the rank-size rule may be rarer than the city size distributions that approximate to it reasonably well, they have provided ground for attacking the rank-size approach as an empirical method. Thus, Allen's (1954) detailed analyses on which much of the data of Table 12.1 rely were criticised by Ward (1963). The criticisms stressed the inappropriateness of the method used to test the accuracy of the parameter, i.e. by its ability to predict cities by size class rather than by individual rankings, too many *ad hoc* exclusions and the failure to test for other distributions, e.g. the lognormal. The fact remains that Allen's study still the most thorough empirical analysis of city size distributions, and the difficulties of handling urban population data drawn from a wide range of countries are immense. A less satisfactory investigation was carried out by Hoyt (1962). He attempted to fit the strict rank-size rule ($q=1$), and not surprisingly came to negative conclusions. He plotted the rectangular hyperbola through the value for the largest city in each case, so that if the population of this city was either too large or too small he missed the 'best' linear fit over the whole range; a more useful procedure would have been to concentrate on the middle range where the best fits usually occur. Furthermore, his samples of cities were too small to obtain a reasonable estimate of the slope. Finally, he considered rank reversals between census periods to be a refutation of the rank-size rule; this converts what was intended as a statistical hypothesis into a deterministic model. The major problem, and partly a question of judgement, is whether the considerable analytical advantage in being able to express the city size distribution in terms of a single parameter is offset by its inaccuracies in cases where 'perverse' distributions occur. In these latter cases, improved results may be obtained by partitioning the frequency distribution curve into sections and estimating the slope for each independently, but the analysis then becomes much more cumbersome.

A problem glossed over here is that it is unclear to what system the city size distribution refers. The preceding analysis assumes the national economy, but there is nothing to preclude extending the analysis of city size distributions up to the largest city in the world, or, at the opposite extreme, truncating the distribution at a regional centre. As is well known, many applications, particularly of hierarchy models, e.g. Christaller (Baskin, 1966), Lösch (1954), Brush and Bracey (1955), Higgs (1970), have been confined to regional not national city size distributions. The regional level undoubtedly places less strain on *hierarchy* models. The reason is that in such models the determinant of the largest urban centre is the size of the largest market area, and this is easier to comprehend at the regional level than in a national or international context where market area concepts become much more imprecise. On the other hand, the introduction of non-nodal functions brings national and world markets into consideration as an influence on the city size distribution. Also, empirical studies of city sizes in a supranational framework (continents, or even at the world level; Zipf, 1949) yield reasonable rank-size fits. Thus, city size distribution analysis is capable of being extended above the national level, though this is unlikely to imply a hierarchical model.

An interesting solution may be obtained if it is assumed that the rank-size distribution applies to the region while the hierarchy model applies to the nation. In the ideal case where all regions were of similar size the rank-size relationships for each region could then be aggregated to yield a national urban hierarchy where the number of centres at the highest level (regional

164

metropolis) was equal to the number of regions in the system. Although this approach may be relevant to an explanation of the national urban hierarchy in very large countries where regions might reasonably be treated as mini-nations,[4] it has certain drawbacks. First, a more common assumption is that the hierarchy model fits better at the regional level while the rank-size distribution works best for nations (or at the supranational level). Second, we need to account for the capital city since this cannot be obtained from a model based on the aggregation of regional rank-size distributions. Possible solutions might be either to assume that one of the regional metropolises wins out in a competitive struggle to become the nation's leading city or to determine the capital city exogenously. Third, this approach could scarcely provide a general model since a geographically large country is probably a prerequisite for deriving *regional* rank-size distributions. Many countries in the world would fall below the minimum critical size to justify a model of this kind.

Two other implications, if not drawbacks, of the single parameter approach to measuring city size distributions are inherent in its nature. First, it concentrates on the *relative* size distribution not the absolute size distribution. It may be capable of shedding light on the questions 'too many?' or 'too few?' but is not equipped to deal with the questions 'too big?' or 'too small?'. Yet explaining the precise shape of the size distribution curve may be less crucial than explaining why everyone does not crowd into one giant metropolis or accounting for the continued attraction of small towns. This, of course, takes us back to the problem of the costs and benefits of urban scale Locational preferences may be very important at the lower end of the scale, but economic factors such as congestion and scale diseconomies are vital to an understanding of the constraints upon agglomeration and why primate distributions are not the universal case.

Second, and inevitably, as a measure of the size distribution q must neglect the spatial distribution. However, the two are interrelated since the size of a city at a particular time depends not only on the size but on the location of all other cities. As pointed out below (p. 169), primate distributions are more common in geographically small countries. This probably reflects a tendency for the spatial sphere of influence of the metropolis to be so large that intermediate size cities cannot get far enough away to experience fast independent growth. It is possible to compute theoretical interurban distances between cities in the same size class,[5] but the value of such an approach is dubious. The initial locations of cities may have been determined by factors other than market area principles (the basis for theoretical distance calculations), and rank-jumping over time will merely reduce not eliminate the distortions of fixed locations. The dispersion around the theoretical average distance increases with city size as the number

165

of observations become few. Interurban distance is affected by population densities and transportation improvements over time.[6] Moreover, as inter-urban distances increase (via upward and downward shifts in city ranks) the theoretical absolute size of equal-ranked cities will also rise. Finally, the theory of interurban distance usually derives from models (e.g. the Löschian model) that assume an equal spread of cities and towns over the whole economy. In reality, the cities may cluster in a small fraction of the available space with the leading city frequently off-centre. The latter reflects the fact that many countries were initially opened up from abroad so that the leading city tends to find its ideal location on the coast or border; the former reflects economies in transport costs to be gained (at least in a large country) by settlement of only part of the area. How important it is to allow for spatial influences depends upon whether the impact of interurban distance is more likely to affect the absolute size of individual cities in particular cases than have major repercussions on the size distribution as a whole. If this is a priority area for future research, there is need for co-operation between economists (hitherto preoccupied with the size distribution) and geographers (equally preoccupied with the spatial distribution).

Primacy

The city size distributions which fail to be satisfactorily described in Pareto, rank-size or lognormal terms are the primate distributions. Primate countries are found in all parts of the world and at all levels of economic development (see Table 12.2). Of the 27 countries in Table 12.2, 13 are in Latin America,[7] 7 in Europe, 6 in Asia and 1 in Africa. Also, despite the variation in their stages of development, very few primate countries are mature highly industrialised economies.

Primacy presents awkward problems for empirical analysis. Sometimes, reasonable rank-size fits are obtained by excluding the leading city,[8] though in other cases the mere existence of the primate city distorts the whole structure of the urban size hierarchy. Occasionally, satisfactory fits are obtained by correcting for primacy, while another alternative is to describe different sections of the hierarchy in terms of separate functions. For instance, Berry (1961) argued that the England and Wales case was made up of primate cities grafted on top of a more or less exact lower lognormal distribution. This might be explained by the fact that the leading cities, and especially London, played key economic roles outside the urban system of the country, i.e. their historical functions as service centres for a world-wide empire.[9]

The causes and interpretation of primacy are very obscure. Jefferson

Table 12.2

Measures of primacy, most primate distributions

Country	Ratio of city 1 to city 2	Percentage of population of four largest cities residing in largest city
Uruguay	10·0	86·7
Hungary	13·2	84·7
Guatemala	12·7	83·9
Paraguay	9·0	83·3
Philippines	9·8	82·0
Peru	7·3	81·7
Argentina	9·1	79·4
Costa Rica	–	78·9
Ceylon	4·6	78·0
Haiti	5·6	77·8
Cuba	7·3	77·3
Austria	7·3	76·8
Denmark	7·7	76·2
Ireland	4·7	75·8
South Vietnam	5·0	75·7
Tunisia	5·9	75·6
Greece	4·9	75·2
France	7·5	74·7
Mexico	7·4	74·3
Thailand	3·5	74·1
Nepal	–	73·9
Rumania	8·0	73·8
Panama	9·3	72·4
Dominican Republic	6·3	72·0
Chile	4·8	71·4
Lebanon	5·5	70·6
Puerto Rico	3·6	70·2

Year of data=1955, except for Thailand (1963) and South Vietnam (1968).

(1939) regarded primate distributions as the typical case by stating a law of primacy: 'All over the world it is the law of the Capitals that the largest city shall be supereminent, and not merely in size, but in national influence. Once a city is larger than any other in its country, this mere fact gives it an impetus to grow that cannot be affected by any other city, and it draws away from all of them in character as well as in size.... It becomes the primate city' (Jefferson, 1939, p. 227). Countries where primate distributions fail to appear such as Italy, Canada, Spain, the USSR and Nigeria are treated as aberrations, to be explained (in the examples quoted) by strong regionalism or by peculiar factors affecting the individual case. Jefferson's analysis can be treated as an accentuated metropolitan–rural version of Friedmann's (1966) centre–periphery model in which resources gravitate towards the centre (or metropolitan core) of the economy. However, the centre–periphery model is placed in the context of economic development with the centre–periphery dichotomy sharpest during the rapid industrial-isation phase. This raises the unsettled question of the relationship between primacy and development. Consistent with Friedmann's hypothesis are El Shaks' findings (1965) that primacy is rare in very underdeveloped countries, rises during the rapid industrialisation phase (take-off) and decreases thereafter. Also, it was argued that this cycle is compatible with time series data available for developed countries. Although Berry (1961) denied that there was any consistent relationship between the type of city size distribution and economic development, he outlined a developmental model in which the city size distribution function progressed over time through a sequence of phases from primacy to lognormality. Nevertheless, the data on measures of primacy support Berry's overall result: that some primate distributions are found in developed countries while there are less developed countries (particularly in the Middle East and with a few notable examples in Latin America) with city size distributions among the least primate of all (see Berry, 1961; Ginsburg, 1961, and International Urban Research, 1959).

The Latin American experience provides an interesting comment on Berry's developmental model of city size distributions from primacy to lognormality. In a study of eight countries,[10] McGreevey (1971) showed that the reverse situation held – a shift over time from a rank-size distribution to primacy. However, the earlier rank-size distributions could not be inter-preted as evidence of an integrated systemic hierarchy but rather suggested the existence of a hierarchical structure of colonial cities in terrain where high communication costs prevented centralisation. The shift towards primacy coincided (apart from the anomalous case of Mexico) with a marked expansion in exports *per capita*. Thus, the 'growing importance of the export sector (and more broadly, international commercial ties) would

168

seem to be a likely cause of increasing primacy' (McGreevey, 1971, p. 123).

Linsky (1965) carried out a more systematic analysis of primate distributions which suggested *some* links between primacy and underdevelopment. He suggested a number of hypotheses: that it is impossible to service a large, spatially extensive country from one city; that high incomes mean more urban services which cannot be supplied in a rich country from a single city; that in a foreign-oriented export economy the profits from commercial development will be heavily concentrated in the capital or leading trading metropolis; that ex-colonial status may affect primacy, though in either direction depending upon how the colony was administered and developed; that industrialisation promotes dispersal via the need of industries and population to be located near raw materials and power sources; and that rapid population growth will be associated with primacy because of both high rates of natural increase in the metropolis and of rural–urban migration. Thus, primacy was tested against size (−), *per capita* income (−), export dependence (+), ex-colonial status (+ or −; found to be +), industrialisation (−), and population growth (+). Some support was found for these hypotheses, but there are doubts about how primacy was measured and the nature of the tests (simple correlation analysis).[11] Also, there are several instances of primacy particularly in the developed countries e.g. France, which cannot be explained in any of these terms.

Other possible impacts upon primacy include whether or not a country's leading city carries out international finance, commercial or entrepôt functions, the top-heaviness of a country's administration and bureaucracy and the degree of integration of its transportation network.[12] The survival of primate distributions may be in some circumstances be related to the continuously increasing returns to scale case in optimal city size discussions. Leven (1969) has pointed out that the limiting case where everyone lives in one great city is a *possible* equilibrium distribution, and to explain why this particular equilibrium never occurs we have to introduce congestion, diseconomies of scale or preferences for living in small towns. Since in some developing countries the diseconomies of urban scale may be less unpleasant than the alternatives, this might help to explain why, for the moment, primacy persists. Another aspect of primacy is that it can be properly understood only in the wider context of the urban system of which the primate city forms a part. Primacy is usually associated with the stunted development of intermediate size cities, but it is unclear whether this retarded growth is due to the inherent unattractiveness of these cities from a growth potential viewpoint or to the fact that natural growth tendencies have been inhibited by the dominance, early start and agglomeration tendencies in the primate city itself. In the words of a UN study (United Nations, 1969); 'The causal relationship, if any, between first-city dominance and regressivity in size-distribution of the smaller cities cannot be determined at present'.

The systemic effects of primacy raise the question of whether or not primate distributions are harmful to national economic, social and cultural development. In many countries where primacy occurs, active policies are pursued (with varying degrees of success) to promote a more dispersed spatial distribution of population, and there is a widespread feeling that the largest city is too big given the level of and the priorities for development. It may well be true that economic and social development may be facilitated, certainly in terms of equity and possibly even in terms of long-run efficiency, if primate tendencies are successfully reversed, but the advantages of primacy have been played down. These include: the observed positive association between the rate of growth in GDP *per capita* and increasing primacy (Mera, 1973); the fact that primate cities are frequently well placed from the transportation point of view, with the result that the social return to further investment there may still be higher than at alternative locations; the economies of concentrating urban services in a capital-poor economy; the role of the primate city as a focus for the diffusion of urban traditions and attitudes; and the existence of other generative functions such as scale economies, the metropolis as a source of innovations and managerial expertise, and as a destination for migrants. The equation of primacy with parasitism is just too simple.

Notes

[1] See p. 140 above.

[2] Simon (1955) suggested that the condition for a steady-state distribution was that $q \leqslant 1$.

[3] Zipf (1949, Chapter 10) has some complicated, suggestive but on the whole unconvincing arguments about bends and shifts in the slope reflecting unstable international and intranational equilibria.

[4] The USSR is the most obvious example. Perhaps this argument explains Clark's *large* 'counter-primacies' such as the Soviet Union and the United States.

[5] Zipf (1949) and Stewart (1959) proposed a rule that distance between two cities of similar size tends to be proportional to the multiple of their populations, while Lösch suggested the equation $d_m = d_{m-1}\sqrt{k}$ where d=average distance between cities of the same rank and k=number of settlements of rank $m-1$ supplied by a city of rank m.

[6] Fox and Kumar (1965) argued that the equilibrium distance is increasing as a result of long-term advances in transportation technology, while Hoover (1970) showed that the result is indeterminate, depending upon the

relative strengths of the income and substitution effects of reductions in transport costs. However, he argued that in a highly developed economy substitution effects will tend to predominate, a finding consistent with Fox and Kumar's.

[7] Latin America is the home of what the Americans have described as 'megalocephalism' and 'hyperencephalisation'. Out of 22 countries, in 16 more than 50 per cent of the urban population is concentrated in one metropolitan area.

[8] For instance, by excluding the primate cities Clark (1967, p. 328) obtains the following estimates for q: Argentina, 0·98 (1947); Finland, 1·21 (1958); France, 1·12 (1954).

[9] Zipf (1949, p. 439) argues that Greater London was even much too large for the rest of the Empire, and represented (c. 1920) the first community of a much wider system.

[10] Mexico, Cuba, Chile, Argentina, Brazil, Peru, Venezuela and Colombia.

[11] In another study Mehta (1964) found no relationship between primacy and level of economic development, urbanisation, international communications accessibility, or population density. There was evidence of a slight positive relationship with export dependence on raw materials and a much stronger negative association with population size and area of the country.

[12] We might expect the integration of interregional transportation channels to be associated with a move towards rank-size and away from primate distributions. Several Latin American examples fail to support this expectation (W. D. Harris, 1971). A possible explanation could be that transportation improvements may promote polarisation rather than dispersal, at least initially. On the other hand, Mehta (1964) found a significant inverse rank correlation between primacy and intensity of use of internal transportation.

13 National Urban Size Policy

Introduction

This chapter is not concerned with the full range of urban policies dealing with poverty, slums, transportation efficiency and congestion, pollution, urban fiscal problems and all the other symptoms of the so-called 'urban crisis'. These are relevant to the discussion only in so far as they have repercussions on or are affected by urban size questions. Where such considerations suggest the possibility of attempting to reduce the size of the large metropolises or, at the other extreme, promoting the growth of smaller cities and towns, their relevance goes without saying. Even in these cases, however, the analysis cannot be focused on the individual urban centre. The obvious reason is that, except in the rare cases where the whims of human fertility happen to coincide with the designs of policy makers, changes in natural increase cannot accommodate desired changes in city sizes. Consequently, policies to change city sizes imply interfering with migration flows and this reverberates on the populations of other places. Since there are multiple origins and destinations for migrants, these reverberations are system-wide. Although, on occasion, attempts are made to close the system at a lower level of aggregation (e.g. an intraregional population distribution policy), the logical context for strategies to hold down the size of large metropolises (or promote small and medium-sized growth centres) is a national urban growth, or settlement, policy.[1] This is consistent with the observation recurrent in this book that the size of each city depends upon the size and location of all other cities and, indeed, on the national population distribution. This means, of course, that city size distribution analysis is an important input into a national urban policy along with economies and diseconomies of urban scale, the relationship between urban–regional strategies and national economic development and so on.

The objective here is to discuss the appropriate scope for a national urban policy in the light of the preceding analysis of the economics of urban size. The level of discussion is predominantly general, focusing on key issues rather than on the details of individual countries. The latter has been more than adequately surveyed for five countries[2] for the period up to the late sixties by Rodwin (1970). Wingo (1972) has chronicled the early – but very recent – steps in the evolution of thinking about a national urban policy in the United States, while its muddled nature has been revealed by Alonso (1971b). It must be stressed at the outset, however, that the choice of an appropriate policy cannot be divorced from the specifics of an individual country – its institutional environment, its level of development, its level and rate of growth of population, its existing urban structure, and many other facets. This point may be illustrated quite easily with one or two examples.

It is doubtful that a *national* urban policy makes much sense in the United Kingdom. The country is already so highly urbanised, the urban infrastructure so highly developed along clearly defined interregional transportation arteries, locational preferences so deeply imbedded that the scope for modifying the urban hierarchy is limited. Most important of all, the forecast increase in population between now and the end of the century, now about seven million or 12 per cent increase – and consistently revised downwards with each projection in recent years, is so modest that almost any conceivable combination of allocating the increase between new towns and cities and/or existing settlements would have little *overall* impact on the city size distribution. This should not be read to imply that the size and spacing of cities is irrelevant to economic policy in the United Kingdom. The question of a reasonable equilibrium size objective for London, its implications for a viable spatial and city size strategy for the South East Region, the revitalisation of the large nineteenth century metropolises of Northern England and Western Scotland, investigation of the feasibility of a growth centre strategy in lagging regions, the problems of how to service the remaining rural areas and of which settlements should be maintained – all these are legitimate inquiries. However, these problems are not closely interconnected, and they do not add up to the skeletal framework of a national urban policy, except in the very loosest sense of the term. Whatever the actual choices under each of these and other headings, the efficiency of the city size distribution and its spatial configuration is unlikely to be drastically altered. The justifications for this are that it is infeasible in the United Kingdom context to readjust city sizes via large-scale movements of population from some city sizes to others, that 'natural' migration rates are quite low, that too many towns and cities are of sufficient size to make them improbable candidates for secular decline and that this will be reinforced by the partial discontinuities and indivisibilities in the replacement of the urban capital stock, and – as pointed out above – that the anticipated new population to be allocated is too small to make much difference. The validity of the argument that countries need a national urban growth and settlement policy cannot be assessed, therefore, by sole reference to United Kingdom experience.

On the other hand, to consider two countries with which I have some slight degree of familiarity, Canada and Spain, the situation is quite different. In both cases, and in many others, e.g. in Latin America, the formation and structuring of the urban hierarchy may be regarded as an *instrument* of national economic development. In Canada, the vast land mass, the rich and relatively unexploited natural resources, the relatively few large cities combined with a forecast doubling of population by the end of the century, the shape of the developed parts of the country and its strong regionalism, these factors make it feasible, and possibly desirable, to develop and implement a national urban growth and settlement policy (for some early suggestions see Lithwick, 1971). In Spain, too, the heavy concentration of development in the North-East quadrant, the spatial dualism characteristic of an intermediate economy, the lack of integration in the national economy, the sparsity of metropolitan centres, the high rates of interregional migration and the associated wide *per capita* income differentials, the geography of the country with its vast inhospitable central mesa, and again a substantial forecast secular expansion in population, all these make a set of background conditions ideal for devising a national urban strategy.

The United States occupies the middle ground. Some preconditions for a national urban growth policy exist, but the high level of urbanisation and the maturity of the economy make it difficult to alter the prevailing patterns and trends in city sizes. This ambivalent position is reflected in the recent arguments as to whether or not a national urban growth strategy is essential for the United States. The closest approximation to a national urban growth policy was the proposals of the National Goals Research Staff for a 'population distribution policy' in 1970.[3] These stressed the need to reverse the trend towards megalopolis, to avoid 'rural desolation' and for a 'strategy for balanced population distribution'. In concrete terms, these aims were translated into three, possibly complementary approaches: the reversal of migratory flows back to the countryside and the development of opportunities in rural areas (the US Department of Agriculture's doctrine of 'urban–rural balance'); the fostering of a great many new towns outside the large metropolitan regions as containers for future urban growth; the promotion of alternative growth centres in non-metropolitan areas. The viability of these strategies has been challenged strongly by Alonso (1970a, 1970b, and 1971b) on the grounds that they are either ineffective or irrelevant. For instance, in regard to the first line of approach, the migration trends from rural to metropolitan areas could not be reversed, and in any event would have no impact on the big city size problem since only 5 per cent of the population increase of metropolitan areas is due to migration from non-metropolitan areas. Moreover, steering industries to rural areas would probably slow down growth in the country as a whole.

The new towns strategy, beloved by planners and others, would also fail to provide a solution to the problem. The Advisory Commission on Intergovernmental Relations (1968), a product of the Johnson regime, recommended a massive programme which was adopted by the National

Committee on Urban Policy in 1969, suggesting 100 new towns each of 100,000 population and 10 new cities each of a million by the year 2000. The resource cost of this would be colossal. Even if it could be implemented, these new communities would accommodate only 20 per cent of the projected increase in population by the year 2000[4] and 7 per cent of that year's national population. There are other objections to a national urban policy for the United States based on new towns. The 100,000 size class must offer a narrower range of economic and social opportunities than the larger metropolitan areas. New towns in an American context with their private developer orientation are not a solution for either the urban or rural poor, whether black or white. For reasons already stated, the need for new towns to divert the rural–metropolitan migrants is out of date. Other arguments are even less convincing: better utilisation of land hardly seems important when 100 million people could be accommodated at suburban densities on 1 per cent of the US land territory; the construction of new towns is too inflexible and indivisible to be used as a cyclical tool; development cost savings assumptions need testing, but in any event could amount to only a tiny fraction of the GNP. The sole saving grace of new towns, in Alonso's eyes, is as experiments in social planning, but this would mean perhaps a dozen certainly not a hundred: 'even if new towns turned out to be wonderful places, this would be almost irrelevant to our present urban problems, and that as sirens of utopia they might distract us from our path' (Alonso, 1970a, p. 54).

The third strategy, that of alternative growth centres, is less easy to knock down. The idea here is to promote the growth of medium-size urban areas, say those over 250,000, with growth potential. This strategy also has more backing from professional economists (e.g. Hansen, 1970; Cameron, 1970). The principles of a growth centre element in a national urban policy are discussed later. Here, we are concerned merely with a few observations on the US situation. The 200 SMSAs smaller than a million could absorb all the anticipated increase in population without any of them getting too big. This would merely be a continuation of past trends. However, this was not the strategy recommended by the NGRS. They were thinking in terms of encouraging smaller urban centres particularly in non-metropolitan areas. The opportunities here are far less obvious, and anticipated results far too small. For instance, SMSAs less than 250,000 account for no more than 10 per cent of metropolitan growth. Although this approach would have negligible effects on national urbanisation patterns, the regional consequences could be significant. The rudiments of such a strategy are already embodied in EDA (Economic Development Administration) policy, but the principles adopted are inappropriate: heavy concentration on too many, very small centres,[5] frequently without growth potential; a public works bias which meant that the aid given primarily related to infrastructure in the narrow sense. In more general terms, the objective of growth centres as a focus for migrants from depressed areas makes better sense than the other aim of hoping to divert population from the large centres and, in particular, from the Atlantic megalopolis and from the Pacific coast (from 'rimland' to 'heartland'). The latter would only be feasible, if at all, with high taxes on living in certain places and controls on particular types of interstate migration. In assessing the so-called disadvantages of megalopolis, it must be borne in mind that many of the SGCs (spontaneous growth centres; Alonso and Medrich, 1972) of the 1960s were located there rather than as free-standing cities in the heartland.

What are the alternatives to strategies of this kind? Friedmann (1971) has argued that the most appropriate choice for America is to take existing major metropolises as given and improve their livability.[6] Alonso (1971b) has suggested that population distribution policy is subordinate to overall national goals, and hence has no independent existence outside the general framework of national economic and social policies. Wingo's position (1972) is that the level of ignorance about the processes that influence the distribution of population is so great that the effects of policy cannot be predicted. This implies a less extreme point of view, since he also accepts that the high migration rate, $6\frac{1}{2}$ per cent of the population per annum, is sufficient to have a more than negligible effect on the national settlement pattern.

Too often, a national urban policy is a euphemism for big city size control. The dangers in this are far more serious than a mere underestimation of personal income gains and consumption externalities in large metropolises and a parallel exaggeration of their social costs. The large city may play a crucial role in the formation of an efficient urban hierarchy, particularly in developing economies. For example, Herrara (1971) has argued that in the larger Latin American countries a minimum size for the leading cities of 5–6 million is necessary if the right conditions are to be created for the development of secondary centres. The innovation diffusion potential of the metropolis may be closely related to its size. Mills (1972b) has argued that in the United States the effect of measures to restrict in-migration into the big cities would be to shut out the blacks from opportunities for self-betterment. In lagging regions boosting the size of their largest city may figure among the sounder strategies for development since the higher the city rises in the national urban hierarchy the greater its tendency to benefit from growth diffusion. On the other hand, it might be argued that big cities benefit greatly, possibly excessively, from central government policies, particularly grant-in-aid programmes. There are two explanations of this: large cities have the technical expertise and the information to take advantage of central government assistance; they find it easier to obtain the fiscal resources to meet the matching requirements of conditional grants. This bias hardly provides a case for intervention, however. Of course, this argument is not a denial of the existence and gravity of big city problems. Yet it would appear to be much more sensible to tackle these problems directly via internalising externalities, controls, taxes and subsidies, social welfare expenditures and other methods rather than the indirect, infeasible and probably irrelevant strategies of urban size control. A qualification of some importance should be noted in respect to rapidly growing cities. Inequities and social problems may be avoided if action can be taken (e.g. land use controls) to regulate the rate at which a particular city grows. However, such a problem should be defined as one of absorption not city size.

Chapters 11 and 12 discussed the theory and some empirical characteristics of city size distributions. A question which needs a little, though does not deserve much, attention is whether or not there is anything optimal about any particular kind of city size distribution, and consequently whether there is any scope for a national urban strategy that aims to mould the distribution. Clearly, of course, any such strategy, if successful, must have some influence on the distribution of city sizes, but it is doubtful if this would have a noticeable impact except where measures were on a large scale and policy objectives persistently pursued over long periods of time. The main justifications for this argument are the high degree of stability of city size distributions and the mixed success of attempts by governments to stop the growth of large cities. However, given the will and the means it would be difficult to argue that it is *impossible* to alter the city size distribution. If this were the case, the question of the desirability and feasibility of a national urban growth policy would not even merit serious discussion.

Some analysis of the problems arising in manipulating city size distributions as represented, say, by the rank-size distribution has been given by von Böventer (1971). His conclusions are very sensible. First, he suggests that for policy purposes the rank-size distribution is too crude a measure to be of any practical value. Second, he argues convincingly that agglomeration economies (in the widest sense) are a key function of cities but that they become effective not only within but between cities, and hence the spatial distribution of cities is no less important than the size distribution. This implies that measures of the city *size* distribution are deficient as a guideline for policy. Third, extending the previous point, von Böventer argues that spatial optima are compatible with widely different city size distributions. There is considerable scope, therefore, for a population distribution policy either regionally or nationally, but more in regard to the spatial aspects than the size aspects. The functional interconnections between cities and intermetropolitan agglomeration economies are becoming increasingly important, and these inevitably blur interpretation of city size

178

measures and their analysis.

The policy implications of these arguments are quite clear. From the growth maximisation objective point of view, it is unnecessary and probably inefficient for large cities to be close together since a single large city may create sufficient agglomeration economies to be shared with smaller urban centres. For small urban centres with few positive hinterland effects a location distant from a large metropolis confers no benefits. Instead, smaller cities thrive best if they are not too far away to profit from the metropolis's agglomeration economies and spillover effects, though it is advantageous if there are no competitors of similar size nearby. Moreover, if there are some diseconomies of urban scale, the small city near the large metropolis gains most of the benefits of agglomeration without the pains of large size. Hence, Alonso's alternatives (1971a) of 'small and near, and big and far'[7] are appealing. In addition, in some situations the adoption of a development axis approach with centres built up along axes from or between metropolitan cities may make it possible to retain access to agglomeration economies without having to sacrifice hinterland effects. In short, a polinucleated megalopolitan structure, far from being an untidy and ugly urbanised sore, is frequently an efficient constellation of urban centres for fostering national growth.

The role of migration in changing the national settlement pattern is crucial, yet this role is not easy to understand because the process is so complex due to the many different types of offsetting flows. In discussing how migration affects the national distribution of population, and in particular the distribution of population between urban centres of different sizes, we must be careful to distinguish between types and directions of migratory flows. This is especially important if one element in a national urban size policy consists of measures to influence and control patterns of migration. The variations in fertility and mortality by size of place are not sufficiently wide for natural increase to bring about much change in the national settlement pattern, and in any event are not necessarily biased in the appropriate (i.e. goal-conforming) direction.

The size of an individual city in population terms may change as a result of any combination of the following effects:

(i)   natural increase (changes in both births and deaths);
(ii) in-migration from other cities and towns: (a) from within the region and (b) from other regions;
(iii) in-migration from rural areas: (a) from within the region and (b) from other regions;
(iv) immigration from abroad;
(v)   an age-distribution bias in any of these in-migration streams that has

repercussions on future rates of natural increase;

(vi)–(ix) the out-migration equivalents to (ii)–(v);

(x) suburbanisation, i.e. outmigration over a legal boundary but where the population remains within the metropolitan sphere of influence.

Of these, only (i), (iv), (viii) and in some cases (x) have no repercussions on the rest of the urban system. All the other elements affect the present or future size of *other* cities. Also, the relative importance of each component varies with the size of the city. In the largest size classes we might expect (x) to be particularly important but the other out-migration streams to be less significant; in smaller size groups, on the other hand, in- and out-migration flows could be equally important. These considerations are reflected in the feasibility of strategies to promote or control changes in city size. For example, controlling the largest metropolises is likely to be easier by stemming the inflow of new migrants rather than by adjusting the rates of natural increase and of out-migration, except in the special case of sub-urbanisation. The rate of suburbanisation is largely a spontaneous flow, though influenced by the incidental effects of other policy measures e.g. central city versus suburban tax rates. Where attempts are made explicitly to raise the suburbanisation rate, the most common and successful policy approach is the indirect one of inducing the decentralisation of industry and economic activity. Of course, in most instances the goal of controlling large size does not involve attempts to accelerate the rate of suburbanisation, since this tends to exacerbate some – but not all – of the metropolitan problems responsible for the worries about large size.

Decomposition of the total migration streams is essential to understanding. For example, it makes a great difference whether the predominant share of in-migration into cities comes from rural areas or from other cities, and many of the prescriptions for a national urban policy in highly developed countries ignore the change from the former to the latter in recent decades. Also, the implications of whether or not the sources of migrants are intra-regional or interregional are also considerable. In many countries intra-regional migration flows are far larger than those between regions. Along with the suburbanisation flow (x), they fall more within the scope of modifi-cations to regional population distribution than adjustments to the national settlement pattern. On the other hand, an intraregional gravitation towards a region's largest metropolis does have direct repercussions on the size distribution of the national urban hierarchy.

Since migration is the most direct influence on city size distributions, it is at first sight surprising that so very few countries use instruments that act directly on the migration streams, in particular, migration subsidies and controls. Migration controls would be very difficult to introduce and to administer, and in any event conflict rather too strongly with prevailing ideology and ethos of the free, democratic or mixed economy. The role for migration subsidies is rather harder to assess. First, the question of a national urban size policy is less likely to arise in a low-mobility economy. In countries where the problem is of importance, the task before policy makers will not be raising the overall migration rate (that is probably already high enough) but influencing where the migrants want to go. On the contrary, *reducing* the overall migration rate may in some circumstances yield results closer to policy objectives (e.g. in the case where the dominant migration flows are to the large cities, and policy makers wish to control their size). Even if a direct migration subsidy were matched by equivalent cuts in indirect subsidies (e.g. investment incentives to firms at particular locations), one of its consequences would probably be a stimulus to the migration rate apart from its effects on the destinations of migrants. In most countries, preference is given to subsidies to job creation at particular places in order to influence migration indirectly.[8] This is consistent with many empirical findings on the determinants of migration suggesting that employment opportunities are a key attracting force. On the other hand, the practice of offering subsidies to industry (either capital or labour) in expanding cities in fast-growing areas is difficult to sell politically, so that this measure is most frequently applied as part of a growth centre strategy in depressed regions rather than as an instrument for a *national* urban policy. Some observers, especially Niles Hansen, have argued that it is possible to achieve a closer link between migration and job creation and between regional prescriptions and a broader urban policy by offering employers in fast-growing cities subsidies related to the employment of migrants from depressed areas. However, it may be difficult to devise a subsidy scheme simple enough to be effective yet precise enough to ensure that the aid is migrant-related. Also, it may be hard to justify aid to prosperous cities on equity grounds,[9] even if there are favourable indirect income effects on depressed regions.

Growth centre strategies

An obvious element in a national urban size policy and one that is pursued in a large number of countries is a growth centre (or growth pole) strategy. The growth centre concept has received much attention in the literature (for recent examples see Hansen, 1972; Kuklinski, 1972; and Kuklinski and Petrella, 1972), and this is not the place to review this nor to discuss the characteristics of growth centres in any depth. However, since growth centre policies are the most common form of government intervention to influence city sizes, a brief commentary is required. The chief feature of a growth centre strategy is to promote the expansion of particular urban centres to the level where their future growth becomes self-sustaining[10] and where they achieve certain policy objectives. These objectives may vary according to conditions and depending on the level of aggregation of the strategy (national, regional or sub-regional). Usually, the strategy involves some spatial gravitation of activities and population towards the centre from a surrounding sphere of influence or hinterland.

Although growth centre strategies are most frequently developed in the context of a regional policy, they may also be relevant to national urban policy (and in some cases to rural development policy). The focus of policy and the characteristics of the country both make a difference to the size of growth centre selected and aimed for. In most cases, even with national growth poles, the size of city designated is usually less than a million. The lower limit varies considerably from one country to another. In most countries, however, the favoured size is in the medium range – Italy, West Germany, the Netherlands, Spain and in some parts of Eastern Europe. In a few areas, however, North America (both the United States and Canada) and Scandinavia being the obvious instances, a growth centre strategy tends to imply very small centres frequently in rural areas. In Sweden, for example, 20 localities were created as growth centres in the north of the country but the minimum size was as low as 30,000. Bylund (in Kuklinski, 1972) reports geographical–sociological research in the 'forest counties' of Sweden suggesting a minimum size of 3,000 to support basic services. Yet only three centres of this size existed, and it was estimated that about thirty were needed. A growth centre policy for this type of area, and the similar attempts in Northern Canada to promote centres in the 15–20,000 range, is of a very different kind from the intermediate growth centre strategy with its minimum critical size of 250,000 urged by Hansen (1970a, 1970b, 1972) and others for the United States. The size criteria are clearly dissimilar in these cases because the policy objectives are not the same. In determining viable service centres for rural areas the emphasis will be placed on service costs. The choice of a larger growth centre in a regional development strategy is based on an evaluation of the city sizes that generate agglomeration and other external economies for stimulating economic growth. The even larger cities designated in those countries pursuing a 'countermagnet' strategy are merely a reflection of the assumption that large size is a necessary precondition for competing with a dominant national capital.

Despite their many forms and objectives, growth centre policies are all directed towards changing the sizes of individual urban centres. To that extent, they represent an attempt to change the city size distribution. It is improbable that they have had noticeable effects on measures of the city size distribution hitherto. The reasons are quite obvious. First, in most countries growth centre strategies have been in operation for less than a decade which is too short a period to have much impact. A generation is a more realistic time horizon for successful promotion of growth centres. Second, the successful strategies have usually been those where resources and policy instruments were concentrated on one or two centres which show themselves merely as a minor kink or as occasional shifts in ranks. To have a noticeable visible effect on the frequency distribution curve it would be necessary to change the size of many cities. However, designating a great many growth centres[11] inevitably means a dissipation of resources and a high failure rate. In this case, too, therefore, the city size distribution remains more or less unchanged. To the extent that the city size distribution is affected, *how* it is affected depends upon the aims and content of the growth centre strategy. If growth centres are intended to divert population and industry from the large metropolises, its success will be reflected in a reduction in the size of the Pareto coefficient. Also, where the growth centres are located in less prosperous areas than the metropolises, regional development and national urban policy goals will converge. The more usual situation occurs at the lower end of the urban hierarchy where the function of growth centres is to attract population from smaller centres within their own region. Occasionally, it may be possible to aim for both objectives simultaneously, via a strategy of fewer small, uneconomic units, more medium-sized cities and controlling the expansion of the largest cities. This is a very ambitious approach to growth centre strategies, primarily because of the difficulties involved in controlling the growth of the largest cities especially via inducing the out-migration of activities to specified alternative centres.

Even in the latter case, it is not always clear that the diversionist strategy is a sound one. Earlier in the book it has been shown that the evidence in favour of the hypothesis that big cities are too big is far from conclusive. To consider a specific example, Higgins (1972) has pointed out the potential dangers of a growth centre strategy in Quebec, Canada, where the establishment of three or four growth centres to the east of the province – though desirable on many grounds – runs the risk of weakening the economy of Montreal. His argument is that the metropolitan area of Montreal with a population of two-and-a-half million is not too big, and may be too small, to be safe in competition with other large North American cities. 'And without a dynamic Montreal the prospects of Quebec are dim. It would be easy enough to convert Montreal into another Quebec City by a policy of neglect; turning Quebec City into a second Montreal will be a long and difficult process' (B. Higgins, in Hansen, 1972, p. 228). The growth centre strategy is more generally valid when conceived as an efficient approach to promoting the development of lagging regions rather than as an instrument for dealing with the problems of large cities. Of course, policies for guiding the growth of a country's largest city frequently involve inducing decentralisation to nearby smaller centres within the sphere of influence of the metropolitan area (e.g. the strategies for South East England). However, it bastardises the term growth centre to describe these areas by that name. They remain within the range of the leading city's agglomeration economies and, therefore, the question of reaching the size needed to generate agglomeration economies independently is of limited relevance. If this argument is accepted, most growth centre strategies fall within the definition of regional policy rather than national urban policy.

It is difficult to offer any conclusive assessment of the effectiveness of growth centre policies. There are many reasons for this: the limited period over which policies have been in operation; the gap between theoretical expectations of dynamic generating effects and massive spatial spillovers and the practical achievements; the difficulties involved in selecting growth centres[12]; the wide variety in experience both between and within countries. On the whole, success had been very mixed. In most of the relatively successful instances, expanding the population and employment opportunities in the growth centres has been easier to achieve than self-sustained growth and spatial polarisation. However, the population increase is the most significant change from the viewpoint of urban size policy though not, of course, for growth centre purposes. In a mature, highly urbanised economy the national urban hierarchy is so developed and structured that it tends to be much more difficult to alter than in countries where the urban hierarchy is very imperfectly developed. On the other hand, the growth centre phenomenon is a product of institutional environments associated with developed industrial economies. The best candidates for growth centre policies tend, therefore, to be countries in the developed world which are not yet fully industrialised, with an imperfectly formed urban structure and a more than negligible rate of population growth.

Goals[13]

Alonso (1970b and 1971b) has argued that the goals of national urban policy are the same as those of other national policies (e.g. growth, efficiency, equity, quality of life, stability, participation). It follows that national settlement policy must be placed in the broader context of general national objectives before useful guidelines and strategies can be developed. In other words, the distribution of national population is seen merely as the projection on the geographical plane of the socio-economic system. While this means that all kinds of social and economic policies have incidental side-effects on the settlement pattern it is wrong to invert the logic and argue that national urban growth strategies can be used to solve general economic and social problems. The solutions to the national crime rate, the race problem, drugs, poverty, even pollution and congestion, are not to be found by altering the national settlement pattern. Even if we wished to change city sizes it is feasible to do this only within narrow limits.

While there is much good sense in these arguments, and Alonso is right in stressing the universality of the overall policy objectives, at bottom his analysis amounts to denying the possibility of a national urban growth policy at all. He may be correct in this in an American context – particularly in terms of the ideology of society and government and the range of feasible instruments available – but it is an extreme position to adopt on a world scale, particularly in less developed countries where the urban hierarchy has still to be formed.[14] If the national urban policy concept has any meaning at all, it is necessary for goal formulation to specify sub-goals that are a little more precisely related to the spatial distribution of population than the general goals cited above. However, as will be seen, it is impossible to base national urban size strategies on a single goal, either because of internal inconsistencies or infeasibility, while changing the distribution of city sizes is too clumsy a policy approach to deal with a broad set of multiple goals other than by attempting to achieve a very general compatibility.

It is possible for a national urban policy to be based on the pursuit of a single objective. Alternative objectives might be:

(i)   minimisation of inter-urban migration;
(ii) prevention of urban imbalance;
(iii) convergence of interregional income and growth differentials[15];
(iv) maximisation of innovation diffusion potential;
(v)   creation of a market for cities;
(vi) equating the private and social costs of urban expansion;
(vii) accessibility to equal opportunities for all citizens.

Many of these are too broad for implementation and need to be translated into a more specific form for the guidance of policy makers. Some are ambiguous. Others are clear but are either too costly or impossible to make operational. These points may be illustrated by commenting on each goal.

In a country without a significant rural surplus of labour, goal (i) implies that each city tends to grow at its rate of natural increase. Although this could alter the city size distribution if there were large interurban differences in fertility, it is unlikely to bring about much change in urban rankings. However, despite locational preferences for a familiar environment, such a goal is unattainable. It may make more sense to modify the objective to minimising 'involuntary' migration, but this raises acute questions of definition. In any event, any policy involving a reduction in the overall rate of migration is likely to interfere with national growth objectives.

Objective (ii) is not very specific, though it clearly implies restrictions on the growth of large metropolises. However, there is no evidence to suggest that a more even size distribution of large cities implies greater efficiency and higher welfare than a skewed distribution. Even if a more even distribution were considered desirable, it is doubtful whether available policy instruments could achieve much by way of cutting down the size of great cities. Moreover, there are political difficulties in the way of strengthening these instruments. Large city governments are powerful, and are unlikely to take kindly to national policy makers who attempt to reduce their territory and tax base. The interference in local autonomy that this national–local conflict necessarily involves is itself a far from negligible social cost.

The third goal is also difficult as long experience with regional policy shows. In regard to urban policy it requires controlling city growth in rich regions and expanding urban centres in lagging regions. If the rich regions contain the largest cities, then operationally this policy becomes similar to the urban growth strategies pursued in most countries. However, as it stands it may be an oversimplification since the argument assumes that income and growth indicators move together. If large cities have high proportions of low income residents the policy implications may be rather different with a possibility of conflict between growth and income equalisation (equity), e.g. high growth rates may require large cities in backward regions but these may create rather than reduce poverty.

The maximisation of innovation diffusion potential, though important, is unlikely to prevail as a single urban policy goal but to be associated with others. We know that realisation of such a goal requires a national hierarchy of cities with strong communication links between them and multiplant corporations operating in or near many centres in the hierarchy. Where our knowledge is deficient is in identifying more precisely the most efficient hierarchical distribution for the diffusion of innovation,[16] technical progress, new management methods, etc. Accordingly, other than investing in the communications networks it is difficult to know what pursuit of this goal implies by way of policy measures.

The argument of goal (v) is that community welfare is increased by offering households and firms a wider freedom of choice in the types of urban centre in which they choose to locate. Pursuit of this goal simply requires the government to stimulate product differentiation in the types and quality of urban living by developing a system of cities of widely different size and with very varied environments and urban life styles. This strategy, the creation of a 'market for cities', is an extension on a wider front of Tiebout's

(1956) case for a varied interurban mix of urban service–tax structures. It probably requires extensive Government subsidies since more product differentiation needs urban experimentation which involves risks and doubtful pay-offs. A serious objection to the relevance of this goal is that an extremely wide choice in urban environments, life styles and service–tax mixes can be found within a very large metropolitan area without having to create a differentiated system of separate cities.

Goal (vi) is a favoured single objective. It requires measures to redistribute interurban population until the private and social costs of urban expansion are matched in each city. The rationale is that the divergence between social and private costs leads to excessive growth of cities. This happens because households and firms make location decisions on the basis of average costs, but the marginal costs of their entry into a city fall on the entire community, and these costs are much higher than average costs because costs curves are rising. Thus, market decisions result in cities becoming too big unless in-migrants can be forced to pay the marginal costs associated with their arrival. The trouble with this objective is that it is incomplete and is non-operational. It is incomplete because it ignores the benefit side of the picture. In-migrants may also create social benefits and these may or may not exceed the gap between social and private costs. It is non-operational because we cannot accurately measure social costs and benefits and hence cannot fix the appropriate levels of taxes (subsidies) even if a marginal cost pricing policy was politically acceptable. Moreover, there are dangers in applying a static pricing framework to a dynamic problem. For instance, rising marginal costs of in-migration might be incurred only in the short run because the rate of in-migration is temporarily too fast to be absorbed. In other words, they may result from inelasticities in short-run functions rather than from higher social costs in the long run.

Goal (vii), the provision of equal opportunities, is unattainable if interpreted literally, but in general terms overlaps with the interregional income convergence goal. From the viewpoint of national urban policy, it implies giving particular attention to the smaller urban centres especially in regard to education, social services and urban amenities expenditure. It demands the setting of minimum standards of social service and urban infrastructure provision even in the smallest urban centres serving predominantly rural populations. In countries where this goal is explicit, e.g. Canada, it is not surprising to find that they operate an interregional fiscal equalisation policy. In city size distribution terms, active pursuit of this goal results in a bolstering of cities and towns at the lower end of the urban hierarchy. This is because it requires the redistribution of resources from large cities to small which eventually has an impact on their relative growth rates.

These comments suggest that the apparent simplicity of a single-goal national urban policy is deceptive. The overall comprehensive goal is often vague and frequently subsumes several other implicit and not necessarily consistent objectives. It is usually not specific enough for us to translate it into clear criteria for action. Many of the dimensions of the goal cannot be quantified, and this means that optimising decisions must be to some extent subjective since they rely on the policy maker's own weights. It follows that a *workable* strategy for a national urban policy is likely to be based on several goals with all the possibilities of conflict that multiple goals imply. The nature of these goals will vary from one society to another according to levels of economic development and socio-cultural values, as will the priorities among selected goals. In most developed economies, however, we would expect to find the following minimum set:

(a) the pursuit of national growth;
(b) the promotion of interregional equity;
(c) a 'quality of life' goal.

There is, of course, the possibility of other goals, either independent from those on the list or subsumed within them.[17]

Goal (a) has implications for the distribution of city sizes, both in regard to the structure and spacing of the hierarchy as a whole and to the importance of leading cities as generators of growth and innovation. Although goal (b) may call for controls on urban growth in prosperous regions, mainly via redirecting expanding industry to lagging regions, its main focus will be on building up smaller urban centres in backward regions to that critical minimum size which guarantees agglomeration economies. The 'quality of life' goal – goal (c) – is possibly the most important component of an urban policy strategy, yet it is the most nebulous. It refers primarily to the possible divergence between productivity and welfare in cities due to non-measurable social costs and intangible benefits. We still know very little about what constitutes a good environment for urban living, though we do know that perception of and response to environment differ a great deal from individual to individual and between groups. Moreover, the social costs, however defined, may be offset by higher real incomes and less quantifiable benefits associated with large city life; how far this is true depends upon whether individuals are 'forced' to live in large cities or whether their residential location decisions reflect a 'free choice' and a personal favourable balance of benefits over costs. Furthermore, if higher social costs are generated in large cities, it is unclear whether this is a direct consequence of size itself or simply reflects remediable managerial and organisational inefficiencies, the absence of pollution control policies, or lags in the response of urban governments to past population pressure. If the former there may be a *prima facie* case for decentralising population into smaller centres, but if the latter factors explain the high social costs the answer may lie in more effective city management and improvements in *intracity* spatial distribution.

The presence of multiple goals and the fact that priorities will differ among national, regional and urban policy makers means that it is difficult to prescribe an optimal strategy to fulfil the stated objectives. Goal conflicts will have to be reconciled, the 'best' technical solutions will have to be modified by the constraints of political feasibility and by the need to satisfy community and individual preferences. Optimisation is scarcely practicable. In particular, it is impossible for all the objectives of urban policy (faster growth, the revival of lagging regions, the control of environmental nuisances, etc.) to be satisfied by a unique optimum in the distribution of cities. For instance, even if it were true that large cities were always more efficient economically than small, this would not rule out the possibility that a hierarchy of sub-optimal cities could be more 'efficient' in relation to goal achievement (including growth goals) than the encouragement of a pattern of a few ever-increasing metropolises. Finally, in a multiple goal framework it is difficult to know whether a particular policy measure works in the right direction since its impact on the attainment of one goal may be offset by unforeseen disturbances on the attainment of others. All this amounts to a plea for very careful pragmatism rather than ambitious and inevitably abortive attempts to optimise the size and spatial distribution of cities.

Instruments

Even if urban policy goals have been precisely specified and it is known what changes will achieve them, there remains the problem of whether the instruments are, or can be made, available to bring about the required changes. It is arguable that a centrally planned economy would be needed to attain a particular distribution of city sizes in a spatial framework, and even in planned economies experience in attempting to halt the growth of large cities has not been very successful. Secondly, and this is the crucial point, the instruments available within the city to change the intraurban spatial distribution of activities are more powerful and their effects more predictable than the instruments available for modifying the interurban spatial distribution. This is primarily because planning, zoning and land-use controls are more effective and their results more predictable (though not necessarily more efficient) than investment incentives, tax-subsidy measures, etc. Moreover, measures to improve the efficiency and organisation of the great metropolises may not only be more practicable than measures to prevent

189

their growth but also more important in the sense that they will affect more people.[18] The arguments for emphasis on metropolitan rather than city size distribution solutions to policy problems should not be interpreted as a case for leaving policy solely in the hands of local governments. For if polinucleated clusters of cities are desirable and efficient (because they create large markets and offer a flexible structure for expansion), they need intermetropolitan and national policies to cope with common problems – transport, water and sewage, open space and recreation requirements and air pollution.

In distinguishing between policy instruments we must be careful to draw the line between those directly and those incidentally related to urban policy. For example, the central government's national policies – industrial policies, monetary and fiscal measures, transport policy, health, education and welfare expenditures – have differential impacts on cities. Regional measures occupy an intermediate role since policies to redistribute industry between regions are bound to have large urban side-effects because most population and economic activity is urban. Measures to influence the inter-regional distribution of industry (investment incentives, tax allowances, payroll subsidies, prohibitive controls such as i.d.c.s) can also be used to implement urban policy goals, but only in rare circumstances will their use in this context be compatible with their role as a regional policy instrument. For instance, controls on office building in Greater London since 1964 have been primarily associated with attempts to persuade firms to relocate in the Outer Metropolitan Area, and this has done nothing to correct imbalance in expanding service industries between the South East and the outer regions of Britain. Other measures, such as the provision of infrastructure and social overhead capital, simultaneously serve national, regional and urban ends. In this sense, decisions on the location of infrastructure might be regarded as the unifying theme in the coordination of national urban policy, except for the facts that infrastructure decisions are taken at different levels of government and that successful realisation of urban goals also requires a sequence of compatible private decisions by households and firms to rationalise and justify the prior (or associated) infrastructure decisions.

Apart from public infrastructure investment, the two most obvious urban policy instruments are (i) planning, land and zoning controls and (ii) pricing methods, such as congestion taxes, user charges for public services, etc. Both can be justified in general by reference to 'externality' arguments. The trouble arises when attempts are made to justify the application of specific measures in relation to the achievement of urban policy goals, especially if these goals include an efficiency in resource allocation component. The repercussionary effects of land use controls are difficult to trace, while the importance of non-measurable social costs makes it impossi-

190

ble to set 'optimal' congestion taxes. In addition, the widespread use of pricing methods to control urban scale is suspect on the grounds of political feasibility. The crudity of our policy instruments once more reinforces the case for pragmatism. In devising an urban growth strategy, goals set as targets are more likely to be attainable than goals expressed in terms of optimal efficiency. The best we can do is to take action in response to specific and clear-cut problems in the hope that we nudge the spatial allocation of resources a little in the desired direction.

In discussing potential instruments for urban size policy, it is useful to draw a distinction between controlling the size of large cities and promoting expansion in smaller cities. Although in some cases the same instrument may be used for both purposes (negatively and positively respectively), e.g. i.d.c.s or land use controls, frequently there is no symmetry in the use of instruments. Thus, to take one example, subsidies to migrants to move to growing towns are much more feasible than taxes or other controls on migration to large cities. Furthermore, it is much easier to encourage an increase in the size of smaller urban areas, provided that they have potential for growth, than to halt or reduce the size of a large metropolis. The major problems in a city-boosting programme are not so much the task itself but the selection of the cities to be expanded and the choice of the instruments that are the most cost-effective. This runs into the complex problem of how to implement growth centre strategies, a topic already briefly discussed.

The choice of appropriate instruments in the expanding city case is tricky, primarily because the rate of in-migration depends most of all on the creation of job opportunities. Accordingly, the key instruments are those that prove to be the strongest attractors to outside industry. Thus, investment in infrastructure may be important if it is believed that public capital investment can generate private investment, though even if this hypothesis is justified it is unclear whether technical infrastructure (such as industrial estates, power and water supplies, roadworks) is more strategic than urban and social infrastructure. Some evidence (admittedly impressionistic) tending to favour the latter is that amenities, interpreted broadly, appear to be an increasingly powerful locational attractor to potentially mobile industries. If this were so, it suggests that policies to encourage amenities could be significant determinants of how fast smaller cities grow. Of course, some amenities (e.g. climate) are unalterable, but many others are subject to intervention. Subsidies to education, medical and entertainment services, the relevance of recreation management and conservation strategies to improving the supply of parks and recreational facilities, environmental quality programmes, these are among the possible policies. Some types of industry will be attracted by amenities, though others may be repelled,

191

primarily because many amenities are expensive and locally financed.[19] On the other hand, if labour supply, its quality and range of technical skills are important locational factors then investment in manpower, training and human resource development programmes could be suitable instruments. Yet again, if location decisions are primarily determined by profit maximisation criteria, investment incentives may be the most useful measure. In many countries, however, such as the United Kingdom, such incentives are offered on a regional rather than a city basis.[20] Another alternative is to operate directly on influencing migrants by direct subsidies to migrants or subsidised housing in cities that are being expanded. However, since it is difficult to synchronise the rates of inward movement of people and jobs it may be more efficient and less socially wasteful to use investment controls and inducements to influence the migration rate indirectly rather than to develop an explicit migration policy.[21]

The instruments potentially available to hold down or reduce the size of large cities are many, but several of them are difficult to implement in some countries on grounds of political infeasibility. The basic choice is between prohibitive controls, whether land use controls or restrictions on location (i.d.c.s or office development permits), and pricing policies – particularly congestion taxes. The latter include road congestion charges, pollution taxes and employment taxes. However, the impact of these on city size is obscure. For example, heavy polluters may be the capital-intensive industries and the reduction in activity in this sector may be more than offset by expansion in labour-intensive sectors such as the service industries; this might increase city size via in-migration. As Tolley (1969) showed, measures to internalise externalities may either increase or reduce city size according to background conditions. Employment taxes are more likely to induce decentralisation of industry and hence stimulate out-migration of population. Similarly, the taxes on metropolitan capital investments recently introduced in Holland and considered in Sweden may be expected to have the same effect. As for the social costs that result from spatial concentration, e.g. pollution, there may be a choice between acting on city size and densities on the one hand and technical solutions or institutional changes (e.g. pollution taxes) on the other. The latter are almost always preferable because the rate of population dispersal following from city size control measures is too slow to have much impact on the social costs.

A possible instrument of urban size policy is the administrative reorganisation of urban areas, either subdivision or consolidation of urban government units, or alternatively the restructuring of multilevel urban service areas. In this sense, city size may be adjustable by institutional change rather than by migration or locational changes. However, this assumes that the problems of large cities stem from public goods provision or the size of the planning unit rather than, say, the spatial concentration of people and activities. Obviously, this is only partly true. On the other hand, there is little doubt that the strengthening of local government has an important role in the formation and implementation of national urban growth policy, particularly once it is recognised that strategies for population distribution must be based on existing settlement rather than on new towns (Alonso, 1970a; Downs, 1970).

The importance of urban government reorganisation, especially in an American context where the multiplicity of local government units is chaotic, has been stressed by Thompson (1972, p. 112): 'the cutting edge of public policy will be less to find an optimum system of cities and more to create an optimum system of governments'. This is partly a question of making the links and cooperation between central and local government more effective. It is even more a problem for restructuring at the urban level. The difficulty here is in reaching a compromise between the utopian notions of an 'optimum' and what is politically feasible. Alonso (1971b) has made his position quite clear: 'current suggestions that all government activities within a region be co-ordinated... are naive and unworkable'. Even in the United Kingdom where the administrative structure is quite simple, the 1969 Royal Commission on Local Government proposals for a two-tier structure with the upper level based on population sizes of about a million were watered down prior to implementation, and the new areas are merely an adaptation rather than a complete restructuring of the existing authorities.

In the United States, the situation is much more difficult. Burton (1971) has made out a strong case for the political decentralisation of State government via the establishment of what he calls Metropolitan States, which would be, in effect, consolidated metropolitan regions with a lower threshold population of about one million. If this is considered too ambitious, his second-best solution is the administrative decentralisation of State government by the establishment of Metropolitan Counties, an extension of the Toronto proposals and the precedents in the United States such as Dade County, Florida. Even these modest proposals seem too ambitious for nationwide implementation given the political climate in the United States. Yet the alternative is the erosion of local government by increasing Federal involvement in the form of the proliferation of grant-in-aid programmes or by the establishment of special purpose area-wide authorities to deal with such questions as transport, water provision and quality, and pollution. The objective of the proposals of Burton and others is that metropolitan-wide government reorganisation is the only way to defend and revive local government, and its theoretical justification is that institutional changes may be capable of dealing with externalities, and their chief manifestation – the complex set of problems described in America as the 'urban crisis'.

Conclusions

If it implies an optimal distribution of national population through the nation's existing and planned urban centres, a national system of cities is not a sensible object of public policy. This is not to say that a national urban policy is undesirable or unnecessary. But such a policy should be goal-oriented, and we can identify several separate if overlapping and frequently conflicting goals. Moreover, the magnitudes of change needed to achieve these goals are in some cases not easily, if at all, measurable. With many goals, and when some of these cannot be translated into quantifiable objectives, the case for optimisation loses much of its strength. Certainly, there is no unique spatial distribution of population which can be said to achieve these goals. Von Böventer (1970) has pointed out that deriving an optimal distribution of population is difficult. I will go further; in a policy context, it is impossible.

A hierarchy of cities is an efficient system for promoting national growth and for producing and distributing goods and services to society. This suggests that it would be foolish to attempt to equalise the size of cities, but it does not help us to decide whether one hierarchical structure is superior to another. There are a few general indications. First, variety in urban form, structure and environment both in regard to differentials in city size and within a specific size-class is probably a good thing because it offers individual households and firms a wider choice. Given heterogeneous tastes, wider choice implies greater welfare. Second, if a first-order metropolis is a seedbed for innovation, managerial expertise and growth and a 'port of entry' for new technology and ideas into a region, then every region should contain a large city (relative to the size of the region). If this condition is fulfilled, a national hierarchy of regional cities will further devolve into sets of central place systems. Third, whatever the size distribution of the top level of the national hierarchy, its efficiency depends as much on the quality of the transport and communications networks linking the major cities as on the balance between agglomeration economies and urban costs within them.

The promotion of growth centres in lagging regions is in many cases a valid policy objective, but it is much more relevant to regional than to urban policy. A growth centre strategy involves an attempt to maximise regional growth potential via spatial concentration of development and to obtain cost-effectiveness in urban infrastructure spending. Much more central to a national urban policy is what, if anything, should be done about a nation's large cities. We know that all is not well, that our great metropolises have generated considerable social costs. The fact that many of these are difficult, or impossible, to measure cannot deny their existence and importance. What we do not know, however, is how far these social costs may be offset by social benefits in the form of higher urban productivity. Some, but not all, of this higher productivity is captured in higher real incomes, but the incompleteness of urban data makes it difficult to quantify precisely the measurable component. If higher costs were outweighed by higher productivity, we would have not a diseconomy of scale question but an income distribution question, since the burden of social costs falls heavily on those too poor to evade them, while the benefits of higher urban productivity are not equally shared but accrue to owners of urban land, business corporations and other monopoly groups (see Kirwan, 1972). Furthermore, it is unclear whether higher social costs are inherent in the phenomenon of large size or whether they might not be transient due, say, to a too fast rate of in-migration relative to the increase in urban capacity, i.e. a problem of absorption rate rather than absolute scale. If so, the appropriate remedies would be to monitor and control the rate of expansion of large cities not to attempt to reduce them in size.

Even if we suspect that the net social benefits of the present distribution of urban population are negative, there are two further considerations. First, the policy instruments available in a mixed economy are probably not strong enough to *reduce* the size of large cities. By influencing the distribution of jobs and the provision of housing and infrastructure, however, it may be possible to alter the spatial distribution of urban population in a period of population expansion by operating on the relative growth rates of individual cities. Second, a danger in pursuing, possibly ineffective, measures to persuade people and activities to leave the large metropolises is that this may provide a pretext for neglecting the pressing problems of improving the urban environment and central city poverty. These problems are not directly related to scale, and will persist even if the size of large cities could be reduced.

Does all this mean that nothing is left of an urban policy strategy? Not at all. However, it implies that such a strategy should be pragmatic, even piecemeal, rather than based on an optimisation approach aiming to achieve a dynamic spatial equilibrium at one stroke. Moreover, a national urban policy ought not to include measures to attain optimal size for an individual city. Optimality in this context has no real meaning. Even if this were not the case, from the viewpoint of national policy an artificial system of cities of 'optimal size' would be less efficient than a hierarchy both for economic growth and for providing an array of different environments for businesses and people. Furthermore, there is not a single unique efficient distribution of city sizes, but many, and given multiple goals we should not be too worried about minor irregularities in the city size distribution.

A pragmatic approach does not rule out measures that affect the national urban hierarchy. These might include action to boost leading cities in backward regions or to bring small cities up to a minimum critical size compatible with efficiency and continued growth. Also, measures to decentralise activities from our largest cities are not inconsistent with a national urban policy. But such measures are unlikely to be successful if they aim at reducing the scale of our metropolitan areas by redistributing population to other distant urban centres in other regions. Better prospects are offered by dispersing population from the central city itself to interconnected smaller centres within the metropolitan region. The promotion of a polinucleated system enables the smaller cities to benefit from the agglomeration economies offered by access to the metropolis. It is also more likely to achieve results since it probably satisfies locational preferences much more than an inter-regional–interurban redistribution.

In some respects, the changes in metropolitan spatial structure (in particular, the horizontal spread of large cities) represent an adjustment of urban scale in the absence of intervention or, at least, in a climate of lukewarm controls. In the United Kingdom, for instance, most of the conurbations are experiencing either population decline or stability, and the same is true of conurbations in many other countries. Also, the formerly strong positive relationship between net migration and city size has disappeared, and a recent British study (Berry, 1973) of selected regions shows that the city size coefficient is actually negative but statistically insignificant. In this case, he reasons appeared to be the shortage of urban land for housing and the opportunities for semi-rural and suburban living combined with jobs in the city offered by the spread of car ownership. However, it is misleading to treat such falls in metropolitan population in the sense of numbers living within defined administrative areas as examples of declining city size. A more accurate interpretation is as a successful adaptation of metropolitan spatial structures, spilling over metropolitan boundaries, to changing social, economic and technical conditions. These spillovers make it difficult to understand what is meant by city size except in the case of the mono-centric city located in the centre of a rural plain. This is yet another argument against the value of the concept of optimal city size.

Most important of all, however, is that the most effective policy, especially if we accept the argument that there are many efficient city size distributions, could well be to improve the efficiency and management of our large cities by acting on the *intra*-city spatial distribution and by correcting the most obvious resource misallocations within the city. The large city is an important engine for growth, and we know that rapid urban expansion may improve welfare rather less than it boosts growth. Is it not, therefore, a sensible urban policy objective to concentrate on improving the urban environment and 'livability' within the city? In this way more people will benefit than by measures to stimulate out-migration from the cities which might adversely

196

affect growth potential without achieving a commensurate reduction in social costs.

Notes

[1] In countries where foreign emigration and immigration are important, the system must be extended beyond national boundaries and a 'national' settlement policy must take account of the decisions and regulations of other governments and the behaviour of potentially migrant foreigners.

[2] The countries were Venezuela, Turkey, Great Britain, France and the United States.

[3] National Goals Research Staff Report (1970).

[4] As the long-run population projections fall, the new towns' share of population increase would grow. By arguing that the decline in the projection extends the scope for absorption in existing cities – a fact true in itself – and by simultaneously adopting the argument in the text, Alonso wants to have it both ways.

[5] By April 1970, 87 Economic Development Districts and 171 Development Centres had been designated. Of the latter, only 30 had a population greater than 50,000 while 13 had a population greater than 100,000; conversely, 42 had less than 10,000 persons.

[6] This view is consistent with my arguments in Richardson (1972), and will be elaborated later.

[7] More recently, Alonso (1972) has argued that the attenuating effects of distance are so strong that even countermagnets are more likely to be successful if they are near to the metropolises from which it is hoped they will attract population.

[8] In a national urban policy context this usually implies attracting migrants to particular cities, but in a policy for depressed areas it usually means checking the rate of out-migration.

[9] The trade-off between efficiency and equity in relation to rural-urban migration has been discussed by Alonso (1968b).

[10] In this sense, the policy involves converting a town or city into what Alonso and Medrich (1972) call a *spontaneous growth centre*, defined in their analysis specifically as an urban centre with a net in-migration rate twice the metropolitan average. It is also interesting that SGCs can be found throughout the urban hierarchy, and that the fastest-growing size classes in the early 1960s were rather larger than those usually associated with growth centre strategies (see above, p. 115).

[11] As Klaassen points out (Kuklinski, 1972, p. 9), there are about 50 designations in Holland and over 300 in West Germany.

[12] Neither 'worst first' nor optimal size criteria will do. Each urban centre must be judged from the point of view of its functions in the wider urban system. However, where the role of growth centres is to boost lagging regions, a simple rule-of-thumb is to examine first of all the region's leading city as a possible choice.

[13] Some of the arguments in the remainder of this chapter are derived from Richardson (1972).

[14] Alonso has expressed doubts in the less developed economy context (Alonso, 1968a), but primarily from the point of view of the difficulties of achieving the development of backward regions by restricting the growth of primate cities. Admitting that there may be a role for national urban strategies does not imply commitment to a policy of restricting the size of the leading city.

[15] A variant of this might be the promotion of income equity within cities. I have not discussed this for two reasons. First, I would argue that the efficiency of the city as an instrument of national economic growth depends on inequities. Second, it is arguable that appropriate policies for dealing with extreme income inequalities are national welfare and social measures more than part of an urban policy. To the extent that urban policies are involved, these arise at the intraurban rather than the city size distribution level. As Mills (1972b) has argued, policies to control the size of large cities are likely to be regressive in income distribution terms.

[16] See Pedersen (1970) and the paper by B. J. L. Berry in Hansen (1972). See also above, pp. 40-3.

[17] For example, in the United States an important social goal might be to attain desirable class–status–race mixes within cities of different size, and this would encompass still other goals, e.g. relating to income redistribution, education, labour markets, etc.

[18] Dissenters from this view may argue that reducing the size of the metropolis will not only raise the welfare of those induced to locate elsewhere but also the welfare of all remaining households and firms in the metropolis. This may be so, but I doubt whether most of the social costs of scale are easily reversible.

[19] See Stanback and Knight (1970a, p. 231): 'for a metropolis to remain competitive and viable, amenities such as pollution-free air and water will have to be given equal or even higher priority than such time-honoured demands for local industry as keeping taxes low. Of course, many amenities have a cost that results in higher tax rates, and firms that cannot afford this cost will be forced to migrate to areas with lower taxes and fewer amenities. Firms and consumers placing a high priority on amenities will converge in the amenity-rich city.'

[20] In countries where narrow definitions of a growth pole are used (e.g.

198

Spain) these incentives are available only for a limited range of cities (i.e. the growth poles themselves).

[21] Inducements to industry may, of course, take the form of employment subsidies which have the advantage that they are not capital-intensive-biased (labour-intensive-biased subsidies would be more appropriate if the main objective of policy is to increase city size).

14 The Case of London

The issues

As a great metropolis, London is admired and loved by many, and particularly by foreigners, for its parklands, its history and its many attractions and
amenities. If excessive size is the great evil, then London (and perhaps some
other capital cities) is testimony to the view that no hypothesis is universally
valid. Of course, London is far from perfect. Its roads can become snarled
up with traffic, its skyline is increasingly spoilt with the products of unimagi-
native architecture, and its inner areas may hide as much poverty, overcrowding and homelessness as many other large cities. Nevertheless, if the
United States cities were no worse than London, there would be very little
talk about 'the urban crisis'.

Attempts to control the size of London have been put into practice
long before the urban crisis became fashionable. It was one of the main
objectives of the Barlow Commission in 1940, though it was unclear at
the time (as with many subsequent inquiries) whether a reduction in size
would be good for Londoners or for the nation as a whole (because of
excessive concentration in the South East). The New Towns policy, over-
praised by observers from overseas, was also closely related to a strategy
for holding back London's growth by accommodating overspill population
in new communities of a much more 'desirable' size. More recently, strategies
for spatial development in the South East – whether in new or expanded
towns at a distance or in the alternative version of much larger counter-
weights developed out of existing towns and circled round London at a much
smaller radius (25–35 miles) – have been partly concerned with reducing the
size of the metropolis. This objective has also figured prominently among
regional policy goals, and many regional policy instruments such as investment incentives, i.d.c. controls and office development permits have been
used to divert industry and population from the South East in general and
London in particular. It is significant that now that these measures are
beginning to bite and out-migration from London has become noticeable
doubts should be raised as to whether size control is an appropriate policy
after all. Although this disagreement partly reflects the growth of strong
vested interests (especially since the establishment of the GLC), it is also
due to lack of clarity about goals and ignorance about the effects of changes
in size.

If London's problems are not due to size *per se*, it is surprising why there has been such a long tradition of size control policy. A major reason must be the ideology and influences on British planners and the extent to which they have been affected, perhaps subconsciously, by Ebenezer Howard's concept of garden cities. The links between the New Town programme and control of London were always strong, though it is significant that the notion of what constitutes a viable size of community has crept upwards over time. Also, the ideal of a desirable town size has been associated in Britain with mobility, meaning the size of place where everybody could go everywhere, as opposed to criteria stressing, for example, the maximisation of employment opportunities for the most people. The benefits of small size have always been taken for granted in the United Kingdom, whereas in the United States the disadvantages of large size were a heresy (though now perhaps the new faith). The emphasis on the benefits of large size in the United States (Winnick in Senior, 1966, pp. 179–80) has probably declined in the last few years, and it is now not so universally held (for instance, a substantial proportion of the American planning profession have adopted the contrary view). In the United Kingdom, on the other hand, the benefits of larger agglomerations are now fully recognised, so that there has been some convergence in attitudes over the last decade. However, in respect to London, this has simply meant a modification in the strategy of how decentralisation should be brought about, not a challenge to the principle of decentralisation itself.

It is not my intention here to chronicle the history of attempts to control the size of London or to analyse the alternative strategies now under discussion. Not only would this stray the argument too far from its path, but such an analysis would be premature. The controversy is still very live, the evidence is not yet fully assembled, the issues remain unclear, the objectives have yet to be finally specified and the effects of changes in size remain nebulous. Our sole concern here is to illustrate that the problem of city size is not an abstract problem but a question for practical economics and politics and to use the London example to show some of the difficulties involved in any analysis of the costs and benefits of city size.

The continued attraction of the London area is beyond doubt, particularly to middle class households with middle class tastes. Peter Hall (1969, pp. 40–1) contrasted Lancashire very unfavourably with the amenities of the London area, particularly in terms of climate[1] and cultural facilities (theatre, music and choice of films). It is questionable, of course, how relevant cultural amenities are to the great mass of the population. However, if groups and individuals vary in their tastes, London remains attractive because of the variety that great size can offer.

At the more mundane level, London offers better economic returns than other places. Incomes are higher, but how far these are offset by higher living costs (especially housing and transport costs) is difficult to measure. Certainly unemployment rates are much lower in the GLC than in the rest of Britain (about 60 per cent of the British average over the last decade) and are lower than in the South East as a whole. The incidence of long-term unemployment is also lower, while vacancy rates are appreciably higher. Moreover, although the evidence on incomes is rather crude, household incomes appear to have increased in the last half of the 1960s faster in the GLC area than in the country as a whole, but slower than in the rest of South East England.

Despite the continued attractions of the capital,[2] London has been losing population primarily as a result of out-migration in recent years. The residential population of the present Greater London has fallen from a peak of about 8·6 million in 1939 to 8·0 million in 1961 and to 7·4 million in 1971. In recent years the net annual average out-migration has been about 110,000 and the net annual population loss about 75,000. The more worrying feature in the 1960s was the relatively poorer economic performance as shown by such indicators as investment, employment and income growth compared to the rest of South East England. The decline in population is expected to continue. The Layfield Panel of Inquiry into the Greater London Development Plan (DOE, 1973) assumed in its analysis that the 1981 population would be in the range 6·37–6·55 million[3] and that in 1991 the population might be 6 million.

The paradox of the attractions of the metropolis and net out-migration is easily explained. For those who are well off, all the benefits of access to London can be enjoyed without living in the London area, so it is possible to move out to suburbs in the Outer Metropolitan Area without having to give up all the advantages of London. On the other hand, for many of the poor trapped in Inner London the attractions of London mean nothing because they lack the income to enjoy them, while living and working conditions may be no better, and in some cases rather worse, than elsewhere in the country. This is the problem of the distribution of benefits and costs once again, and it is difficult to ignore it in any assessment of what is an appropriate size for London. In other words, population size cannot be discussed adequately without specifying more about its composition and income distribution. *Tomorrow's London* expressed this view very well indeed for a popular document (GLC, 1969, pp. 36–8): 'There is no "capacity" for London in terms of numbers. People are not like eggs, eighteen score to a crate'. For a high income population 4 million might lead to overcrowding; for a low income population capacity might be as high as 12 or even 14 million.

Both market forces and the effects of policy have had the result of stimulating out-migration from the Greater London area, both directly (the

202

movement of households) and indirectly (the decentralisation of work-places). However, some observers have argued that the out-migration has been selective, in the sense that the relatively well-off figure disproportionately among out-migrants, with the corollary that the distribution of income in the city itself worsens. If this were so, the question would arise whether the gains from reduced size (e.g. a lower degree of congestion) are outweighed by costs associated with the effects of a deterioration in the income structure of the remaining population. However, the Layfield Panel (DOE, 1973) found no evidence that out-migration was biased in this way. Selective out-migration is much more likely to take place at the neighbourhood than the city level, especially if suburbanisation is income elastic and if there is a direct association between the income levels of the replacement in-migrants and the quality of neighbourhood housing stock. In the case of London, this latter assumption may be invalid as the scarcity of housing and the desire for accessibility induce the relatively well-off to infiltrate into poor neighbourhoods.[4]

The case for retaining London's population at as high a level as possible has been put by the GLC itself (GLDP, May 1971) and its spokesmen (e.g. Eversley, 1972a). The argument is that a decline in population and employment is not matched by an equiproportionate fall in commitments. London's international, national and regional role remains undiminished. Tourism, despite its seasonal character, also demands additional infra-structure.[5] Moreover, the departure of more relatively well-off leaves a higher proportion of the remaining population needing subsidised housing, additional educational and welfare services and more public service provision of all kinds. Meeting these commitments is made more difficult by soaring investment and construction costs and by the effects of selective out-migra-tion on rateable capacity. Eversley pointed out that rateable revenue in London has been increasing at only about one half of the national rate, and the GLC view is that rateable income is bound to fall if selective out-migration continues at a time when the *per capita* cost of running public services will increase.[6] It is sometimes suggested that this process could adversely affect private as well as public investment, and set in motion a cumulative, reinforcing decline. A subsidiary argument is that the effects of out-migration of this type would be to accentuate social polarisation within London.

It is not easy to evaluate the strength of these arguments. If trends continue and we extrapolate sufficiently far ahead, it is possible that these predictions might be confirmed, but there are some offsetting advantages which are insufficiently taken into account. The rateable income point of view is a very narrow way of looking at the problem of London's size, particularly since there might be methods of dealing with the situation if the problems were solely fiscal. For instance, either by more central government support[7] or by devising new forms of local taxation to tap income and wealth created but not spent in the city, it might be possible to redistribute fiscal resources in favour of London and, at the same time, to ensure that these were used to benefit the relatively deprived communities and individuals.

During the course of the Layfield Panel Inquiry, the GLC shifted its ground from the vulnerable proposition that a fall in the level of Greater London's population would have deleterious effects on incomes and welfare to the much more acceptable view that it was the rate of decline which was the worrying feature. The Layfield Panel explicitly rejected both views: 'We emphatically recommend rejection of the GLC view that there is any particular danger in either a lower level of population, to which the present rate of decline of population is likely to lead, or the particular rate of change itself. The arguments put forward in support of the view that the decline should be retarded are either, in our view, illogical or are unsupported by evidence. In any case, we see very little likelihood that policies could be successful in restraining any particular rate of change' (DOE, 1973, para. 25.8). There is much to be said in favour of this scepticism. Too many of the evils of population decline as perceived by the GLC depend on the unproven assumption of selective out-migration. Others could be dealt with by a parallel decentralisation of jobs, but this is even more unpalatable to the GLC than out-migration of population. Once the present and future size of London is put in its place as an irrelevancy in the pursuit of improving the quality of life for Londoners, it enables the analysts and planners to turn to the more important problems of spatial structure and resource allocation, e.g. the selection of strategic growth centres within the London area and the amelioration of London's housing and transport problems.[8] At the same time, the resources and powers of metropolitan and local authorities need not be dissipated in a fruitless attempt to control population size.

Despite the soundness of these opinions, the Layfield Panel abandoned healthy scepticism when it argued that the continued decline of London was desirable. There is as little evidence to support this view as that in favour of the GLC's arguments. The argument[9] is based on the view that the social costs of a higher population exceed the private costs whereas the social benefits *do not* exceed the private benefits. This sheds light on the question of whether a higher or lower population is desirable only if we can specify the relationship between total (or marginal) social benefit and social cost functions. Also, the Panel gave some attention to non-monetary social costs (e.g. traffic congestion, noise, pollution) but restricted its discussion of social benefits to purely monetary items such as higher productivity, export potential and higher incomes. Finally, to argue that a population for

London of 6–6½ million is more desirable from a welfare point of view than a population of 7 million is no more sensible than the original GLC position that London had to be held at a population of 7·3 million. Within these size ranges, the correlation between population and welfare means very little. Since many of the Panel's arguments are consistent with this conclusion, it is a pity that it equated a smaller London population with improved welfare. Its justification of this is based on a simplistic association between overall population city size and overcrowding and between overcrowding and higher social costs.[10]

A recent study by Foster and Richardson (1972) illustrates the tremendous problems involved in examining the impact of declining city size in relation to London. Part of the difficulty lies in ambiguity in the goals, part in data problems and inadequacies in the theory. Even if we assume a simple straightforward goal such as maximising the real *per capita* income of the relevant population, all kinds of problems arise. What is included in real income? How do we define the relevant population? To what extent should we introduce equity considerations into the income maximisation goal? Foster and Richardson suggest that the goal might be to maximise real income *per capita* (narrowly defined) of residents at the beginning of the planning period *plus* in-migrants, subject to the constraint that the city's poor should not be made worse off in absolute terms, but many alternative specifications are possible. In evaluating impacts of a population decline, they compare the effects of a balanced reduction (a representative cross-section of the population) with those of an unbalanced reduction (a population loss disproportionately weighted with upper income groups and highly skilled workers).

The results of their analysis are very unclear, reflecting the complications of the problem. Assuming that the emigrants themselves gain, the effects on those that remain may be summarised as follows. With a balanced reduction, in the housing market renters gain but owner-occupiers lose, in the labour market there will tend to be gains to workers as unemployment falls while vacancies and average earnings rise, the effects on public services are very unclear depending on production technology, factor prices, inherited infrastructure and rating provisions, while the effects on congestion will be insignificant given the rate of decline. An unbalanced reduction in population will generate qualitatively similar effects, but with some additional problems. Obviously, the housing market effect will be concentrated in the higher quality segment of the owner-occupied sector. The labour market impacts depend on the complementarity or substitutability for emigrants of those who remain; on the whole, employees gain relative to employers so that there might be secondary repercussions via workplace emigration though these are most unlikely to degenerate into an emigration

205

spiral. The congestion and pollution impacts are again likely to be insignificant, except that to the extent that there is any effect at all an unbalanced reduction will result in a more spatially uneven distribution of gains and losses. The public service effects are even more complicated than in the balanced reduction case. Too little is known about the income elasticity of demand for public services; Foster and Richardson guess at a high elasticity for refuse disposal and education and a low elasticity for public housing and some welfare and social services. The more a service faces a low income elasticity of demand the less can government expenditure fall (while meeting the original commitment) under conditions of unbalanced emigration. This possibility puts the stability of the local government budget at risk.

The more favourable unemployment situation in the London area suggests that the outmigration of workplaces has not been the chief independent variable in the decline in employment and population. Household migration decisions have been more important; also, there has been some decline in fertility and a falling off in the rate of in-migration. It is difficult to generalise about the overall impact of the fall in population because the unemployment data are the only hard evidence available. Insufficient is known about relative wages, housing costs, the availability of urban services, commuting costs and externalities. The general conclusion was that 'it is not easy to discern extensive hardship in London arising from declining city size... there is not yet visible to us a strong empirical case which would justify a dramatic change in policy designed to alter the nature of existing emigration forces' (Foster and Richardson, 1972, p. 30).

Even were more data available, it is still doubtful whether the results of such a study would be any more conclusive, To examine the city size problem in terms of whether 6½ million or 7 million is the most appropriate size is somewhat unreal from the point of view of analysis of the costs and benefits of urban scale. It is most improbable that there could be substantial net economies attainable at the population level of 7 million which cannot be gained at 6½ million; a question of this kind makes much more sense when we are comparing populations of, say, 250,000 and a million. Of course, the problem of London is a real problem, but it is not due to size but to the difficulties of adjustment and to the special problems arising from the need to finance non-local functions. It is arguable that the London problem is a fiscal problem which could be solved if radical fiscal changes were politically feasible rather than one arising from the maldistribution of resources spatially.[11] Yet the London case has been virtually the only serious instance of concern at the practical policy level with city size in the United Kingdom.[12] To some extent, it reflects a myopic preoccupation in Britain with the problems of London to the exclusion of the difficulties facing other cities and the question of a national urban policy. There is still no prescription in the United Kingdom for the urban growth pattern of the nation as a whole. Moreover, if by the end of the century England and Central Scotland is to form one vast linear megalopolitan complex with London closely linked to Birmingham, Liverpool, Manchester and Glasgow, the question of the population size of those households who happen to reside within a geographically defined London area is for all intents and purposes irrelevant. The key problem will be the efficiency of the spatial structure of the economy as a whole and the political organisation needed to harness the country's resources in a manner consistent with this efficiency.

Controlling the growth of London

Despite the absence of anything that might pass for a national urban growth policy in Britain, there has been a long history of attempts to influence the settlement pattern indirectly via operating on the location of employment. The Greater London experience shows how distribution of industry policy runs into urban size strategies. The principle of decentralisation was first expounded by the Barlow Commission in 1940 in order to relieve the congestion of Greater London and the South East. The congestion argument was not established at the time, and has not been conclusively substantiated since. At the regional level, Holmans (1964) argued in a provocative article that there was plenty of scope and space for further development in South-East England, and that the congestion case was unclear. Similarly, I suggested around the same time (Richardson and West, 1964) that congestion was an intraregional rather than an interregional problem. The Barlow Report, however, analysed the situation in interregional terms.

After the war, a spate of planning legislation in the period 1945–52 provided the controls needed to give some teeth to decentralisation objectives embodied in the Greater London (Abercrombie) Plan of 1945. In particular, the instrument of i.d.c. (industrial development certificate) control introduced by the Distribution of Industry Act of 1945 provided a potentially crucial measure for influencing the location of employment. This was to prove to be the lynchpin of interregional distribution of industry policy in the United Kingdom in the postwar period, and relocation of employment out of London was primarily conceived of in interregional terms. The more immediate effects on decentralisation within the region were concentrated on an 'overspill' policy to redistribute population from London itself to relatively nearby new towns, eight of which were established under the Town and Country Planning Act of 1947. Despite these policies, the population of the Metropolitan Area actually increased by 800,000 between 1951 and

1961, and the 1945 Plan was in any event made obsolete by an unanticipated increase in national population.[13]

The major steps forward in strategies for controlling London's growth and bringing about a reduction in the size of Greater London came in the 1960s. *The South East Study, 1961–81* (published in February 1964) proposed a second generation of new towns and major town expansions in the region. This was reinforced by measures to draw commercial growth from London with the introduction of office development permits under the Control of Office and Industrial Development Act of 1965. The change in strategy from the 1950s was the shift away from a nearby ring of new towns to new and expanding towns further away (e.g. 50–100 miles from Central London), some of which might be built up into large population concentrations. The possibility was envisaged that these might become major cities in their own right and act as counter-magnets for people and jobs that might otherwise be drawn towards London. Examples were Milton Keynes, Northampton and Peterborough – the first a new town, the others major expansions. Revisions to the *South East Study* in January 1966 adjusted for changes in the population forecast and its distribution, and predicted a higher rate of movement out of London, a smaller rate of in-migration into the region, and still greater emphasis on development outside the Metropolitan Area. Also, in 1966 the South East Economic Planning Council was established with the express aim of assisting in the formulation of strategies placing London's growth (or, more accurately, decline) in the framework of a regional strategy. The prime result was *A Strategy for the South East* published in 1967 which carried on the dominant principles of decentralisation and the development of cities to absorb the relocating activities and population.[14] However, a new theme was added – the idea that the greater part of the development should be located on the main lines of radial communication out of London.

Throughout this period the main objectives in a strategy for dealing with London remained more or less the same: arresting London's growth in employment; containment of London within the same spatial area already developed, combined with redevelopment within inner London; the promotion of relatively self-contained towns, including new towns, beyond the green belt; preserving the distinction between urban and rural areas. The two major modifications in strategy were: the extension of employment control measures to cover office developments; the switch from small new towns (say 50–60,000) close to London, typically 20 to 30 miles from the centre, in favour of cities larger than a quarter of a million, usually based on an important existing town, at greater distances – in the range 60–100 miles. This latter change is a striking example of the use of a growth centre strategy to attack directly the phenomenon of large metropolitan size. However, given the limited supply of mobile industry, it must be remembered that i.d.c. controls were strictly in force not merely as an instrument of decentralisation but rather to induce the relocation of industry to the lagging regions of the economy, particularly the development areas. The office development controls, on the other hand, have, in practice, operated primarily as a measure to promote decentralisation within the region.[15]

The most recent attempt to deal with Greater London's problems in a *regional* context is the *Strategic Plan for the South East* commissioned in 1968 and reporting in 1970. The South East Joint Planning Team responsible for this plan was appointed as a result of dissatisfaction in many quarters with the failure to explore alternative strategies in the 1967 SEEPC study. Also, it was widely recognised that events had changed quickly in the late sixties. Population projections for the country as a whole were almost continuously being scaled down; the long historical trend of net in-migration into the South East had come to a halt; the demand for labour in London continued unabated but the supply was falling as the population of London declined; on the other hand, population pressure remained strong in the OMA (Outer Metropolitan Area): it became clear that it was necessary to extend the planning period towards the end of the century.

After exploring ten alternative spatial strategies, the Strategic Plan came down in favour of a scheme under which five major growth areas were proposed supplemented by a number of medium growth areas.[16] It was very much the same mixture as before: a flexible strategy designed to accommodate the region's population growth; recognition of the advantages of urban concentration by making provision for agglomeration at selected growth areas at varying distances from London; preservation of the green belt and conservation of extensive countryside areas; proposals for a regional communication network to link the more important centres in the region with each other and with the rest the country; the belief that continuing the decentralisation strategy would relieve the housing, social and congestion problems of inner London.

Although the Government and all the participating bodies accepted the Strategic Plan in principle, how it can be implemented remains in doubt. The Government's view is that this will depend on the investment plans of central and local government and on the very large number of private investment decisions (by firms and households). While retaining the overriding aim of inducing industry to the development areas and to the more recent intermediate areas, the Government intends to take the Plan into account in its investment decisions. It is argued that local government, particularly in the post-reorganisation era,[17] will be the prime agency responsible for implementing the strategic plan at the local level, which is the level at which it can be made most effective.

The first stage in this process is the preparation of structure plans in the major growth areas. For instance, the *South Hampshire Structure Plan* published in September 1972 provided for a potential 62·5 per cent increase of population over the period 1966–2001. Eight broad objectives (environment, economy, conservation, choice, image, mobility, feasibility and implementation) were subsumed within an overall aim of 'social and economic need' – to provide for the social and economic needs of the present and future forecast population within the planning area. This led to the examination of four alternative strategies: A. creation of a semi-independent third city to rival Southampton and Portsmouth; B. substantial commercial development in existing cities combined with other development in areas least likely to harm conservable resources; C. creation of separate and partly independent satellite urban areas, but linked to one another and to the existing cities; and D. new industrial and commercial developments at centres along a linear axis parallel to the planned M27 motorway, surrounded by areas of residential growth set deeper into the countryside. Evaluation of the four strategies revealed that they were all too expensive, primarily because of heavy road investment. Accordingly, the strategies were revised to make more provision for public transport. It was then found that C and D conferred similar net social benefits (using the Planning Balance Sheet approach; Lichfield, 1966, and Lichfield and Chapman, 1970); both were marginally better than B and far superior to A. The preferred strategy was a variant of alternative C, partly on the grounds of cost savings – lower operational costs, lower initial, committed expenditures on development, and the best prospects for economical planning. It involved the selection of 6 principal growth sectors which would also accommodate the bulk of residential development. The essence of the structure plan approach is to concentrate on the broad, overall strategy designed to achieve specified objectives, and to retain maximum flexibility in order to be able to adjust the details of the strategy in response to changing conditions, revised population targets, etc.

A general worry about the Strategic Plan and its antecedents is that it is unclear where the responsibility for implementation lies and how the Plan could be implemented. It can function as a basic information input to be taken into account in public (central and local) decisions, and hopefully in private decisions, to increase the prospects that such decisions are made consistent with each other. This is to some extent analogous to internalising externalities, except for the fact that some of the external investment decisions affecting a particular decision are yet to be made. In other words, the time phasing of investment decisions, on top of their spatial interdependence, is a complicating feature. The main instruments for implementing a regional strategy in the South East England context must be physical planning in-

210

struments. These act only indirectly on the location of employment and one of the problems arising from strategies to deal with London is that it is much easier in the United Kingdom to implement *inter*regional than *intra*regional policies.

The final question is whether there are lessons to be learnt from London's experience about national urban size strategies. If we include the inter-regional aspects, the London metropolitan area has been subject to a wide range of decentralisation inducements – prohibition, financial incentives and exhortation – over a long period of time. For a non-centrally-planned, i.e. a mixed, economy the controls have been quite strong. To some extent, the size of Greater London has been brought under control which suggests that, given the will, a size strategy is feasible. On the other hand, particularly in regard to office developments and population shifts, spatial readjustment *within* the region has been more striking than any effects on the *national* settlement pattern. This might be regarded as an illustration of adaptation of the form of the metropolitan area and a change in its spatial structure rather than a decline in absolute size, since the number of people living inside the GLC boundaries has no economic significance. Moreover, the anxieties felt by the GLC and some other groups about population decline in this arbitrarily defined area suggest that once we begin to tamper with the size of an urban area it may become difficult to choose the appropri-ate size target and impossible to 'fine-tune' to achieve this target. The message remains the same: structure rather than size is the key to efficiency and the quality of urban living.

Notes

[1] For instance, Burnley has double the rainfall of London and only two-thirds the hours of sunshine.

[2] These attractions apply to firms as well as households: 'there are great advantages in London for firms: even for those which do not have close ties with other enterprises, there are large external economies of commercial and professional services, a very large choice of skills, the port and airports, rail terminals, hotels, exhibition centres – and an easy journey for executives from country homes to head offices. What drives them out are high rents or land costs, road congestion, and shortages of certain kinds of labour' (GLDP Inquiry, Stage I, 1971, para. 1.50).

[3] Both these forecasts assume that the current rate of out-migration will continue. They differ in their assumptions as to whether the fall in fertility will continue or level out.

[4] An analysis of London boroughs in the period 1961–6 failed to reveal any

trend towards social polarisation (Layfield Panel, Supporting Papers, S11/113).

5 The number of overseas tourists visiting the United Kingdom doubled between 1965 and 1971 reaching a total of over 7 million (GLC, 1972, Table 3.27).

6 Costs do not decline along with population because of diseconomies associated with lower densities and decentralisation and because of indivisibilities in public utilities and the transport system.

7 As Kirwan (1972) points out, special weight is given to some London costs in the Rate Support Grant, but no mechanism exists for directing these additional resources to the most needy groups.

8 In the main report of the Layfield Panel, 275 out of 657 pages were devoted to transport.

9 See particularly DOE, Vol. 2 (1973), Appendix H, pp. 1021–36.

10 See DOE (1973), Vol. 2, Appendix F.2, para. 3.15: 'There are very good arguments for thinking that London is, by modern standards, still over-crowded and that if a good proportion of its citizens were to move, through their own efforts or with help from the Council, to areas outside London, both they, and those who remain, would benefit. Such a decline in population, should make it easier to deal with environmental problems and will probably, in the national context, save a substantial amount in social costs.'

11 Of course, there are some lower level problems which are very important. London's housing problem is the most obvious example.

12 The second instance is in the context of new towns. At the unofficial level, an interesting if impressionistic study of Swindon relying on interview data by Hudson (1967) argues that many of the town's problems are the result of its 'awkward size' – just over the 100,000 level.

13 Similarly, the sub-regional strategies developed in the late 1960s are in danger of being made redundant by the downward revisions in future population projections.

14 By the end of 1971 about 132,000 Greater London Families had been accommodated in new and expanding towns. Between 1952 and 1971 (primarily in the 1960s) 46,100 'overspill' dwellings had been built and 784 factories (covering more than 25 million square feet) completed. See GLC (1972), Table 8.15.

15 The Layfield Panel's views on employment controls are of some interest. It rejected, quite rightly, the GLC's reliance on planning permission for floorspace on the ground that floorspace-employment ratios are highly unstable. It was very critical of ODPs (Office Development Permits) and other negative controls, and came out in favour of taxes, probably on employment, as a method of bringing private costs into approximate alignment with social costs. It also argued that i.d.c. controls should be relaxed

to permit relocation within London as a possible solution to the problem of how to revitalise stagnating areas.

[16] The major growth areas were: South Hampshire; Milton Keynes – Northampton – Wellingborough; South Essex; Crawley – Burgess Hill; and Reading – Wokingham – Aldershot – Basingstoke. The medium growth areas were: Maidstone – Medway; Ashford; Eastbourne – Hastings; Bournemouth – Poole; Aylesbury; Chelmsford; and Bishops Stortford – Harlow. All these were endorsed apart from Bishops Stortford – Harlow.

[17] This refers to the consolidation of local government areas, the introduction of a watered-down version of the Redcliffe-Maud Commission's proposals of 1969.

Bibliography

Abbreviations

AAAPSS	*Annals of the American Academy of Political and Social Science*
AER	*American Economic Review*
ASR	*American Sociological Review*
Bm	*Biometrika*
EDCC	*Economic Development and Cultural Change*
EJ	*Economic Journal*
Em	*Econometrica*
GR	*Geographical Review*
JAIP	*Journal of the American Institute of Planners*
JET	*Journal of Economic Theory*
JPE	*Journal of Political Economy*
JRS	*Journal of Regional Science*
LE	*Land Economics*
MLR	*Monthly Labor Review*
NTJ	*National Tax Journal*
PPRSA	*Papers and Proceedings of the Regional Science Association*
RE&S	*Review of Economics and Statistics*
RS	*Regional Studies*
RUE	*Regional and Urban Economics*
SCB	*Survey of Current Business*
SJPE	*Scottish Journal of Political Economy*
US	*Urban Studies*

References

Aitchison, J. and Brown, J. A. C. (1957), *The Lognormal Distribution*, Cambridge UP.

Allen, G. R. (1954), 'The "Courbe des Populations": a Further Analysis', *Oxford Bulletin of Statistics*, 16, 179–89.

Alonso, W. (1968a), 'Urban and Regional Imbalances', *EDCC*, 17, 1–14.

Alonso, W. (1968b), 'Equity and its Relation to Efficiency in Urbanisation', Institute of Urban and Regional Development, UCLA, Berkeley, WP 78.

Alonso, W. (1970a), 'What are New Towns For?', *US*, 7, 37–55.

Alonso, W. (1970b), 'The Question of City Size and National Policy', IURD,

UCLA, Berkeley, WP 125.

Alonso, W. (1971a), 'The Economics of Urban Size', *PPRSA*, 26, 67–83.

Alonso, W. (1971b), 'Problems, Purposes and Implicit Policies for a National Strategy of Urbanisation, IURD, UCLA, Berkeley, WP 158.

Alonso, W. (1972), 'Policy Implications of Intermetropolitan Migration Flows', IURD, UCLA, Berkeley, WP 177.

Alonso, W. and Fajans, M. (1970), 'Cost of Living and Income by Urban Size', UCLA, Berkeley, WP 128.

Alonso, W. and Medrich, E. (1972), 'Spontaneous Growth Centres in Twentieth-Century American Urbanisation', 229–64, in N. M. Hansen (ed.), *Growth Centres in Regional Economic Development*, Free Press, New York.

Armen, G. (1972), 'A Classification of Cities and City Regions in England and Wales, 1966', *RS*, 6, 149–82.

Bahl, R. W. (1969), *Metropolitan City Expenditures: A Comparative Analysis*, Kentucky UP, Lexington.

Bahr, R. C., Meiners, M. R. and Nakayama, T. (1972), 'New Consumer Price Indices by Size of City', *MLR*, August, 3–8.

Barnett, H. J. (1968), 'Discussion of Part I', 229–34, in Perloff, H. S. and Wingo, L. (eds), *Issues in Urban Economics*, Resources for the Future, Johns Hopkins Press, Baltimore.

Barr, J. L. (1970), *Transportation Costs, Rent and Intraurban Location*, Department of Economics, Washington University, St. Louis.

Barr, J. L. (1972), 'City Size, Land Rent and the Supply of Public Goods', *RUE*, 2, 67–103.

Baumol, W. J. (1967), 'Macroeconomics of Unbalanced Growth: the Anatomy of Urban Crisis', *AER*, 57, 415–26.

Baumol, W. J. and Oates, W. E. (1971), 'The Use of Standards and Prices for Protection of the Environment', 53–65, in Bohm, P. and Kneese, A. V. (eds.), *The Economics of Environment*, Macmillan.

Beckmann, M. J. (1958), 'City Hierarchies and the Distribution of City Sizes', *EDCC*, 6, 243–8.

Beckmann, M. J. (1968), *Location Theory*, Random House, New York.

Beckmann, M. J. and McPherson, J. (1970), 'City Size Distributions in a Central Place Hierarchy: An Alternative Approach', *JRS*, 10, 25–33.

Bell, C. S. (1970), *The Economics of the Ghetto*, Pegasus, New York.

Bergsman, J., Greenston, P. and Healy, R. (1972), 'The Agglomeration Process in Urban Growth', *US*, 9, 263–88.

Berry, B. J. L. (1961), 'City Size Distributions and Economic Development', *EDCC*, 9, 573–87.

Berry, B. J. L. (1964), 'Cities as Systems within Systems of Cities', *PPRSA*,

13, 147–63.

Berry, B. J. L. (1968), 'A Summary – Spatial Organisation and Levels of Welfare: Degree of Metropolitan Labour Market Participation as a Variable in Economic Development', *EDA Research Review*, June, 1–6.

Berry, B. J. L. (1972), 'Hierarchical Diffusion: The Basis of Developmental Filtering and Spread in a System of Growth Centers', 108–38, in Hansen, N. M. (ed.), *Growth Centers in Regional Economic Development*, Free Press, New York.

Berry, B. J. L. and Neils, E. (1969), 'Location, Size and Shape of Cities as Influenced by Environmental Factors: The Urban Environment Writ Large', 257–302, in Perloff, H. S. (ed.), *The Quality of the Urban Environment*, Resources for the Future, Johns Hopkins Press, Baltimore.

Berry, B. M. (1973), 'Migration Analysis for Sub-Regional Planning in England and Wales', Ph.D. thesis, Cambridge University.

Borsky, P. N. (1971), 'Theoretical Framework of Factors Influencing Human Annoyance and Complaint Reactions to Environmental Noise', paper for 4th Karolinska Institute Symposium on Environmental Health, Stockholm.

Borts, G. H. and Stein, J. L. (1964), *Economic Growth in a Free Market*, Columbia UP, New York.

Bos, H. C. (1965), *The Spatial Dispersion of Economic Activity*, North-Holland, Amsterdam.

Bostick, T. A., *et al.* (1954), 'Motor Vehicle-Use Studies in Six States', *Public Roads*, 28, 99–126.

Brackett, J. C. and Lamale, H. H. (1967), 'Area Differences in Living Costs', *American Statistical Association, Proceedings of Social Statistics Section*, 144–8.

Branch, Jr., M. C. (1942), *Urban Planning and Public Opinion*, Bureau of Urban Research, Princeton University.

Brazer, H. E. (1959), *City Expenditures in the United States*, National Bureau of Economic Research, Occasional Paper No. 66.

Breese, G., ed. (1969), *The City in Newly Developing Countries*, Prentice Hall, Englewood Cliffs, New Jersey.

Breton, A. (1965), 'Scale Effects in Local and Metropolitan Government Expenditures', *LE*, 41, 370–2.

Brown, A. J. (1972), *The Framework of Regional Economics in the United Kingdom*, National Institute of Economic and Social Research, Economic and Social Studies XXVII, Cambridge UP.

Brown, L. A. (1969), 'Diffusion of Innovation: A Macroview', *EDCC*, 17, 189–211.

Brush, J. F. and Bracey, H. E. (1955), 'Rural Service Centres in Southwestern Wisconsin and Southern England', *GR*, 43, 559–69.

Buchanan, J. M. (1969), *Costs and Choice: An Inquiry in Economic Theory*,

Markham, Chicago.

Burton, R. P. (1971), 'On the Relevance of Governmental Reorganisation to National Urban Growth Policy', paper prepared for Resources for the Future – University of Glasgow Conference on National Urban Development Strategies.

Calhoun, J. B. (1962), 'Population Density and Social Pathology', *Scientific American*, February, 139–49.

Cameron, G. C. (1970), 'Growth Areas, Growth Centres and Regional Conversion', *SJPE*, 17, 19–38.

Carlestam, G. and Levi, L. (1971), *Urban Conglomerates as Psycho-Social Human Stressors*, Swedish Preparatory Committee for the United Nations Conference on the Human Environment, Stockholm.

Champernowne, D. G. (1953), 'A Model of Income Distribution', *EJ*, 63 318–51.

Chinitz, B. (1961), 'Contrasts in Agglomeration: New York and Pittsburgh', *AER*, Papers 51, 279–89.

Christaller, W. (tr. by Baskin, C. W., 1966), *Central Places in Southern Germany*, Prentice Hall, Englewood Cliffs.

Clark, C. (1945), 'The Economic Functions of a City in Relation to its Size', *Em*, 13, 97–113.

Clark, C. (1967), *Population Growth and Land Use*, Macmillan.

Clemente, F. and Sturgis, R. B. (1971), 'Population Size and Industrial Diversification', *US*, 8, 65–8.

Curry, L. (1964), 'The Random Spatial Economy: An Exploration in Settlement Theory', *Annals of the Association of American Geographers*, 54, 138–46.

Czamanski, S. (1964), 'A Model of Urban Growth', *PPRSA*, 13, 177–200.

Dacey, M. F. (1966), 'Population of Places in a Central Place Hierarchy', *JRS*, 6, 27–33.

Davis, E. and Swanson, J. G. (1972), 'On the Distribution of City Growth Rates in a Theory of Regional Economic Growth', *EDCC*, 20, 495–503.

Davis, K. (1969 and 1972), *World Urbanization, 1950–70*, 2 volumes, UCLA Press, Berkeley.

Department of the Environment (1973), *Greater London Development Plan, Report of the Panel of Inquiry*, 2 volumes, HMSO.

Dohrenwend, B. P. and Dohrenwend, B. S. (1972), 'Psychiatric Disorder in Urban Settings', in Caplan, G. (ed.), *American Handbook of Psychiatry*, Vol. III, Basic Books, New York.

Downs, A. P. (1970), 'Alternative Forms of Future Urban Growth in the United States', *JAIP*, 36, 3–11.

Duncan, O. D. (1956), 'The Optimum Size of Cities', 372–85, in Spengler, J. J. and Duncan, O. D. (eds.), *Demographic Analysis*, Free Press.

Duncan, O. D. (1959), 'Service Industries and the Urban Hierarchy', *PPRSA*, 5, 105–20.

Duncan, O. D. and Reiss, Jr., A. J. (1956), *Social Characteristics of Urban and Rural Communities, 1950*, Wiley, New York.

Economists Advisory Group (1971), *An Economic Study of the City of London*, Allen and Unwin, London.

Edel, M. (1972), 'Land Values and the Costs of Urban Congestion: Measurement and Distribution', 61–90, in École Pratique des Hautes Études, VIe Section, *Political Economy of Environment: Problems of Method*, Mouton and Co., The Hague.

Ellickson, B. (1971), 'Jurisdictional Fragmentation and Residential Choice', *AER*, Papers 61, 334–9.

El Shaks, S. (1965), 'Development, Primacy and the Structure of Cities', Unpublished Ph.D. dissertation, Harvard University.

Engels, F. (1892), *The Condition of the Working Classes in England in 1844*, Swan Sonnenschein, London.

Evans, A. W. (1972), 'The Pure Theory of City Size in an Industrial Economy', *US*, 9, 49–77.

Eversley, D. E. C. (1972a), 'Old Cities, Falling Populations and Rising Costs', *GLC Intelligence Unit Quarterly Bulletin*, No. 18, March, 5–17.

Eversley, D. E. C. (1972b), 'Urban Problems in Britain Today', *GLC Intelligence Unit Quarterly Bulletin*, No. 19, June, 53–61.

Eversley, D. E. C. (1972c), 'Rising Costs and Static Incomes: Some Economic Consequences of Regional Planning in London', *US*, 9, 347–68.

Fano, P. (1969), 'Organisation, City Size Distributions and Central Places', *PPRSA*, 22, 29–38.

Federal Bureau of Investigation (annual), *Uniform Crime Reports for the United States*, Washington, D. C.,

Flaim, P. O. (1968), 'Jobless Trends in 20 Large Metropolitan Areas', *MLR*, 91, No. 5, 16–28.

Foster, C. D. and Richardson, G. R. J. (1972), 'Employment Trends in London in the 1960s and Their Relevance for the Future', Centre for Environmental Studies Conference on the Inner City, Oxford.

Fox, K. A. and Kumar, T. K. (1965), 'The Functional Economic Area: Delineation and Implications for Economic Analysis and Policy', *PPRSA*, 15, 57–85.

Frech III, H. E. and Burns, L. S. (1971), 'Metropolitan Interpersonal Income Inequality: A Comment', *LE*, 47, 104–6.

219

Fried, M. and Gleicher, P. (1970), 'Some Sources of Residential Satisfaction in an Urban Slum', 334–5, in Pröshansky, H. M., Ittelson, W. H. and Rivlin, L. G. (eds.), *Environmental Psychology*: *Man and his Physical Setting*, Holt, Rinehart and Winston, New York.

Friedmann, J. (1966), *Regional Development Policy: A Case Study of Venezuela*, MIT Press.

Friedmann, J. (1971), 'The Feasibility of a National Settlement Policy for the USA', *Growth and Change*, 2, 18–21.

Fuchs, V. R. (1967), *Differentials in Hourly Earnings by Region and City Size, 1959*, National Bureau of Economic Research, Occasional Paper No. 101.

Gibbs, J. P. and Martin, W. T. (1962), 'Urbanisation, Technology and the Division of Labour: International Patterns', 27, 669–72.

Ginsburg, N. (1961), *Atlas of Economic Development*, Chicago UP.

Girard, A. and Bastide, H. (1960), 'Les problemes demographiques devant l'opinion', *Population*, 15, 287.

Glaser, D., ed. (1970), *Crime in the City*, Harper and Row, New York.

Goldner, W. (1955), 'Spatial and Locational Aspects of Metropolitan Labour Markets', *AER*, 45, 113–28.

Graham, Jr., R. E. and Coleman, E. J. (1968), 'Metropolitan Area Incomes, 1929–66', *SCB*, 48, No. 8, 32–7.

Greater London Council (1969), *Tomorrow's London*.

Greater London Council (1971), *Greater London Development Plan: Public Inquiry*, Subject Evidence – Stage 1, General Strategy and Implementation.

Greater London Council (1972), *Annual Abstract of Greater London Statistics, 1971*, Volume 6.

Greater London Group, London School of Economics (1968), *Local Government in South East England*, Research Studies No. 1, Royal Commission on Local Government in England.

Greenwood, M. J. (1970), 'Lagged Response in the Decision to Migrate', *JRS*, 10, 375–84.

Groom, P. (1967), 'A New City Worker's Family Budget', *MLR*, November, 1–8.

Gupta, S. P. and Hutton, J. P. (1968), *Economies of Scale in Local Government Services*, Royal Commission on Local Government in England, Research Studies No. 3.

Hägerstrand, T. (1966), 'Aspects of the Spatial Structure of Social Communication and the Diffusion of Information', *PPRSA*, 16, 27–42.

Hägerstrand, T. (translated by Pred, A., 1967), *Innovation Diffusion as a Spatial Process*, Chicago UP.

Hägerstrand, T. (1968), 'Methods and New Techniques in Current Urban and Regional Research in Sweden', *Tidskrift for Plänering av Landsbygd och Tätorter*, 22, 3–11.

Haggett, P. (1968), 'The Spatial Structure of City Regions', SSRC/CES Joint Conference on the Future of the City Region, Vol. 2, Centre for Environmental Studies, WP 6.

Haldane, J. B. S. (1942), 'Moments of the Distribution of Powers and Products of Normal Variates', *Bm*, 32, 226.

Hall, P. G. (1969), *London 2000*, 2nd ed., Faber and Faber, London.

Hamburg, D. A. (1971), 'Crowding, Stranger Contact, and Aggressive Behaviour', 209–18, in Levi, L. (ed.), *Society, Stress and Disease: The Psychosocial Environment and Psychosomatic Diseases*, Oxford UP.

Hansen, N. M. (1970a), *Rural Poverty and the Urban Crisis*, Indiana UP, Bloomington.

Hansen, N. M. (1970b), 'A Growth Centre Strategy for the United States', *Review of Regional Studies*, 1, 161–73.

Hansen, N. M., ed. (1972a), *Growth Centers in Regional Economic Development*, Free Press, New York.

Hansen, N. M. (1972b), 'Criteria for a Growth Centre Policy', 103–24, in Kuklinski, A. (ed.), *Growth Centres in Regional Planning*, United Nations Research Institute for Social Development, Mouton and Co., The Hague.

Harris, C. D. (1970), *Cities in the Soviet Union: Studies in their Functions, Size, Density and Growth*, Rand McNally, Chicago.

Harris, C. D. and Ullman, E. (1945), 'The Nature of Cities', *AAAPSS*, 242, 7–17.

Harris, W. D. (1971), *The Growth of Latin American Cities*, Ohio UP, Athens.

Haskell, M. R. and Yablonsky, L. (1970), *Crime and Delinquency*, Rand McNally, Chicago.

Hawley, A. H. (1951), 'Metropolitan Population and Municipal Government Expenditures in Central Cities', *Journal of Social Issues*, 7, 100–08.

Herrara, F. (1971), 'Nationalism and Urbanisation in Latin America', *Ekistics*, 32, 369–73.

Higgins, B. (1972), 'Growth Pole Policy in Canada', 204–28, in Hansen, N. M. (ed.), *Growth Centers in Regional Economic Development*, Free Press, New York.

Higgs, R. (1970), 'Central Place Theory and Regional Urban Hierarchies: An Empirical Note', *JRS*, 10, 253–5.

Hirsch, W. Z. (1959), 'Expenditure Implications of Metropolitan Growth and Consolidation', *RE & S*, 41, 232–41.

Hirsch, W. Z. (1960), 'Determinants of Public Expenditures', *NTJ*, 13, 29–40.

Hirsch, W. Z. (1968), 'The Supply of Urban Public Services', 477–525 in Perloff, H. S. and Wingo, L, (eds.), *Issues in Urban Economics*, Resources for the Future, Johns Hopkins Press, Baltimore.

Hoch, I. (1972), 'Income and City Size', *US*, 9, 299–328.

Holmans, A. E. (1964), 'Restriction of Industrial Expansion in South East England: a Reappraisal', *Oxford Economic Papers*, 16, 235–61.

Hoover, E. M. (1969), 'Some Old and New Issues in Regional Development', 343–57, in Robinson, E. A. G. (ed.), *Backward Areas in Advanced Countries*, International Economic Association, Macmillan.

Hoover, E. M. (1970), 'Transport Costs and the Spacing of Central Places', *PPRSA*, 25, 255–74.

Hoover, E. M. (1971), *An Introduction to Regional Economics*, Alfred A. Knopf, New York.

Hoover, E. M. and Vernon, R. (1959), *Anatomy of a Metropolis*, Harvard UP, Cambridge, Mass.

Hoyt, H. (1962), 'World Urbanisation', Urban Land Institute, Technical Bulletin No. 43, Washington D. C.

Hoyt, H. (1966), 'Growth and Structure of 21 Great World Cities', *LE*, 42, 53–64.

Hudson, K. (1967), *An Awkward Size for a Town: A Study of Swindon at the 100,000 Mark*, David & Charles, Newton Abbot.

Hughes, J. T. (1967), 'Economic Aspects of Local Government Reform', *SJPE*, 14, 118–37.

Inbau, F. E. and Carrington, F. G. (1971), 'The Case for the So-Called "Hard Line" Approach to Crime', *AAAPSS*, 397, 19–27.

International Urban Research (1959), *The World's Metropolitan Areas*, UCLA Press, Berkeley.

Isard, W. (1956), *Location and Space–Economy*, MIT Press.

Isard, W. (1960), *Methods of Regional Analysis*, MIT Press.

Jacobs, J. (1961), *The Death and Life of Great American Cities*, Random House, New York.

Jaksch, J. (1970), 'Air Pollution: Its Effects on Residential Property Values in Toledo, Oregon', *Annals of Regional Science*, 4, 42–52.

Jefferson, M. (1939), 'The Law of the Primate City', *GR*, 29, 226–32.

Johnson, M. (1964), 'On the Economics of Road Congestion', *Em*, 32, 137–50.

Kapp, K. W. (1963), *The Social Costs of Business Enterprise*, 2nd ed. Asia Publishing House, Bombay.

Kapp, K. W. (1970), 'Environmental Disruption and Social Costs: A Challenge to Economics', *Kyklos*, 23, 833–48.

Kermack, K. A. and Haldane, J. B. S, (1950), 'Organic Correlation and Allometry', *Bm*, 37, 30–41.

Kirwan, R. (1972), 'The Contribution of Public Expenditure and Finance to the Problems of Inner London', Centre for Environmental Studies Conference on the Inner City, Oxford.

Klaassen, L. H. (1965), 'Regional Policy in the Benelux Countries', in United States Department of Commerce, *Area Redevelopment Policies in Britain and the Countries of the Common Market*, Washington DC.

Klaassen, L. H. (1972), 'Growth Poles in Economic Theory and Policy', 1–40, in Kuklinski, A. and Petrella, R. (ed.), *Growth Poles and Regional Policies*, United Nations Research Institute for Social Development, Mouton & Co., The Hague.

Koupernik, C. (1968), 'Psychiatry and the Great City', in Documenta Geigy, *Man and Megalopolis*, Basle.

Krapf, E. E. (1964), 'Social Change in the Genesis of Mental Disorder and Health', in David, H. P. (ed.), *Population and Mental Health*, Hans Huber, Berne and Stuttgart.

Kuklinski, A., ed. (1972), *Growth Poles and Growth Centres in Regional Planning*, United Nations Research Institute for Social Development, Mouton & Co., The Hague.

Kuklinski, A. and Petrella, R., eds. (1972), *Growth Poles and Regional Policies*, United Nations Research Institute for Social Development, Mouton & Co., The Hague.

Kuznets, S. (1955), 'Economic Growth and Income Inequality', *AER*, 45, 15–19.

Lampard, E. E. (1968), 'The Evolving System of Cities in the United States – Urbanisation and Economic Development', 81–139, in Perloff, H. S. and Wingo, L. (eds.), *Issues in Urban Economics*, Resources for the Future, Johns Hopkins Press, Baltimore.

Lave, L. B. (1970), 'Congestion and Urban Location', *PPRSA*, 25, 133–49.

Lave, L. B. and Seskin, E. (1970), 'Air Pollution and Human Health', *Science*, 169, 723–32.

Lave, L. B. and Seskin, E. (1971), 'Health and Air Pollution', 119–38, in Bohm, P. and Kneese, A. V. (eds.), *The Economics of Environment*, Macmillan.

Leven, C. L. (1969), 'Determinants of the Size and Spatial Form of Urban Areas', *PPRSA*, 22, 7–28.

Lichfield, N. (1966), 'Cost-benefit Analysis in Town Planning: a Case Study, Swanley', *US*, 3, 215–49.

Lichfield, N. and Chapman, H. (1970), 'Cost-benefit Analysis in Urban Expansion', *US*, 7, 153–88.

Lichtenberg, R. M. (1960), *One-Tenth of a Nation*, Harvard UP, Cambridge, Mass.

223

Lillibridge, R. M. (1952), 'Urban Size: An Assessment', *LE*, 28, 341–52.

Lindburg, D. (1969), 'Observations of Rhesus Macaque in Natural Habitats', paper presented at Department of Psychiatry, Stanford University.

Linsky, A. S. (1965), 'Some Generalisations Concerning Primate Cities', *Annals of the Association of American Geographers*, 55, 506–13.

Lithwick, N. H. (1971), *Urban Canada: Problems and Prospects*, Central Mortgage and Housing Corporation, Ottawa.

Livesey, D. A. (1973), 'Optimum City Size: A Minimum Congestion Approach', *JET*, 5.

Lomax, K. S. (1943), 'The Relationship between Expenditure per Head and Size of Population of County Boroughs in England and Wales', *Journal of the Royal Statistical Society*, 106, 51–9.

Lösch, A. (1954), *The Economics of Location*, Yale UP, New Haven.

Lydall, H. F. (1968), *The Structure of Earnings*, Clarendon Press, Oxford.

Madden, C. H. (1956a), 'On Some Indications of Stability in the Growth of Cities in the United States', *EDCC*, 4, 236–52.

Madden, C. H. (1956b), 'Some Spatial Aspects of Urban Growth in the United States', *EDCC*, 4, 371–87.

Madden, C. H. (1958), 'Some Temporal Aspects of the Growth of Cities in the United States', *EDCC*, 6, 143–70.

Marler, P. and Hamilton, W. J. (1966), *Mechanisms of Animal Behaviour*,

Martin, J. E. (1966), *Greater London: An Industrial Geography*, Bell.

Mathur, V. K. (1970), 'Occupational Composition and its Determinants: an Intercity Size Class Analysis', *JRS*, 10, 81–91.

McClintock, F. H. and Avison, N. H. (1968), *Crime in England and Wales*, Heinemann.

McGreevey, W. P. (1971), 'A Statistical Analysis of Primacy and Lognormality in the Size Distribution of Latin American Cities, 1750–1960', 116–29 in Morse, R. M. (ed.), *The Urban Development of Latin America*, Center for Latin American Studies, Stanford University.

Mehta, S. K. (1964), 'Some Demographic and Economic Correlates of Primate Cities: A Case for Revaluation', *Demography*, 1, 136–47.

Mera, K. (1970), 'On the Concentration of Urbanisation and Economic Efficiency', International Bank for Reconstruction and Development, Economics Department, WP 74, Washington DC.

Mera, K. (1973), 'On the Urban Agglomeration and Economic Efficiency', *EDCC*, 21, 309–24.

Meyer, J. R., Kain, J. F. and Wohl, M. (1965), *The Urban Transportation Problem*, Harvard UP, Cambridge, Mass.

Milgrim, S. (1970), 'The Experience of Living in Cities', *Science*, 167, 1461–8.

Mills, E. S. (1972a), *Urban Economics*, Scott, Foresman and Co., Glenview,

Illinois.

Mills, E. S. (1972b), 'Welfare Aspects of National Policy Toward City Sizes', *US*, 9, 117–24.

Mills, E. S. (1972c), *Studies in the Structure of the Urban Economy*, Resources for the Future, Johns Hopkins Press, Baltimore.

Mills, E. S. and de Ferranti, D. M. (1971), 'Market Choice and Optimum City Size', *AER*, Papers 61, 340–5.

Ministry of Housing and Local Government (1964), *The South East Study, 1961–81*, HMSO.

Mirrlees, J. A. (1972), 'The Optimum Town', *Swedish Journal of Economics*, 74, 113–35.

Mitchell, R. E. (1971), 'Some Social Implications of High Density Housing', *ASR*, 36, 18–29.

Morgan, J. N., Sirageldin, I. A., and Baerwaldt, N. (1966), *Productive Americans*, Survey Research Center, Monograph 43, University of Michigan, Ann Arbor.

Morse, R. M. (1962), 'Latin American Cities: Aspects of Function and Structure', *Comparative Studies in Society and History*, 4, 473–93.

Morse, R. M. *et al.* (1968), 'Costs of Urban Infrastructure as Related to City Size in Developing Countries: India Case Study', Stanford Research Institute. Partially reprinted in Berry, B. J. L. and Horton, F. E. (eds), *Perspectives on Urban Systems* (Prentice Hall, Englewood Cliffs, New Jersey, 1970).

Mumford, L. (1961), *The City in History*, Harcourt Brace, New York.

Muth, R. F. (1969), *Cities and Housing*, Chicago UP.

National Goals Research Staff (1970), *Toward Balanced Growth: Quantity with Quality*.

Netherlands Economic Institute (1961), *Eerste Resultaten van het voor West-Duitsland Verrichte Agglomeratieonderzoek*, Rotterdam.

Neutze, G. M. (1965), *Economic Policy and the Size of Cities*, Australia National University, Canberra.

Nicholson, R. J. and Topham, N. (1972), 'Investment Decisions and the Size of Local Authorities', *Policy and Politics*, 1, 23–44.

Ogburn, W. F. and Duncan, O. D. (1964), 'City Size as a Sociological Variable', 129–47, in Burgess, E. W. and Bogue D. J. (eds.), *Contributions to Urban Sociology*, Chicago UP.

Olsson, G. (1967), 'Central Place Systems, Spatial Interaction and Stochastic Processes', *PPRSA*, 18, 13–45.

Ornati, O. A. (1968), 'Poverty in the Cities', 335–62, in Perloff, H. S. and Wingo, L. (eds.), *Issues in Urban Economics*, Resources for the Future,

Johns Hopkins Press, Baltimore.

Orshansky, M. (1965), 'Counting the Poor', *Social Security Bulletin*, 28, 3–29.

Osborn, F. J. and Whittick, A. (1969), *The New Towns: the Answer to Megalopolis*, Leonard Hill, London, 2nd ed.

Packer, H. L. (1970), article in *Crime Control Digest*, March 25.

Pahl, R. E. (1971), 'Poverty and the Urban System', 126–45, in Chisholm, M. and Manners, G. (eds.), *Spatial Policy Problems of the British Economy*, Cambridge UP.

Parr, J. B. (1970), 'Models of City Size in an Urban System', *PPRSA*, 25, 221–53.

Pedersen, P. O. (1970), 'Innovation Diffusion within and between National Urban Systems', *Geographical Analysis*, 2, 203–54.

Perloff, H. S. and Wingo, L. (1968), *Issues in Urban Economics*, Resources for the Future, Johns Hopkins Press, Baltimore.

Phillips, B. D. (1972), 'A Note on the Spatial Distribution of Unemployment by Occupation in 1968', *JRS*, 12, 295–8.

Popp, D. O. and Sebold, F. D. (1972), 'Quasi Returns-to-Scale in the Provision of Public Services', *Public Finance*, 27, 46–60.

Poveda, T. G. (1972), 'The Fear of Crime in a Small Town', *Crime and Delinquency*, 18, 147–53.

Pred, A. (1966), *The Spatial Dynamics of United States Urban-Industrial Growth, 1800–1914*, MIT Press, Cambridge, Mass.

President's Commission on Law Enforcement and Administration of Justice (1967), *The Challenge of Crime in a Free Society*, Washington DC.

Price, D. O. (1969), *A Study of the Economic Consequences of Rural to Urban Migration*, OEO Migrant Study, Tracor Sociometric Research, United States Department of Commerce, PB 188–655, 658, 659.

Racionero, L. (1972), 'El Tamaño Optimo de la Ciudad', *Boletin de Estudios Economicos*, 27, 365–85.

Rashevsky, N. (1943), 'Contribution to the Theory of Human Relations: Outline of a Mathematical Theory of the Size of Cities', *Psychometrika*, 8, 87–90.

Rashevsky, N. (1947), *Mathematical Theory of Human Relations*, Principia Press, Bloomington.

Rashevsky, N. (1951), *Mathematical Biology of Social Behaviour*, Chicago UP.

Redcliffe-Maud, Lord (1969), *Royal Commission on Local Government in England*, Cmnd. 4040, HMSO.

Regional Plan Association (1967), *The Region's Growth*, New York.

Registrar-General (annual), *Statistical Review of England and Wales*, Part 1. *Medical Tables*.

Richardson, H. W. (1971), *Urban Economics*, Penguin.

Richardson, H. W. (1972), 'Optimality in City Size, Systems of Cities and Urban Policy: A Sceptic's View', *US*, 9, 29–48.

Richardson, H. W. (1973a), *Regional Growth Theory*, Macmillan.

Richardson, H. W. (1973b), 'Some Uses of Mathematical Models in Urban Economics', *US*, 10, 259–66.

Richardson, H. W. and West, E. G. (1964), 'Must We Always Take Work to the Workers?', *Lloyds Bank Review*, No. 71, 35–48.

Richter, C. E. (1969), 'The Impact of Industrial Linkages on Geographical Association', *JRS*, 9, 19–28.

Ridker, R. G. and Henning, J. A. (1967), *The Economic Costs of Air Pollution*, Praeger, New York.

Rodwin, L. (1970), *Nations and Cities: A Comparison of Strategies for Urban Growth*, Houghton Mifflin, Boston, Mass.

Rogers, A. (1966), 'A Markovian Policy Model of Interregional Migration', *PPRSA*, 17, 205–24.

Rothenberg, J. (1970), 'The Economics of Congestion and Pollution: An Integrated View', *AER*, Papers 60, 114–21.

Roy, A. D. (1950), 'The Distribution of Earnings and Individual Output', *EJ*, 60, 489–505.

Royal Ministry of Foreign Affairs, Sweden (1972), *The Human Work Environment: Swedish Experience, Trends and Future Problems*, Stockholm.

Ruiz, E. (1972), 'Urban Family Budgets Updated to Autumn 1971', *MLR*, June, 46–50.

Schmandt, H. J. and Stephens, G. R. (1960), 'Measuring Municipal Output', *NTJ*, 13, 369–75.

Schmandt, H. J. and Stephens, G. R. (1963), 'Local Government Expenditure Patterns in the United States', *LE*, 39, 397–406.

Schmid, C. F. (1960), 'Urban Crime Areas', *ASR*, 25, Part I, 527–42, and Part II, 655–78.

Schmitt, R. C. (1966), 'Density, Health and Social Disorganisation', *JAIP*, 32, 38–40.

Schnore, L. F. (1963), 'Some Correlates of Urban Size: A Replication', *American Journal of Sociology*, 69, 185–93.

Schultz, T. W. (1953), *The Economic Organization of Agriculture*, McGraw-Hill, New York.

Scott, S. and Feder, E. L. (1957), *Factors Associated with Variation in Municipal Expenditure Levels*, Bureau of Public Administration, UCLA, Berkeley.

Seeley, J. R. (1968), 'Remaking the Urban Scene', *Daedalus*, 97, 1124–1139.

Senior, D., ed. (1966), *The Regional City*, Longmans.

Shapiro, H. (1963), 'Economies of Scale and Local Government Finance', *LE*, 39, 175–86.

Shefer, D. (1970), 'Comparable Living Costs and Urban Size: A Statistical Analysis', *JAIP*, 36, 417–21.

Shindman, B. (1959), 'An Optimum Size for Cities', 257–60, in Mayer, H. M. and Kohn, C. F. (eds.), *Readings in Urban Geography*, Chicago UP.

Simmel, G. (1957), 'The Metropolis and Mental Life', 635–47, in Hatt, P. K., and Reiss, A. J. (eds.), *Cities and Society*, Free Press, New York.

Simon, H. (1955), 'On a Class of Skew Distribution Functions', *Bm*, 42, 425–40.

Singer, H. W. (1936), 'The "Courbe des Populations". A Parallel to Pareto's Laws', *EJ*, 46, 254–63.

Smith, D. M. (1971), *Industrial Location*, Wiley, New York.

Smith, W. F. (1970), *Housing: The Social and Economic Elements*, UCLA Press, Berkeley.

Smith, W. S., Schueneman and Zeidberg, L. (1964), 'Public Reaction to Air Pollution in Nashville, Tennessee', *Journal of the Air Pollution Control Association*, 14, 418–23.

Smolensky, E., Tideman, N. and Nichols, D. (1971), 'The Economical Uses of Congestion', *PPRSA*, 26, 37–52.

Solow, R. M. and Vickrey, W. S. (1971), 'Land Use in a Long Narrow City', *JET*, 3, 430–47.

South East Economic Planning Council (1967), *A Strategy for the South East*, HMSO.

South East Joint Planning Team (1970), *Strategic Plan for the South East*, HMSO.

South Hampshire Plan Advisory Committee (1972), *South Hampshire Structure Plan*, SHPAC.

Stanback, Jr., T. M. and Knight, R. V. (1970), *The Metropolitan Economy: The Process of Employment Expansion*, Columbia UP.

Stewart, Jr., C. T. (1959), 'The Size and Spacing of Cities', 240–56, in Mayer, H. and Kohn, C. F. (eds.), *Readings in Urban Geography*, Chicago UP.

Streit, M. E. (1969), 'Spatial Associations and Economic Linkages between Industries', *JRS*, 9, 177–88.

Strotzka, H. (1964), 'Town Planning and Mental Health', in David, H. P. (ed.), *Population and Mental Health*, Hans Huber, Berne and Stuttgart.

S.V.I.M.E.Z. (1967), *Ricerca sui Coste d'Insediamento*.

Taylor, Lord and Chave, S. (1964), *Mental Health and Environment*, Longmans, London.

Thompson, W. R. (1965a), 'Urban Economic Growth and Development in a National System of Cities', 431–90, in Hauser, P. M. and Schnore, L. F. (eds.), *The Study of Urbanisation*, Wiley, New York.

Thompson, W. R. (1965b), *A Preface to Urban Economics*, Resources for the Future, Johns Hopkins Press, Baltimore.

Thompson, W. R. (1968), 'Internal and External Factors in the Development of Urban Economies', 43–80, in Perloff, H. S. and Wingo, L. (eds.), *Issues in Urban Economics*, Resources for the Future, Johns Hopkins Press, Baltimore.

Thompson, W. R. (1972), 'The National System of Cities as an Object of Public Policy', *US*, 9, 99–116.

Tiebout, C. M. (1956), 'A Pure Theory of Local Expenditures', *JPE*, 64, 416–24.

Tinbergen, J. (1961), 'The Spatial Dispersion of Production: A Hypothesis', *Schweizerische Zeitschrift für Wolkwirtschaft und Statistik*, 97, 412–19.

Tinbergen, J. (1964), 'Sur un Modèle de la Dispersion Géographique de l'Activité Economique', *Revue d'Economie Politique*, 74, 40–44.

Tinbergen, J. (1968), 'The Hierarchy Model of the Size Distribution of Centres', *PPRSA*, 20, 65–8.

Tolley, G. S. (1969), 'The Welfare Economics of City Bigness', University of Chicago, Urban Economics Report No. 31.

Treuner, P. (1970), 'An Infrastructure Cost Model of a System of Central Places', *PPRSA*, 24, 85–101.

Ullman, E. L. (1962), 'The Nature of Cities Reconsidered', *PPRSA*, 9, 7–23.

Ullman, E. L. and Dacey, M. F. (1960), 'The Minimum Requirements Approach to the Urban Economic Base', *PPRSA*, 6, 175–94.

United Nations (annual), *Demographic Yearbook*, UN, New York.

United Nations Bureau of Social Affairs, Population Division (1969), 'World Urbanisation Trends, 1920–60', 21–53, in Breese, G. (ed.), *The City in Newly Developing Countries*, Prentice Hall, Englewood Cliffs, New Jersey.

United States Advisory Committee on Intergovernmental Relations (1968), *Urban and Rural America: Policies for Future Growth*, Washington DC.

United States Bureau of the Census (1972), *Statistical Abstract of the United States, 1971*, US Government Printing Office, Washington DC.

United States Congress, Joint Economic Committee, Sub-Committee on Urban Affairs (1967), *Urban America: Goals and Problems*, evidence of W. Z. Hirsch, 8–11.

United States Department of Health, Education and Welfare (1968), *Air Quality Data*.

United States Department of Labor (1966), *City Worker's Family Budget*,

Bureau of Labor Statistics, Bulletin No. 1570–1.
United States Department of Labor (annual), *Handbook of Labor Statistics*, Washington DC.

Vernon, R. (1960), *Metropolis 1985*, Harvard UP, Cambridge, Mass.
Vickrey, W. S. (1969), 'Congestion Theory and Transport Investment', *AER* 59, 251–60.
Vining, R. (1955), 'A Description of Certain Spatial Aspects of an Economic System', *EDCC*, 3, 147–95.
Vipond, M. J. (1974), 'City Size and Unemployment', mimeo.
von Böventer, E. G. (1969), 'Determinants of Migration into West German Cities, 1956–61, 1961–6', *PPRSA*, 23, 53–62.
von Böventer, E. G. (1970), 'Optimal Spatial Structure and Regional Development', *Kyklos*, 23, 903–24.
von Böventer, E. G. (1971), 'Urban Hierarchies and Spatial Organisation', *Ekistics*, 32, 329–36.
Voorhees, A. M. *et al.* (1966), 'Factors in Worktrip Lengths', *Highway Research Record*, 141, 24–6.

Walker, M. (1930), *Municipal Expenditures*, Johns Hopkins Press, Baltimore.
Walters, A. A. (1961), 'The Theory and Measurement of Private and Social Cost of Highway Congestion', *Em*, 29, 676–99.
Walters, A. A. (1968), *The Economics of Road User Charges*, Johns Hopkins Press, Baltimore.
Ward, B. (1963), 'City Structure and Interdependence', *PPRSA*, 10, 207–21.
Warren Spring Laboratory (1972), *National Survey of Air Pollution, 1961–71*, HMSO.
Webber, M. (1968), 'The Post-City Age', *Daedalus*, 97, 1091–1110.
Weiss, H. K. (1961), 'The Distribution of Urban Population and an Application to a Servicing Problem', *Operations Research*, 9, 860–74.
Will, R. E. (1965), 'Scalar Economies and Urban Service Requirements', *Yale Economic Essays*, 5, 3–61.
Wilson, A. G. (1969), 'Notes on Some Concepts in Social Physics', *PPRSA*, 22, 159–93.
Wingo, L. (1972), 'Issues in a National Urban Development Strategy for the United States', *US*, 9, 3–27.
Winsborough, H. H. (1959),'Variations in Industrial Composition with City Size', *PPRSA*, 5, 121–31.
Winsborough, H. H. (1970), 'The Social Consequences of High Population Density', 84–90, in T. R. Ford and G. F. Dejong (eds.), *Social Demography*, Prentice Hall.
Zimbardo, P. G. (1969), 'The Human Choice: Individuation, Reason and

230

Order versus Deindividuation, Impulse and Chaos', 237–307, in Arnold, W. J. (ed.), *Nebraska Symposium on Motivation.*

Zipf, G. K. (1949), *Human Behaviour and the Principle of Least Effort,* Addison Wesley, Cambridge, Mass.

—— (1940), *Report of the Royal Commission on the Distribution of the Industrial Population* (Barlow Report, Cmnd. 6153), HMSO.

—— (1960), *Report of the Royal Commission on Local Government in Greater London* (Cmnd. 1164), HMSO.

—— (1969), 'Metropolitan Area Income in 1967', *SCB*, 49, No. 5, 19–33.

—— (1970), 'Personal Income in Metropolitan and Nonmetropolitan Areas', *SCB*, 50, No. 5, 22–35.

—— (1971), 'Personal Income in Metropolitan and Nonmetropolitan Areas', *SCB*, 51, No. 5, 16–31.

—— (1972), 'Metropolitan Area Income in 1970', *SCB*, 52, No. 5, 27–44.

—— (1972), 'A Blueprint for Survival', *Ecologist*, January.

—— (annual), *Statistisches Jahrbuch Deutschen Gemeinden*, Bonn.

Name Index

Abercrombie, P. 207
Aitchison, J. 140
Allen, G. R. 161, 162, 163
Alonso, W. 3, 4, 10, 20, 58, 59, 68, 83, 103, 115, 119, 130, 131, 137, 173, 175, 176, 177, 179, 184, 193, 197, 198
Armen, G. 82
Avison, N. H. 97, 99

Bahl, R. W. 86, 87, 95
Bahr, R. C. 67
Barlow, M. 200, 207
Barnett, H. J. 90, 126
Barr, J. L. 20, 44, 122, 127, 128, 133
Baskin, C. W. 164
Bastide, H. 104
Baumol, W. J. 18, 24, 35, 126
Beckmann, M. J. 142, 143, 152
Bell, C. S. 68
Bergsman, J. 72, 77, 79
Berry, B. J. L. 41, 42, 43, 46, 131, 147, 148, 152, 158, 166, 168, 198
Berry, B. M. 196
Borsky, P. N. 107
Borts, G. H. 68
Bos, H. C. 73, 144
Bostick, T. A. 55
Bracey, H. E. 164
Brackett, J. C. 54
Branch, Jr., M. C. 55
Brazer, H. E. 86, 95
Breese, G. 119
Breton, A. 86
Brown, A. J. 122, 123, 125, 136
Brown, J. A. C. 140
Brown, L. A. 43

Brush, J. F. 164
Buchanan, J. M. 24
Burns, L. S. 54
Burton, R. P. 193
Bylund, E. 182

Calhoun, J. B. 105, 106, 109
Cameron, G. C. 46, 75, 86, 131, 176
Carlestam, G. 104, 105, 109
Carrington, F. G. 101, 109
Champernowne, D. G. 139, 157, 160
Chapman, H. 210
Chave, S. 104
Chinitz, B. 46
Christaller, W. 141, 142, 145, 158, 164
Clark, C. 27, 28, 85, 131, 133, 135, 162, 163, 170, 171
Clemente, F. 81
Curry, L. 147, 153
Czamanski, S. 82

Dacey, M. F. 81, 143
Davis, E. 148
Davis, K. 113, 119
de Ferranti, D. M. 21, 23
Dohrenwend, B. P. 107
Dohrenwend, B. S. 107
Downs, A. P. 193
Duncan, O. D. 3, 9, 41, 50, 53, 63, 81, 82, 83, 85, 103, 120, 135, 156, 158

Edel, M. 4, 5, 19, 20, 43, 48, 127, 128, 136, 145
Ellickson, B. 91, 95
El Shaks, S. 158, 168

233

Subject Index